Inside the Star Wars Empire

Inside the Star Wars Empire

A Memoir

Bill Kimberlin

Guilford, Connecticut

An imprint of Rowman & Littlefield

Distributed by NATIONAL BOOK NETWORK

British Library Cataloguing in Publication Information available

Library of Congress Cataloging-in-Publication Data available

ISBN 978-1-4930-3231-0 (hardcover)
ISBN 978-1-4930-3232-7 (e-book)

∞™ The paper used in this publication meets the minimum requirements of American National Standard for Information Sciences—Permanence of Paper for Printed Library Materials, ANSI/NISO Z39.48-1992.

Printed in the United States of America

We know the pharaohs well, but not the men who built their tombs.

—Anonymous

CONTENTS

Foreword . . . viii

The Gilded Cage . . . 1
Mrs. Hickman . . . 6
The Droid Olympics . . . 15
High School Reunion . . . 22
What's It Like? . . . 26
Hollywood . . . 33
The Cutting Room Floor . . . 40
Film School . . . 45
"Francis Coppola Wishes to Speak with You" . . . 50
Mike Medavoy . . . 57
Chan Is Missing . . . 65
American Nitro . . . 67
The Screamer . . . 80
The Players . . . 85
What Do You Do? . . . 91
The Oracle . . . 94
The Smell of Napalm . . . 97
Roger Rabbit . . . 102
Back to the Future . . . 109
Pixar . . . 114
A Jolt of Money . . . 121
The Mask . . . 126
Off the Ground . . . 132
Defining Myself . . . 137
Jurassic Park . . . 142

Schindler's List 146
The Intern 151
Acting Out. 155
Earthquake. 159
Finding Boonville 163
Are You OK?. 167
Mason's Distillery 169
Kimberlina 173
The UFO Detector. 177
Criminal Behavior 183
The China Girl. 190
The Distraction. 194
Digital City 203
The Stone Age Institute 206
Dropping Dead 211

Index 220
About the Author 232

Foreword

I WAS ONE OF THOSE NAMES ON THAT ENDLESS LIST OF CREDITS AT THE close of blockbuster movies. From *Star Wars* to *Star Trek, Back to the Future* to *Forrest Gump, Roger Rabbit* to *Schindler's List, Saving Private Ryan* to *Jurassic Park*, from *Gangs of New York* to others I sometimes forget, I was one of those interminable people thanked as Oscars are collected by dazed winners, clutching that surprisingly heavy gold statue as they try not to leave out anyone that helped them.

I was an employee at Lucasfilm, and not an especially important one. The supervisors of projects like my boss, Ken Ralston, or Dennis Muren and many others were the stars. I did, however, work at Lucasfilm's Industrial Light and Magic (ILM) for twenty years, and ran a department for almost a decade.

This book is not a history of ILM or Lucasfilm, nor is it a biography of George Lucas. It represents my own personal views and experiences from a life in the movie business and is told in a narrative of vignettes that, like a script, sometimes flash either forward or back.

When I started at Industrial Light and Magic, the receptionist answered the phone saying, "Lucasfilm." Later that changed, but I refer to them both interchangeably in this book. Also, when I write "we" I mean the company, which may or may not include myself.

—Bill Kimberlin, California, 2016

The Gilded Cage

It is May 1982, Marin County, California. I am in George Lucas's editing room with a small group of production people sitting around a KEM film editing machine (a viewing device for the physical editing of picture and sound). George is explaining to us what he wants to happen in the space battle sequence of *Revenge of the Jedi,* the third in the original Star Wars series. I have been hired as the visual effects editor for this space battle.

The phone rings and we wait patiently. It is Steven Spielberg, and George starts describing how he wants the next Indiana Jones movie to open. "It should be a big Busby Berkeley–type dance number," he says and then proceeds to describe in detail what is to become the opening to the sequel of the wildly successful *Raiders of the Lost Ark.* How can he handle all of this at the same time? I'm thinking. We are all under intense pressure to finish this *Star Wars* sequel, and he is deeply involved in yet another blockbuster.

A few weeks earlier I had walked into a company of about 120 people called Industrial Light and Magic (ILM), where a lot of very smart people were working. There was, naturally, a lot of competition. You could feel the tension. For some, this would be a launching pad for their careers. This division of Lucasfilm alone would spawn at least two major directors, David Fincher (*The Social Network*) and Joe Johnston *(Honey, I Shrunk the Kids*); two major producers, Steve Starkey (*Forrest Gump*) and Colin Wilson (*Avatar*); and the creator of Photoshop, John Knoll. There were many others as well. I had survived in the independent film world, but could I survive here?

There is a term in motion picture production slang for a movie failing at the box office; it's called "dropping dead." I had directed one feature film of my own, *American Nitro,* which had gotten national distribution, and McGraw-Hill had released my documentary on the famous black boxer Jack Johnson (*Jeffries-Johnson 1910*; more on this later), and I hadn't dropped dead, at least not yet.

Here I was, thrust into the center of this movie moguldom, and my head was spinning ever so slightly. That was because the company ethos was to hand people buckets of responsibility and trust them to pull it off. The result for everyone was a perfect act of spine straightening. To paraphrase a famous line from *Star Wars*: "Do or do not." At ILM, there was no try.

At this point in his career, George had made *American Graffiti* in praise of his generation's cultural roots in cruising and rock 'n' roll music. While not an immediate smash hit, it was one of those pictures that just sat in theaters all across the country pumping out cash, week after week. Made for just $750,000—a rounding error in today's movie production world—it went on to earn $50 million. This picture alone made George and his wife, Marcia Griffin, independently wealthy. This was not supposed to happen: New directors are given a salary and perhaps a small percentage of the net profits of their film. However, the way Hollywood accounting is structured, there are almost never any net profits, no matter how successful the film. Yet this film cost so little, and made such huge profits, that there was no place left to hide them, and it paid off for the director like a slot machine.

George followed *Graffiti* with an ode to the old Flash Gordon movie serials that reran on suburban televisions in the 1950s. He called it *Star Wars*. In fact, he had tried to secure the rights to Flash Gordon at first, but finding them unobtainable, he wrote and directed his own version. While his friend Steven Spielberg had set a high bar with his movie *Jaws*, *Star Wars* soon surpassed it in both box office and cultural impact.

It was these two movies that changed the Hollywood business model forever. They proved that it was possible to sell just the sizzle. In many ways this was a positive change. The sheer power of the filmmaking itself came to the forefront with rapid editing, roaring soundtracks, and explosive visual effects, and the audience couldn't get enough of it. It now appeared plausible to adjust the calculus of what could be expected of motion picture entertainment investments. This is not to say that these particular films were not good movies, or even great movies—it was the opportunity to try to mimic their success that changed the dynamic of how Hollywood studios began to operate.

When asked once why Hollywood doesn't make good movies anymore, one candid movie producer remarked, "Because good movies are very, very hard to make. There is no formula for a good movie; it is a crap shoot at best." Hollywood would rather gamble ten times the money on a potential monster film with big stars and boatloads of special effects. Even if the movie isn't really any good, your odds of returning your investment are much, much higher. If the movie fails the producer is unlikely to be blamed too harshly, because they all would have bet on that same horse.

The game had changed for George Lucas as well. He had shrewdly bargained with the 20th Century Fox studio to retain the toy rights from the movie for himself, a tradeoff in exchange for a lower salary. Toy rights had been traditionally worthless, and the studio gladly gave most of them up. But there was one more thing George wanted after his most recent spectacular success: He wanted to own his own movies. Charlie Chaplin and Harold Lloyd owned their movies, but that other film genius of the silent era, Buster Keaton, did not and suffered as a result. Michael Jackson had purchased the Beatles song library after Paul McCartney passed on it, and those ownership rights helped him become a billionaire. Ownership was the model George wanted to follow.

The way for him to do this was to finance his own films from now on. In this way he, not the studio, would control the vast majority of any future profit from the two *Star Wars* sequels. The studio would receive a mere distribution fee. This act set the die for George and Marcia's future, but it also risked everything they had worked for. These movies would cost millions and millions of dollars to make.

By the time I entered the picture, George had made the *Star Wars* sequel (and arguably the best of the entire series) *The Empire Strikes Back* and had, with director Stephen Spielberg, cooked up an entirely different homage to old movie serials, *Raiders of the Lost Ark.* Now, with their combined power, Spielberg and Lucas offered a record-breakingly bad deal to the studios vying for the rights to distribute the new *Raiders,* and the studios eagerly accepted. All of this made for an exciting place to work. Silicon Valley hadn't really happened yet, and this felt like the center of the universe for anyone interested in motion pictures.

The ILM movie compound, where I worked, was spread out over several acres with different departments located in a cluster of industrial buildings. I always thought the name Industrial Light and Magic came from the real estate itself. When searching for a location where the messy end of filmmaking could take place (we blew things up), George must have encountered the term "light industrial," which is exactly how this area (and the original location in L.A.) would be described on the local county zoning maps. All he had to do was add the "magic." In any case, this was the industrial district, and you could pretty much do what you liked. If you needed to blow up a Star Destroyer, in all its wide-screen glory, this was the place to do it.

At about this time, George had decided to consolidate all of his filmmaking divisions into what would become Skywalker Ranch, a 5,000-acre movie ranch, at an eventual cost of at least $100 million. This ranch was in an isolated valley about a twenty-five-minute drive from ILM. It would include a $3.5 million recreational building for his employees with an Olympic-size swimming pool, indoor handball courts, and a restaurant. Across a lake from that complex would be a huge technical building with a sound stage large enough to record a hundred-piece symphony orchestra, multiple editing and sound mixing rooms, and a giant movie theater.

Somewhat removed from all of this would be George's office, a 50,000-square-foot building that looked like a Victorian hotel. This building would have an even larger restaurant with two dining rooms and a magnificent two-story library crowned with a stained glass dome. The artist who created all this stained glass would eventually break up George's marriage and run off with his wife, Marcia.

However, all of this was a long way, in both time and distance, from where I sat pondering my new life in this Marin industrial district. What we did here was far too offensive in dirt, dust, and noise; we were quarantined so as not to infect the moviemaking Shangri-la that George was building. We would be free to visit the Ranch whenever we wanted, and I would often take friends or family there for lunch and they would all be astonished. But in time the Ranch, while beautiful, began to seem very isolating. It was so far out of town that you couldn't reach any other lunch places in the time you had available. So essentially, no one could leave. For many of those who worked there, it came to represent a gilded cage, and we who worked in the real world eventually began to become cynical about the Ranch's splendor.

Those of us at ILM were the barnacled hull, and the Ranch was the part that stuck out of the water. Beautiful Lake Ewok, we renamed "Butthead Lake" among ourselves. Some of us even started calling the whole operation "Lucasland." But not yet. That was to come. Those early years still remain amazing to me—magical almost.

Decades later I would come across F. Scott Fitzgerald's description of Hollywood.

> *Under the moon the back lot was thirty acres of fairyland, not because the locations really looked like African jungles and French chateaux and schooners at anchor and Broadway at night, but because they looked like the torn picture books of childhood, like fragments of stories dancing in an open fire.*

His description was something like what I would experience. I would be introduced to fragments of fantasy, stored in the real world and this is something hard to forget.

Mrs. Hickman

My first few weeks were a blur of the new, and I had to get used to the ILM system. I worked as an editor in Special Visual Effects. It was our job to layer up shots, like making Dagwood sandwiches. Backgrounds, star fields, spaceships, monsters, explosions, actors—whatever the script called for. We worked off guides called storyboards. These were drawings showing the contents of the scene and the action expected. Every department had walls lined with hundreds of these cartoonlike visuals. Each one had a sequence title, like "Space Battle," and a scene number. Every day thousands of feet of motion picture film would arrive, either from the six large shooting stages at Elstree Studios in Great Britain, where the full-size *Millennium Falcon* was parked, or from any of the other more exotic locations around the world.

For the special effects shots we didn't use ordinary movie film—we used the huge images produced by an all-but-dead Hollywood format called VistaVision. Each frame was four times the size of a regular movie film frame, which gave us a tremendous advantage in retaining quality in the extensive duplicative processes we used to create the impossible.

During the years when television was threatening to take away the Hollywood moviegoing audience, all the major studios fought back with something that television could not compete with: wide-screen formats such as Cinerama and VistaVision. George rounded up the old cameras and projectors so he could shoot, project, and edit VistaVision right alongside the standard cameras.

George differed from the rest of Hollywood in that he not only made movies, but also wanted to advance the technology. Hollywood wasn't interested in investing in better equipment and methods. Their attitude was that if someone came up with something useful, they would just buy it. George, on the other hand, was developing a completely new electronic editing system and a better sound system for theaters, and was taking the early steps toward digital cinema.

We worked ten-hour days and fifty-hour weeks. These were all union jobs except for the executives, producers, and clerical staff. That meant you were paid a minimum of at least ten hours a week of overtime beyond your normal salary. Unlike the current high-tech world, we got paid for our endless hours. As the number of calendar days to the movie's release shrank, we would begin working six days a week and then seven, clocking dozens of hours of overtime and sometimes even double time. Also, at least in the early days, every worker's family shared in all the special Saturday screenings of the films we worked on and all of the gifts and lavish holiday parties, as well as the organic Thanksgiving turkeys that were handed out each year by the truckload.

Perhaps more than any of this was just the feeling that you belonged to something, something the world thought important. When one of the chief model makers got sick after flying to England with a bad cold that infected his brain, we got bulletins on his condition every morning before dailies, until it was announced that George showed up at the hospital and was "on the case." It was as if one were now part of a wealthy family—a third cousin at best, but still a part.

We laughed on seeing any new executive arrive all dressed in a suit and tie. That never lasted long. The poor guy would look around, see George Lucas in a flannel shirt and jeans, and quickly decide he was overdressed. Also, the executives were a little afraid of us. We knew how to make movies and they didn't. Their jobs depended on how well we did ours. We called them the "green carpet boys," as the front office was the only place in our building that had any carpet. My building, Building D, was basically a warehouse with tilt-up walls and roll-up doors that had been severely modified over the years to accommodate our needs.

Everything we did was done in secret. It had to be. The world at that time was crawling with *Star Wars* fans. Our buildings had no signs that would indicate who we were or what we were doing. The front door had lettering that said "The Kerner Company. Optical Research Lab." We left the sign as a kind of puzzle. We were located on Kerner Boulevard and we used optical printers for compositing our effects shots. Since one of our printers had been used to open the Red Sea in Cecil B. DeMille's *The Ten Commandments,* we thought of ourselves as just researching better ways to perform miracles.

We outfitted our crews with signs and T-shirts that had phony film names on them, like *Blue Harvest,* for our location shoots. People always ask what movie you are shooting, and since we couldn't say *Star Wars,* we came prepared with cover names, and that seemed to satisfy them.

Still, people showed up, having driven clear across the country just for a glimpse of anything related to their passion for the movies we made. One fan even entered our reception area and inquired suspiciously about the sign on our door, "What do you actually do here?" To which our resident former Marine replied, "We manufacture and *test* rectal thermometers."

They would go through the garbage and climb over the fences. To me it was living proof of the power that motion pictures have over people. It could be annoying, but it was also thrilling to watch all the madness.

One Saturday, things were kind of slow around the studio, so when I saw an outside telephone repair guy had brought his kids with him, I decided to have some fun. "Would you guys like to see Darth Vader?" Their dad said it was OK, so I took them over to the model shop, which had a fully costumed seven-foot-tall Darth Vader on a hidden mannequin. Also, R2-D2 and C-3PO were there. This was long before any commercial mock-ups of these characters were out in the real world. They were getting the "A" tour that hordes of movie fans only dreamed about. They were impressed, but I could tell that they were also slightly disappointed. The thrill we seek comes in darkened movie theaters. Without the lighting and music, without James Earl Jones's thundering Darth Vader voice, it was just an empty suit. This was an important lesson for me to learn, and there would be many more in the years to come.

It was George's birthday on the week I started. We were all in Building D's screening room watching what in filmmaking are called "dailies"—the raw, unedited footage that comes back from the lab every morning. George would sit in the center flanked by his key supervisors and his art director, Joe Johnston (now a major director). I would sit just behind his right shoulder to hear his instructions. Someone took detailed notes of everything we said as we viewed the footage. These notes, called the "Daily Report," were published and distributed to everyone an hour or so after the screening ended.

As we sat watching miles of VistaVision footage for what would eventually become the "Bike Chase" in *Jedi*, several Ewoks suddenly entered screen right holding a huge banner that said "Happy Birthday George." It got a big laugh and George kept saying, "Make sure that is in tonight's dailies at my house so Marcia can see it." George's wife Marcia was every bit a full partner in both the moviemaking and the empire-building. She was a first-rate film editor in her own right, having cut *Taxi Driver*, the seminal 1976 film directed by Martin Scorsese. In fact, I once saw her fashion an emotional scene out of some almost-scrap footage of two Ewoks talking. When she gave her opinion, people listened.

There was a small restaurant, more of a coffee shop really, close to my building, and some of us would walk over there after dailies in search of a donut or bagel. On about my second day on the job, I'm sitting there when George walks in, grabs a Styrofoam cup, and starts pouring himself some coffee. I remember thinking, doesn't this guy have anyone to go get coffee for him? But that wasn't it. He just wanted to lead a normal life like everyone else. I remember being with him in the screening room the morning that *ET* had surpassed *Star Wars* as the all-time box office champ. Someone asked him about it and he said, "Good, now maybe they will leave me alone."

Even though he had become wealthy and famous, and was becoming more powerful with every new film, George remained uncomfortable around people he didn't know. My friend Tim, who was a gentle soul, also worked for ILM and he told me that he walked up to George in the hallway once and stuck his hand out, saying something like, "Hello, Mr. Lucas, I've worked for you for over two years and I still haven't met you." Tim said that George almost leaped backwards in shock. Awkward moment. Even the elaborate Christmas parties were always slightly awkward, because they seemed to have no host. A simple "Thanks for coming" from George would have done the trick, but that never happened.

What George may have lacked in social skills, however, he more than made up for in his ability to make decisions on the spot, sometimes with millions of dollars at stake. Whenever George was around, the whole movie had a direction and could move forward, but when he was off in England or somewhere, the decisions would pile up. Should we tear that set down? We need the space for the next setup. Are we done? Does the cutting room have enough to work with? I remember him returning to our screening room after a couple of weeks' absence. There had been a lot of hand-wringing by producers because we were getting behind schedule. This was explained to him and he said, "You want decisions? Bring the lights down and roll the film, I'll give you decisions."

Believe me, not all directors can do that. Some are almost paralyzed with indecision. On *The Hunt for Red October*, ILM had picked up the underwater submarine work after some other effects company ran out of ideas on how to make it work. We were going over the deep-ocean sub tests we had faked with smoke and miniatures when the director, John McTiernan, starts into a speech about how "there is actually no light at all down at this depth, you know." Good lord, I thought, you've been on this movie a year now and you're still talking about that? Hey, guess what, there is no sound in space either. What do you want us to do, withdraw *Star Wars* from distribution? It's called suspension of disbelief. It is the anchor of all theatrical drama. No wonder you are behind. Let's get on with it. Of course, I kept my mouth shut.

I always felt that directors that came to ILM for their effects work were like kids being handed the keys to a Ferrari. Some could handle it and we made them rich. Others couldn't handle it and they ran off the road, crashed, and burned. But even some of these got rich as well. It got so that just having our logo on a film was a draw. It became like having the name Dolby Stereo on a theater marquee—the audience didn't really know what it meant, but if your theater didn't have it, you lost out.

But all of that was still in my future. For now I was walking down the hallway of Building D dodging the little people that we had hired to play Ewoks as they swarmed toward the big stage in their costumes. I saw a lot of things in that hallway. One time I was coming back from lunch and I was wearing a felt hat that I had bought. It looked a little like the famous Indiana Jones hat from the *Raiders* movies. Well, Harrison Ford was coming the other way. He smiled at me and started to turn into editorial, when all of a sudden he turned back to me in a classic double take. It was the hat, and for once in his life he was the one staring.

The whole star thing must be annoying. I remember seeing Red Skelton in San Francisco once. I was crossing the street just past I. Magnin, a luxury department store, and Skelton was walking right towards me. I didn't notice him at first, but when I did, he saw it in my eyes and beamed at me. The very famous spend their lives anticipating you are going to notice them. They know it's coming and they wait for it, and it's a small relief to them when it arrives.

I had grown up in this same Marin County where the Lucasfilm empire was now located. It was always a well-to-do suburb of San Francisco, just across the Golden Gate Bridge from the city. I remember my introduction to motion picture magic was when my mother took me to see the set of the movie *Blood Alley,* starring John Wayne and Lauren Bacall and directed by William Wellman, in about 1954. The movie scouts had located an old Chinese fishing village called "China Camp," which was actually not far from Lucasfilm's Industrial Light and Magic, where I now worked. The thing I remember is that as my mother and I walked into the camp, which had been dressed to look like it was actually in China, I saw a large stack of boulders piled up to one side, but when I brushed against them, they moved. It surprised me. How could they move, I barely touched them? Ah, they are fake. The movie guys had made them out of paper and expertly painted them to look real. I was struck with the idea that adults actually had jobs doing things like this, and they worked in the make-believe world of motion pictures. I was seven. Duly noted.

By the time I was twelve years old, I was still in Marin but my parents were both dead. My father had died of a stroke, or so I thought, and then when I was maybe seven or eight, I started to realize that my mother was terribly ill. She had acquired hepatitis during my birth, but while my father was alive she had been able to keep it in check. Now it started to worsen, and her doctors advised selling the big old San Francisco house with its three floors of stairways. So she moved back to Marin to be close to her family. She bought a single-level house in an exclusive area of

Kentfield that had servants' quarters and was a short drive to her brother and her aunt, who everyone called Aunt Bobbitt.

My brother wouldn't say it, but he knew she was going to die. We had arguments about it where I maintained that she could still get well. How dreadful and fearful those conversations were. I remember thinking, what will we do, what will happen to us?

She was in and out of the hospital and spent a lot of time in bed. I remember coming home from summer vacation and visiting her bedroom where she spent most days now, lying down. I was happy to be home and almost skipping around the house when I heard her say, "If he would slow down for a minute, I would give him a kiss."

That was a shock—our family was not huggers and kissers. My mother never kissed me or held me. She would use her handkerchief, wet by her tongue, to clean my face if it was dirty, but that was about as intimate as it got. It never bothered me. It was normal—she loved us but just didn't outwardly show it. I had slept over at a friend's house one time and told him about all this, and his mother came in and kissed me good-night that evening. She must have overheard me.

The worst part came one evening when I was watching television and the news came on. During the newscast the anchor said, "We are sending out an appeal. Please give blood for Margaret Kimberlin, who needs it very badly." I couldn't believe my ears. He was talking about my mother!

She died the day before my birthday. I received all these presents that I was so anxious to get, yet I was riddled with guilt for caring more about my toys than my mother. Our sheltered life evaporated quickly as the high walls of a relatively wealthy family began to dissolve.

Slowly, everything in the house got sold or was given away, including my dog. They told me she went to a ranch family, but I never believed that. All my toys, everything was gone, including the house, which was sold at a slight loss. That house is still there today, and when I worked in Marin, years later, I used to drive over and sit in front of it. It was like waking up from a bad dream, but it wasn't a dream. Somehow my connection to generations of family had been wiped out here, and it had taken me decades to understand the power of that.

My brother Jimmy and I were split up. He went to live with our Uncle DeWitt, who had six children, and I went to live with our Great-Aunt Bobbitt. We made the best of it. I didn't like living with my great-aunt because she just seemed so ancient. She had never learned to drive, which was unusual for California, and she always referred to a car as "the machine." She would say, "Jimmy, bring the machine around."

I slept in the living room in her small one-bedroom apartment. We lived right next to the hospital where my mother had died. This was good and bad. It brought back painful memories for me, but there had been a good side to my mother's last months. Bobbitt had been a professional nurse, and she could walk to mother's room every day to make sure she was properly cared for. Also, near the end, she made sure the will was correct and that a guardian was selected to take care of us.

Years later I worked with a woman who, having heard a little about my childhood, said to me, "You are remarkably unscrewed up for having gone through that." This surprised me because I guess it had never occurred to me that I might have been "screwed up" by this. She also said, "I envy you because you know exactly what you want, and I have no idea of what I want." She was right: I did know what I wanted, and it started with my second encounter with the movie business.

Great-Aunt Bobbitt had a next-door neighbor in the apartment building named Mrs. Hickman who left her television running day and night. Like my great-aunt, this neighbor just seemed to be another little old lady to me. Whenever I went over to her place to bring things my aunt wanted her to have, the TV was always blaring. One day I asked my aunt about this and she said, "Oh, she doesn't want to miss the broadcast of any old movies. You're too young to remember, but do you know who she is? That's Bessie Barriscale and she was the biggest silent-screen star in the country in 1910, and for a few years afterward. Her husband was a film director."

In the 1950s television was relatively new and they filled airtime with hundreds of old movies, which they could get for practically nothing. The TV stations broadcast them almost randomly. You never knew when something might appear, as the TV schedules were sketchy at best. So

Bessie ran the television day and night, to catch not only her old films, but those of all her movie pals.

She was a major star for Thomas Ince and was directed by Cecil B. DeMille in *Rose of the Rancho*, which was a hit in 1914. Bessie had played opposite William Desmond Taylor in *Not My Sister,* and in later years her friend Mary Pickford cast her as her daughter in *Secrets*.

When I started studying film in college, I began to learn who some of these people were. Thomas Ince commanded a large Hollywood studio, and some say he was murdered by William Randolph Hearst, on the Hearst yacht. And when the great *Sunset Boulevard* was made, with Gloria Swanson playing the faded silent film star, she was given the composite screen name of Norma Desmond as an echo to great silent star names of the past, including Bessie's former costar, William Desmond Taylor.

It was this long-ago neighbor, Mrs. Hickman, that introduced me to the idea that a person could actually work in motion pictures.

The Droid Olympics

Along with the amazing roster of talented people that worked at Lucasfilm when I started in 1982 was an even larger group of people who might otherwise have been canning peas or working as secretaries. They had no film background or motion picture experience of any kind. Yet, through happenstance or pure luck, they had been swept into this relatively new and hugely successful company in every conceivable position from receptionist to horse wrangler at the Ranch. After a few months many of these employees would conclude that they were now in the motion picture business and that there should be no limit to their ambitions. Indeed, over the years there appeared to be no limit. One of the original receptionists became the head of all production. A woman that started off on the maintenance crew, empting the trash baskets, became a top digital engineer that now works at Pixar, the hugely successful animation company.

In part, the company was a meritocracy where anyone who was smart and ambitious had an opportunity to advance. As with most companies, the tone was set from the top, and that was George Lucas. He had come from nowhere, and the message to the employees was that you could come from nowhere too and still succeed. There was no better example of this than Chris, a young fellow I came to know while helping him get a small film made for a college project.

Years earlier, George had been looking for someone to watch over his enormous Skywalker Ranch property as it was being developed, and Chris related to me how he came to be that person. He met for his interview with George and Marcia Lucas at their home in San Anselmo, California. They had purchased the oldest house in Marin County after the success of *American Graffiti* and had returned it to the elegant mansion it once had been. Sometime late in the interview, Chris, who was only twenty-three or so, asked whether, if he were hired, his friends could visit. "Of course," George said. "This will be your home."

Just at that moment there was a light knock on the door and George's executive secretary and gatekeeper, Jane Bay, stuck her head in and said, "I'm sorry to bother you, George, but I have Sir Laurence Olivier on the phone, and he wishes to speak with you." What happened next still puzzled Chris a little bit as he related, "George said to her, 'I'm talking to Chris right now. Tell him I'll call back.'" That doesn't happen in Hollywood.

The flip side of this field of opportunities was the minefield of ambitions it set off in some, and I would have plenty of firefights with these individuals in the days and years to come.

Early on, the big question in my mind was whether I could compete in the deep end of the pool where the highly skilled people swam. I was about to find out.

Every year there was an event called the Droid Olympics, pitting the editorial staff of all the local film companies against each other. On a given weekend we would gather at Walter Murch's house in Inverness. Walter is a legend in the film business for his talents as an editor, sound designer, and author. He represents those amazingly talented people that make directors' movies so much better than they otherwise would have been. His editing and sound design work on *Apocalypse Now* and *The Godfather*, to name just two, is a large part of what makes such an indelible impression on everyone who sees the films. What really sets him apart, however, is his ability to write and lecture on filmmaking. He is the only film professional I have ever met who not only excels at the craft, but can also give an explanation of the intellectual framework of making movies that is profound and effective.

The Friday before the event, George came by the effects editorial department at ILM to deliver the T-shirts he designed for us to wear as part of his team. Whenever I got the chance, I always tried to say something provocative to him just to see if I could get him to talk or tell moviemaking "war stories" like we all did when we got together outside of work. Sometimes it worked, sometimes it didn't. This time I said something stupid like, "With these shirts, how can we lose?" He turned to me with a weird look and said, "At my rate, those are the most expensive T-shirts you will ever own."

In the movie business everyone has a rate—that is, if they are not studio staff people. They work by contract for a given period of time at their given rate. A feature film editor in those days might have made $10,000 a week, which sounds like a lot of money except for the fact that months can go by without any work. This feast-or-famine style of income makes it hard for many people to handle their finances. In a sense, if you work in production, you are fired every Friday. That's payday. You get paid every week and if they are going to let you go, that's when it happens. Your goal is to keep getting jobs one after another. This often means no vacations because you are afraid if you turn work down, the next time they won't call you. You are like an actor, waiting for the phone to ring. This became my life.

I don't know what George's rate was or how he calculated it back then, but for a guy worth about $100 million, it had to be substantial. Still, except for his building sprees, he wasn't ostentatious. After the *Empire Strikes Back* came out and was a big success another employee told me, "We all noticed that George got new tires for his Camaro."

Oh, and I still have the T-shirt.

The Droid events were inspired by cutting room tasks that we were all way too familiar with. For instance, who could run the fastest time across the yard and back carrying and not dropping an impossibly high load of empty cardboard trim boxes (used to hold film trims or clips) in their arms. Or who could spin the highest number on the footage counter that is attached to a film synchronizer (which holds picture and soundtrack in sync when winding film). Silly stuff like that.

When my turn came, I did all of the tasks fairly well except one: running an upright Moviola editing machine, blindfolded, and stopping it when you thought one minute on the time counter had passed. I did it perfectly. I hit the brake on exactly one minute, which shot my score up. All our names were up on a big blackboard and the scores were updated immediately. When I hit the highest score on the board, George, who at that time barely knew who I was, walked over and said, "Nice job." This from a man who never talked to anyone he didn't know very well.

This was a lesson. This guy was so competitive that he could rise out of his reticence if he spotted a winner. My score subsequently sank and I turned back into a pumpkin, but it was fun while it lasted. Now he knew who I was.

Originally, *Return of the Jedi* was called *Revenge of the Jedi*. George had decided to change the name of the movie reportedly because some little kid wrote and reminded him that Jedis don't seek revenge. Whether they do or not, I have no idea. We all admired and respected George Lucas as a brilliant filmmaker, but after months of work in the trenches trying to pull this movie off, the fantasy stuff had rubbed us a little raw. When the executives and lawyers at the Ranch asked the employees to come up with a name for the company's central computer system, my department suggested Rochester, after the famed black character portrayed by Eddie Anderson on the old Jack Benny television program. Rochester was supposed to be a valet to Benny but he always got the better of his boss. We hoped for the same results. Instead they chose Endor, which was the moon where the Ewoks lived in the redwood forests. Yikes.

Still, if we thought something was so strained as to be camp, we would adopt it ourselves. We found many uses for the line "Many Bothans died to bring you this information." I still like the sentiment in "Do. Or do not. There is no try," because that comes directly out of George's personality. He had spent his entire early career with people, sometimes important people, telling him, "You can't do that." Henry Ford had said it before, in a slightly different way: "Whether you think you can, or you think you can't—you're right." I was the recipient of some of this Lucas wisdom one day when I wasn't expecting it.

I was still pretty green when George wandered into editorial looking for my boss. "Where's Ken?" he asked. "They've all gone to lunch," I said. He asked if I could show him the shot, so I took him into the room we called "line-up" where we fashioned the effects shots on these huge old VistaVision editing machines. You could stack multiple layers of movie film, each with its own fighter craft, and run them all at once on these machines. You could also make drawings on clear acetate animation cells for planning modifications, like making all the spaceships fly in patterns. I ran the shot for him and he said something like, "Take this X-wing and blow him up, right at this frame." For some reason I opened my mouth and said, "I don't think we can do that." Wrong answer. George turned to me and said, "Of course we can," with such force that I instantly glimpsed what had got him where he was. Absolute certainty.

What did I know about blowing up spaceships? This guy had probably blown up hundreds of them, as well as destroying thousands of stormtroopers. George hadn't been angry and he didn't shout, but he woke me up. I had things to learn.

Most of what I learned was from my boss Ken Ralston. He was a tall, somewhat thin, twenty-eight-year-old effects director, who at first seemed somewhat young to handle all the responsibilities George had given him. He had an almost goofy cartoonist's sense of self-deprecating humor, and he effectively shielded that he was as ambitious as any of the other star employees. He was an artist who could draw well and he always sat a drawing board, not a desk. He was quite smart and would memorize every shot, its description, and shot number on whatever movie he was working on. He won five Oscars while at ILM.

When Ken was finally hired away after twenty years by Sony Pictures Imageworks, they made him president and creative head, with what would become a multimillion-dollar salary. The head of Sony, remarking about Ken, said, "Talent loves him." Translated from Hollywood-speak, that means that all the top directors (somewhat dismissively referred to here as "talent") liked and respected him. Some of us noticed that the Oscars we were accustomed to winning abated for a while after Ken left.

What Ken was doing was mounting models of spaceships or even the DeLorean from *Back to the Future* on mechanical stands that could be controlled both by hand and by computer while filming. Our cameras rode on dollies mounted on tracks so they could swoop past, say, a mounted fighter aircraft from *Star Wars* or the steam engine in *BTTF* while the models themselves sat still, yet moved their wings or tilted.

Each frame of motion picture film was shot in a timed exposure with our camera shutters open for perhaps a second or more to capture enough light—all this in front of a large screen that was backlit a bright blue. We could then optically suck out the blue, leaving just the model to be placed against whatever background we wished. As the audience would have no frame of reference as to size, we could make believers of them when we placed, say, a star field for a space movie or a street scene for the flying car behind our models. One documentary film about how we did our work was called *How to Film the Impossible,* and that was about the size of it.

There was one monster shot in *Return of the Jedi* that I worked on with Ken that first year, called SB19. It was the nineteenth shot in the space battle and is pictured on the cover of this book. This was the shot that George had told Ken that he wanted to be a "wow" shot. Ken had set up four camera crews shooting the battling spaceships for three months just to get this shot. It contained sixty-three separate elements. I've never researched it, but it may have been the most complicated effects shot ever optically composited. It would take about ten hours when it came time for the final printing onto a blank piece of raw film negative as spaceships, planets, star fields, laser cannons, explosions, etc., were burned in, one at a time, rewinding the raw stock after each addition. If even the slightest error was made, you had to start all over again.

Why go to these lengths? It was a calculation. George knew how to entertain an audience and hold their attention. He would open a movie with either an action sequence like the chase in the original *Raiders of the Lost Ark* or the seemingly endless underbelly of the Star Destroyer in the original *Star Wars* to give the audience a wonderful shock of seeing what seemed to be just a glimpse of the amazing visual treats in store for them. Once the audience felt they were in the safe hands of a movie master, George could afford to introduce his characters and story points without fear of losing them. When it worked correctly, he owned the audience.

I had boxes and boxes and more boxes of film on my desk, all pieces of a giant jigsaw puzzle called SB19. I hadn't designed it or shot it; that was George, Ken, and the art director Joe Johnson's work. But I had to put it together and some of the spaceships wouldn't work as shot, so I manipulated them by turning their flight paths upside down. In other cases, I borrowed ships from other shots or other movies. We had tons of reusable elements from the two earlier *Star Wars* films. This was long before computer graphics or digital filmmaking. In a way, we just hammered on stuff until we made it work.

It took about two weeks to come up with a rough black-and-white temporary composite of the shot. We were all a little nervous about how this might go over with George. Art, who ran the editorial department at the time, said he thought we would be chewing over this shot for a long time. One of the many coordinators called George's cutting room in the adjoining building, and he walked over to take a look. I ran it for him and he said, "Great." That was it. His most frequent expression of approval, and I was glad to get it.

Now the arduous color compositing process began, using all the original camera negatives that had been shot, but that was someone else's job. It took two tries to get it right, and there is still a tiny flaw in it which no one will ever see but me. It took almost a year to get that shot from start to finish, so keep that in mind if you ever see the movie. Oh, and look quickly, because it's only two seconds long.

I had slowly started to rise out of obscurity at the company. The BBC came by and used my SB19 shot to illustrate the world of special effects in a nationally telecast program both in Britain and in the United States. They filmed Ken and me reenacting our roles. I was at the editing machines and Ken was the creative mastermind. This show helped demonstrate the complexity of creating this movie magic that was starting to change the way that motion pictures were made, marketed, and financed.

High School Reunion

I WAS SITTING IN SCREENING ROOM D WAITING FOR *JEDI* DAILIES TO begin. George had just taken his usual seat in the center of the second row, just to the right of a small control panel that held a shaded lamp and some lighted pointers that were used by directors and supervisors to point out any details on the projected images that might be up for discussion.

We were all watching VistaVision foreground plates of Admiral Ackbar. We were basically looking over the shoulder of a guy with a rubber head sitting at some kind of spaceship controls as he gazed out into space. Of course, there was no space to look at yet because we hadn't added it. No stars, no planets, nothing but a giant blue screen. There were miles of this footage and George was looking for a section he wanted to use in *Jedi*. One of the supervisors, probably Richard Edlund, asked George what the window Akbar was looking out of was made of. George said, "Well, that hasn't come up. When it does come up, we will figure out an answer."

So *that* was it, I thought. That was the whole thing! We were all sitting here participating in a story that George was making up as we went along. When you are telling a made-up story to children, you only add certain details. The others you wait for the children to ask about.

This was the Monday after George had gone to his high school reunion in Modesto, California, where he grew up. Who hasn't fretted about, or dreamed about, going to their high school reunion? What would it be like to return to your small rural school as one of the richest, most celebrated people in the world?

While we had always joked among ourselves about the movie business being "high school, with money," with this visit somehow George had tied the two together and I began to wonder, who is this guy, anyway? Why is he so different? How did a D student from Modesto, California, become the biggest director and movie mogul of all time? So I drove down to Modesto one weekend to see what I could find out.

I saw the town, the high school, the family home, etc. But to me it was the store that told the most. There it was in the downtown area, the family business, an office supply store run by George's father. I had seen the father once out at the Ranch wandering around with a huge smile on his face. He certainly must have been a proud father. I imagined that the Modesto store told the whole story. It could not have been more mid-America looking, run by a hard-working businessman who had spawned a dutiful son.

I had read that George, at first unhappy with college, had called his father asking how long he had to stick it out. It struck me that it was the father who had cast the die for this talented young man. Just as all the male characters in *American Graffiti* were different facets of George, his father's rock-solid, small-town business acumen loomed over his creative work and his ability to build what would eventually become a multibillion-dollar empire.

His wife Marcia often said that George was "centered," meaning he was comfortable with himself and his ability to achieve his goals. But there was much more. After achieving success, he had deliberately left Hollywood and moved to Northern California, away from the creative echo chamber of the studios that were fraught with gossip, celebrity, and trend-followers. That was the opposite of what almost everyone else did.

George also made smart business deals, passing over short-term gains and investing in long-term ones instead. He built his own studio and staffed it with an army of creative people who were happy to work outside the rigid studio systems of Los Angeles. He wrote and developed his own projects, hiring screenwriters to help structure the stories. He invested in new technologies designed to enhance the moviegoing experience as well as simplify the production processes that would speed things up and save money. Above all, he avoided debt like the plague, remembering how it had once brought down and almost destroyed the dreams of his friend Francis Coppola.

In addition, George was able to identify trends and evaluate their worth. I remember one time when there was a lot of talk in Hollywood about bringing interactivity to movies and it being suggested that the audience be allowed to choose, for example, how a film would end. George's remark was succinct and accurate: "Interactive is games. How hard is that to figure out?" Soon we had a Games Division.

These attributes set him apart from most of Hollywood and the rest of the business world as well. I would argue that not since Thomas Edison and Henry Ford have we seen a more ambitious creative artist. And for these characteristics to be part of an artist is, I think, even more unusual. So far, it seems that Steve Jobs is the one to have received most of the plaudits, but I think the more Lucas's accomplishments are recognized, the higher his stock will rise.

On top of all this, George was just a good filmmaker. I've seen his student films and they all showed talent. It's true that he barely escaped high school, but once he got to college and found he could make movies, he just got better and better at it.

None of the great directors of the past had gone to film school, yet our generation of filmmakers had. While attending my school I always wondered what effect our little films, and all the underground films, art films, and independent films, would have. Would they survive? Would they be saved and someday be of any note, however small? As yet, they are neither saved nor recognized. However, they did influence Hollywood theatrical movies, especially in the 1970s. The film-school era replaced what were in large part filmed plays with an almost silent-era style of filmmaking that had been lost since the advent of sound. Suddenly we saw camera work, editing, and sound design with the same enthusiasm as that of pioneers like Abel Gance, Sergei Eisenstein, and Erich von Stroheim. There was a reason that on the wall in back of my editorial department bench there hung a huge black-and-white photograph of Eisenstein hard at work editing one of his films.

While George's locating a motion picture company in Northern California may have seemed like a crazy idea to Hollywood, there was in actuality a precedent. This was where, in 1872, Eadweard Muybridge took his famous series of stop-motion photographs of Leland Stanford's trotting horse, Occident, that when projected became animated photographic movement, leading eventually to the invention of motion pictures. This was where, in 1916, Leon Douglas invented and patented the first natural-color motion picture method which later became Technicolor. It's where Charlie Chaplin, also in 1916, filmed the most famous exit in cinema history: the last shot in *The Tramp*, where he walks away from the camera down that lonely dirt road. Lastly, it is where, in 1927 in San Francisco, Philo T. Farnsworth invented the first television. All of this far from the movie capital of Hollywood and the financial center of New York.

It has been said that George was trying to escape the trade unions by coming north; however, he quickly signed up with the local unions and we were all members. I think it was mostly to get away from the stifling atmosphere of Hollywood. Here in Northern California one was freer to create new things and try out new ideas. Coming to the Bay Area meant entering the triangle of creative technologies that exists between the University of California at Berkeley, the juggernaut of Stanford University and Silicon Valley, and the soon-to-be-center of digital creativity, San Francisco.

The author Rebecca Solnit has observed that "the two industries that have most powerfully defined contemporary life . . . Hollywood and Silicon Valley . . . are responsible for that part of a new world made from an amalgamation of technology and entertainment. We live today in the future launched there."[1]

All of these elements led to the birth of digital filmmaking, not in Hollywood or New York, but in the Bay Area, and I think George deserves credit for that. The goal is to always understand the present, not to predict the future.

1. Rebecca Solnit, *River of Shadows: Eadweard Muybridge and the Technological Wild West* (New York: Viking, 2003).

What's It Like?

I WAS PART OF A CROWD ONE TIME THAT WAS WATCHING A FEATURE film being shot in San Francisco. After a while a guy in the crowd turned to his wife and said, "Oh, I get it. They film just a little bit at a time and then they put it all together." A lot of people probably think that the camera crew just follows the actors around filming them until they have a two-hour movie. That is, if they think about it at all, which most don't. And why should they? It would just spoil the fun.

Still, I am often asked, "What's it like to work in the movie business?" Well, it is a lot like the construction business. You gather a group of skilled workers together for a given project and you create a skyscraper in one case, or a motion picture in the other. People work in specialties just like any other business: soundman, cameraman, script writer, computer graphics artist, supervisor, director, editor, etc. You either work freelance or for a studio of some type, large or small.

I went to film school to get started. They had equipment you could check out and an audience to show your work to, and hopefully learn from. That's the thing—you need a group of like-minded people to make films. It's a collaborative process. No matter how many big-shot movie directors you hear talking about making their latest film, just remember they had a lot of help. When you see a lousy film by an otherwise great director, chances are he changed his crew. He was no longer working with the writer, cinematographer, editor, and producer he worked with on his better films.

My experience was that I made documentaries and then, in 1970, got a job at a small production company that did everything from processing film to shooting and editing them for clients. I started in the sound department and worked my way up to film editor while making my own movies on the side. Eventually I was invited to screen my only feature film, *American Nitro,* at ILM, and about one minute into it, someone in the audience yelled out, "Has George seen this?" I was working there about a month later. Lucas at the time was an important director who was building his own studio. It turned out that I would go on to work in special visual effects on a lot of famous motion pictures, from *Star Wars* to *The Gangs of New York*.

Movie productions can be a lot like battle zones. There are days of intense boredom shockingly interrupted by incoming mortar rounds landing in your camp. In my case, the incoming ordnance that set off our firefights were cases of motion picture film. It all has to be screened, organized, and cataloged so it can be retrieved instantly. The director watches all the film with his team of editor, producer, cinematographer, and script supervisor. He notes the scenes and takes that he especially likes, and those are sent to his cutting room, where his editor and assistants are assembling a rough cut of the film shot so far. They are guided by the film script only in a general sense, as the story may have been seriously altered during shooting. Sometimes the script is thrown out entirely and the movie is made in the cutting room.

Occasionally the director will schedule a screening room and project his first rough edit to see how it hangs together. This is the moment of truth: Is it working or not?

These are confidential closed screenings with very few people attending because the film is in its most raw state, with no music, no visual or sound effects, rough unpolished dialogue, and a continuity that may need weeks or months of further editing to make it work. The slightest rumor of troubles with a picture at this point could send ripples back to the studio that financed the movie, returning as a tidal wave of trouble for the director. So it is a delicate time for all the creative workers involved.

Just to give you an idea of what these early versions of films are like, I remember being at the ILM studio one time looking through boxes of old archived film footage when I ran across the work print and soundtrack from the original *Star Wars*. This was a reel of picture and a reel of sound from one sequence in the first film. It comprised some of the opening scenes inside a spaceship with Princess Leia trying to escape some stormtroopers. I threaded it up on my KEM film editing machine to have a look. This was not the finished movie—it was the final edit but the music, sound mix, visual effects, color grading, etc., were all not present. It just had the raw sync soundtrack that was recorded when the images were shot. You could hear the actors but the dialogue was intended to be replaced by rerecording the same actors later in a sound studio. That is why Hollywood movies sound so good and your home movies don't.

Watching it was an eye-opener. Without the final polish it looked awful, worse than amateurish. The prop guns made fizzing and popping sounds when fired, with fake-looking sparks spitting out the front of them. The actors were yelling and it was hard to hear what they were saying, and on top of that you could hear George from somewhere behind the camera yelling, "Look to your left! Look to your left!" It was like seeing the picture of Dorian Gray as a dissipated wreck while Dorian the man lived on as a perpetually fresh-faced young fellow. It is no wonder that directors are very selective about who sees these early primitive cuts. A whole production crew can get soured on any given movie if word leaks out that "the part I saw looked terrible."

The original *Star Wars* crew was no exception, and I could see why it was rumored that they didn't expect much from it. A similar thing happened to George at a major screening of *American Graffiti*. The film was almost finished but the head of the studio pronounced it "unreleasable."

Famously, Francis Coppola was just short of being fired on the original *Godfather* because the early rushes looked bad to the studio and his crew was primed to revolt, having been egged on by his first cinematographer who, thank God, Francis fired on a Friday knowing the studio couldn't find a replacement director until Monday, by which time Francis had regained control.

The difference between the rough early assemblage of a movie and the final polished version released to theaters is, to borrow a phrase from Mark Twain, "the difference between the lightning bug and the lightning."

That is partly why George Lucas called the division of Lucasfilm that I worked for "Industrial Light and Magic." Because moviemaking is a craft at its base, which with the right collaboration of artists, can become art. But it takes a kind of *magic* to make it all happen—that rare mix of technology, money, business acumen, talent, and luck.

So that is the general landscape of one part of the movie business. The director John Huston once described it as "an adventure shared by desperate men that finally comes to nothing." That may be a little grandiose, but it still has the ring of truth to it. There is a story that when Huston was directing Marilyn Monroe, she was so distraught about something at one point that he had to remind her, "Marilyn, it's only a movie." It's true, we aren't saving lives here, we are just making entertainment.

One other thing about the movie business that most people don't know is that many famous film directors don't actually know how to make a movie. This is something that movie critics never seem to understand. There is a certain amount of craft to moviemaking, technical stuff that not many directors know about. I am not saying that great filmmakers are not great just because they are not expert in cinematography and editing. What I am saying is that there is a difference between directors and filmmakers. If you gave George Lucas two months and a hundred pounds of film, he could deliver you a movie. He could write, shoot, and edit it himself. Steven Spielberg can direct brilliant movies, but he once said that when he tried to edit something himself, he was all thumbs and chasing the splicing tape under the editing table.

Part of this is because Lucas was one of the first big-time directors to come out of a film school. John Ford didn't go to film school. Like Sergei Eisenstein before him, George picked up on using the strengths of pure filmmaking to bring a fresh experience to movies. He used cutting and sound as dramatic elements, much as Eisenstein had used rhythmic editing in the famous "Steps" sequence in *The Battleship Potemkin*. This was movie school stuff brought to Hollywood pictures.

This slightly different way of doing things had benefits. Before the spaceships had been shot for the original *Star Wars,* George used old World War II dogfight footage from a battle-for-the-Pacific-type documentary and cut in the footage almost like a musician "samples" other music for their compositions. The footage added excitement and helped to block out the needed action. It also made it easier to test-screen the movie, eliminating "scene missing" titles for the audience. Even as late as *The Phantom Menace,* he was having us send him clips from famous movies that we pulled off of videos in a library of classic movies that I had put together. He wanted to scrape them for ideas. It was the filmmaker in him. He knew exactly what he could get away with and he actually cut some of this stuff into what was by this time a digital movie, as temporary ideas. Several years earlier he had shot the whole *Young Indiana Jones* TV series in 16mm. Nobody in Hollywood would do that because they didn't know that, technically, 16mm was perfect for television.

By the time I got to Lucasfilm, it was the early 1980s and everyone was still working with film. *Jedi* was shot on film, so we used what were called "work prints" to edit and project. The main elements of filmmaking had not changed much over the past seventy-five years or so, and I knew a lot about film because I had been working with it every day for the past twelve years. It was said at the time that if a person were to load up one of the old studio cameras from the silent film days, film a scene, and then project it, except for advances in film emulsions and camera lenses, the projected image would look every bit as good as any modern-day film, possibly even better.

If there was a "golden era" in our pre-digital blockbuster factory, it was probably while I was there during the 1980s through most of the 1990s. We were holed up in warehouses creating major movie entertainment, while Silicon Valley seemed to prefer garages for their work. We used old tilt-up industrial buildings that we expanded as if we were constructing the home of the haunted armaments widow who was afraid that if she stopped building her Winchester Mystery House, she would die. Like her, we dared not stop building and expanding. There were actually abandoned second-floor doors that now only opened to air. We simply nailed them shut. There was just no time for architectural nuances—those were for George and the Ranch. We had to just keep going, nonstop. It was somewhat frantic, yet it could be compelling as well.

We were characterized by men, models, and machines. We did it by hand. We built stuff, and flew stuff, and blew stuff up. Once, to get an effect, my boss, Ken Ralston, trained a high-speed camera on a fat yellow pumpkin which he then exploded with a double-barrel shotgun blast. We literally made these movies using whatever was available to us. The model shop would buy plastic model kits by the truckload and scour them for usable parts. It was called "shopping it." If it could be found in a store, we grabbed it.

Back then we were, of course, exposing our images on celluloid that was coated with a light-sensitive emulsion. We then edited that celluloid film by feel and by rhythm as much as anything else. You may not have realized what you just did in editing, but when you screened it and your physical splices ran through a film projector, you could hear a click at every edit, which brings an unintentional beat that you could sense. That beat revealed a pace and structure that lay underneath, unseen and independent of the finished movie, with its soundtrack, that you would later watch. But during assembly it was a clue to creating a compelling experience for the audience.

To some extent, these are just little creative accidents that you become aware of in any physical process of making art. It's not that they are totally lost today in digital filmmaking or computer graphics—they are just different now. New things are discovered, but these were some of ours.

Since *Jedi* was the third *Star Wars* film in the original series, we would often go back and use elements from the two earlier films to build scenes for the new one. We were just copying what we had learned working for George: Films are made in the editing room, and you can do any damn thing you can get away with. We kept all kinds of things that had been expensive to shoot originally, like explosions and clouds. We had rented a huge auditorium called the Cow Palace in San Francisco during the making of *The Empire Strikes Back* to shoot large explosions. High-speed cameras were mounted on the floor, looking to the rafters, while firebomb explosives were dropped toward them from the ceiling far above. The idea was to capture pure slow-motion explosions in all their colorful glory. The extreme slow motion gives the explosions scale. They looked huge. Hundreds of them had been shot with these cameras, and they were now all carefully filed away in our film vaults for reuse in current projects.

In another case a Learjet was rented that had a belly-mounted VistaVision camera. This was used to get huge puffy clouds that all kinds of model aircraft could be made to seem to fly through. We used these expensive-to-shoot elements over and over again. Later, when I ran the ILM feature editorial department, I remember selling $50,000 worth of cloud elements to Disney. So the payoffs of this kind of filmmaking could extend for years.

I had finally gotten far enough to be actually working on big-time movies, and although I was just a minnow compared to the directors, I still had some things in common with them. I *also* knew how to make a movie, and I was delighted one day when George was at the KEM editing machine reviewing a shot and someone said, "That cut crosses the arch" (a slight continuity error in an image sequence), and George replied, "That's film school stuff—we're making a movie here." Once you learn the rules, then you can break them. That's what filmmakers do, and that's what was starting to happen for me working in the movie business.

Hollywood

When Lucasfilm sneaked *Star Wars: Return of the Jedi* in early 1983, it was done a little differently. They arranged with a large theater to run it without any advance notice. Once the audience was seated, an announcer walked up to the front of the theater and apologized that the film they had bought tickets for was unavailable, so there would be a substitution. There was an audible moan of disappointment. "However, in its stead we are going to run the new *Star Wars* film." The entire audience erupted in a cavalcade of cheering the likes of which I had never experienced. It was hard to imagine another sentence in the English language that could have been uttered, at that particular time in history, that would have elicited as great a response. The only one I could think of was the old Ed Sullivan introduction, "Ladies and gentleman, the Beatles."

After *Jedi* was finished, we boxed everything up and were about to be laid off when an opportunity arose for some of us to go down to Los Angeles and supervise the making of the 70mm prints. Key cities across the United States would have a few theaters that could run 70mm. These were the prestige outlets in cities like New York, Chicago, Los Angeles, and elsewhere around the globe. These prints were actually made from blow-up negatives and were not superior in any way except for their soundtracks. Every standard 35mm projection print carried a soundtrack that was composed of a squiggly and jagged-looking photographic image that could be read by the optical sensors on projectors. It was an ancient and inexpensive system, but it could only produce a limited dynamic range from the lowest volumes (whispers) to highest volumes (explosions). Every sound had to be compressed into a range optical sound could handle, but it worked pretty well until the print got old and scratchy, at which time the sound got a little muddy and scratchy as well.

With 70mm prints there was enough room to use multiple magnetic sound stripes to carry full stereophonic and even surround sound. This presented the opportunity for filmmakers to fully exploit the raw power of filmmaking. Huge screens, full symphonic scores, thunderous sound effects—who could resist? Of course, only major studio releases were afforded this opportunity; Joe Blow filmmakers had to make do with an optical track until the advent of digital sound.

They flew us to L.A., rented us hotel rooms and cars, kept us on salary, and gave us per diem (spending money). It was like a paid vacation, Hollywood style. We buddied up with some of the lab guys at Deluxe who were making the prints. They all drove beautiful new European sedans, like the 700 series BMWs. In Northern California you can drive anything you want. One of us had an old Edsel, the famously failed Ford car named in honor of Henry Ford's only son. In fact, we nicknamed this guy "Edsel." I drove an old Alfa Romeo, one of about 600 ever imported. But in Southern California you needed an elegant ride. It had to be freshly new and obviously expensive. Without an impressive car you were like a mobster without a pinky ring. You were an outcast.

Whether they could afford them or not, they had them, and we would drive around Hollywood at night seeing the sights. Brother, did they know L.A. Whether to take the surface streets or the 405 freeway, and the exact time to switch from one to the other, was in their DNA.

We did the all-night hamburger joints with no indoor seating and Cantor's twenty-four-hour deli on Fairfax. We did them all. On my own, I did Musso & Frank's on Hollywood Boulevard. It's the oldest restaurant in Hollywood, opened in 1919. Chaplin, Fairbanks, Pickford, Swanson, Cagney, Lombard, Gable, Howard Hughes—they all dined and socialized there. Everybody went to Musso's and still does. Their menu goes on forever. If you can think of it and it's vaguely Italian, it's on their menu. Bouillabaisse Marseillaise with Shrimp, Lobster, Mussels, Clams, and Cod? Got it. Flannel cakes? How many you want? With a long, ancient oak bar, red leather banquettes, and old-time waiters in black suit and tie, it's a time capsule from the past.

This wasn't Raymond Chandler's L.A. or my L.A., it was just L.A., like Hollywood is just Hollywood. If you've ever been there, it's not *Hollywood.* But there was a beauty to it, a beauty you could only see at night. "This was a town where people used to sleep out on porches," Chandler had written, and I could see that. It wasn't all freeways; there were leafy neighborhoods that residents rarely ever needed to leave. I had stayed for a time in a Craftsman bungalow in Silver Lake not far from the old movie ranch of cowboy Tom Mix. The area was as rural as a TV Western set in the 1950s where as kids we tried to spot airplanes and power poles in the distant backgrounds of Hopalong Cassidy episodes.

It was summer and it was hot. We worked nights mostly. We were not screening the movie, we were screening reels of the movie. Whatever the lab finished printing that day. Originally films were one reel long. That was ten minutes in screen time. Then the "two-reeler" was introduced. Chaplin made "two-reelers"—twenty minutes in screen time. By 1924 the great Erich von Stroheim had made his masterpiece, *Greed*, in forty-two reels. It was nearly eight hours long and that got him fired. The severely edited version we have left has fired the imaginations of film historians for decades about what might be in those other, by now long lost, thirty-six reels.

The industry eventually settled on roughly two hours as a feature length. This meant that a 35mm movie was sent to theaters on six projection reels. Each reel comprised a two-reeler, or twenty minutes of film.

So when I say we were watching reels, not the whole movie, I mean we were perhaps screening an entire evening of reel six only. It was boring, yet somehow being in the belly of the beast, the place that manufactured prints of movies we all loved at one time or another, was, with a little imagination, kind of exciting. This was the steamy hot machine room of the dream factory.

The town has always been magic for me. If you wanted to make movies, where else in the world could you walk into a coffee shop and see Sally Kellerman from the movie *M*A*S*H* getting coffee or ordering breakfast with her agent, like I had? Where else could you find motion picture rental houses where you could get any production equipment you could imagine from 10K movie lights to Panavision cameras? People used to ask, "Why Hollywood?" and the answer was, "If you need fifty cop cars on a set tomorrow, you can get them with a phone call." Today, in Silicon Valley or San Francisco, it's the same thing. Need fifty programmers? They are a phone call away.

I loved just being a part of it. What's the old joke about the kid asking for directions in New York? "How do I get to Carnegie Hall?" "Practice, son, practice." Well, Hollywood was my Carnegie Hall, and whether I was in the bowels of a motion picture lab or at Du-par's restaurant across from Universal Studios, I might as well have been on Broadway in New York. This was where I thought I belonged.

Eventually Oscar night rolled around, and Ken Ralston picked up the Oscar awarded to our crew for best achievement in visual effects. Rushing through the names to thank, he mentioned mine. Let me tell you, when your name is mentioned before a viewership of several hundred million people . . . your phone rings. I don't know how they get the number, but it does ring. I wish I could say it was an old girlfriend calling to apologize for dumping me, but it wasn't. More than likely it was an old landlord, but I can't remember. I do remember that one of our guys who was nominated got sent two tickets to the Oscars and took an ad out in the *San Francisco Chronicle* asking for a date. He had his pick.

Several months after *Jedi* was released to theaters, instructions came to the then-manager of ILM editorial, Howie, to take a plane and supervise the transfer from a specially made, low-contrast dupe negative to a videotape master for duplicating the massive number of home videos that would be sold worldwide. We were all expecting this, except we were not expecting the job to be done anywhere else but in Hollywood. Instead, Howie flew to Farmington, Michigan—a most unlikely destination for such an important transfer process. I wondered why this was happening and researched the matter. If I was going to be in the motion picture business, I had to learn how it worked.

In 1976 Universal and Disney studios sued Sony for manufacturing video recorders capable of recording and playing copyrighted material. They eventually lost in a Supreme Court decision. An additional decision that same year upheld the first-sale doctrine, which basically states that something purchased legally can be either resold or rented without infringing on the creators rights under the copyright law.

In 1977 a man from Farmington, Michigan, named Andre Blay came up with the idea to release prerecorded motion pictures on videocassette. That year, he licensed fifty films from 20th Century Fox for home video release and set up a transfer system. Blay paid a fee of $300,000 plus $500,000 yearly to Fox to license movies from their catalog. By the mid-1980s his operation was so successful that Hollywood's major studios were going to him for the home video releases of their movies. By 1987, with sales of videos surpassing movie theater grosses, Fox simply bought him out for $7.2 million rather than trying to build their own facility. That was a classic Hollywood move—don't build it, just buy it.

It was in this environment that Howie flew off to the unlikely destination of Farmington, where the video transfers were made *in real time,* with hundreds of video recording machines all rolling in tandem for the two-plus hours it took to record the movie.

The fact was that home video, which Hollywood had been forced to embrace after kicking and screaming to try to stop it, was now driving movie ticket sales at the box office because the more movies people saw that they liked, the more movies they wanted to see. It also allowed all kinds of forgotten films to have a new life and to be introduced to newer generations. Home video became the babysitter for a nation's children and also kept franchises like *Star Wars* alive as people actively awaited new episodes.

Somehow the flood of home videos across the country and around the world had not only enriched the filmmakers, but also embedded movies even more deeply into the American culture. The public became more interested in movies than ever. I would go so far as to argue that they had become even more popular than in the heyday of the big studios when people were seeing two or three movies a week. The technology had changed but the audience was again watching that many or more movies a week, only now it was on home video. In turn this seemed to prompt reporters from all the major newspapers and magazines to take more interest in how blockbusters were made. Part of that story had to do with the field of visual effects due to the fact that our work was having such a big impact on the motion picture business, both in the way these effects were being deployed and the impact their success was bringing to the business of making movies itself.

At first, nothing we were doing was really new besides applying some newer technology to age-old techniques, like controlling cameras with some early computers for instance. Miniatures, matte paintings, moving cameras, sound effects, and music had all been used for decades by filmmakers to round out their arsenal of dramatic devices for telling stories. Most of this was behind-the-scenes stuff, only of interest to a limited a number of people. Then slowly the men behind the curtain became of interest.

We had done amazing things in movies like *E.T.* or *Indiana Jones* or *Star Wars* long before we had anything to work with beyond models and optical printers, but when computer graphics started to arrive, whole new worlds of possibilities started to open up. If, as it has been written, there are really only thirty-six dramatic situations, thirty-six story lines that everyone from the ancient Greeks to Spielberg have been buffing up and presenting as new for centuries, then special visual effects were a welcome aid to yet another re-spinning of these old tales. A kingdom's princess is threatened by an evil lord? We can help you reset it as a space opera. Our computer division had made a planet transform in *Star Trek II: The Wrath of Khan* using computer graphics as early as 1982.

The fact that these reporters were showing up to do stories on us reflected the public's interest in what was formerly the somewhat arcane world of movie technicians. This kind of surprised me and also reminded me of a much earlier change I had noticed.

In 1975 Rona Barrett, a Hollywood gossip columnist, was hired to do a segment on the national morning news show *Good Morning America*. To my astonishment she had started to announce the weekend take of the newest movie releases in *dollars*. I was intensely interested in this kind of stuff, but I just couldn't imagine how someone in Podunk, Arkansas, would be interested. But everyone loved it. The studios could use it for advertising: "Our movie is the number one movie in the nation." This kind of publicity couldn't be bought. Or could it?

No one was interested in announcing the number of tickets sold or how many theaters were running a given film (fifty theaters or a thousand?), just the dollars received from the theaters by the distributors. Journalists were careful to never ask too many questions about who was providing these numbers and if they were accurate. It was media/studio back-scratching at its finest. Even today, every Sunday afternoon the top-grossing movies make the national news and the public thinks, "Well, if it made that much money, it must be good." In at least one case when the numbers submitted by the studio for *Forrest Gump* left it short of another studio release, new numbers were submitted after the discovery that two theaters in San Francisco had receipts that weren't counted. Those new numbers converted *Gump* from number two to "the number one box office hit in the nation," or so they said.

The questions the reporters asked us were interesting as well. "When will you be able to create digital actors?" Our answer was always the same: "Why bother? Actors come fairly cheap." We would use face replacements or whole head replacements where we wanted to use a stunt double in place of the star for making, say, a famous actor look like he was doing something too dangerous for him to actually do. We were trying to help directors tell stories rather than just show some flashy technique. Not that we were above doing flashy—it's just that most of these were scripts that were brought to us from outside. We were guns for hire when George wasn't using us. Doing research on building a digital actor would only happen when a client had to have one. Besides, as George has said, "You can't replace actors. We've created duplicates, clones, but they can't act. They're a computer, for God's sake."

We avoided research for a time, and this became almost a company mantra in the sense that we didn't want to do tests in the abstract. Give us real problems and we will solve them for any given movie. We would, of course, bring out our reels of past shows to try to sell clients on using us, but not years' worth of R&D. "Here is some cool stuff we've done in the past," we would say, "and we can do even better cool stuff for you now, because we are smarter than when we learned how to do that."

The Cutting Room Floor

We were nominated for an Academy Award for visual effects nearly every year and we won our share.[1] One of our supervisors, Dennis Muren, has won nine Oscars alone for visual effects. Dennis holds more Oscars than anyone alive.

The way it worked was that the nominated effects studio was asked to present a film reel of about twenty minutes or so of just the effects from the movie. This reel had to be cut from a standard projection print, so it could not be altered or dressed up in any way from what was in the theaters. Well, this presented problems, because the soundtracks on movies, at least back then, were from an optical stripe printed alongside, but not in sync with, the film images. For technical reasons the sound came about a foot ahead of the images. This meant that when we chopped the picture where we wanted to make a picture cut, we were possibly chopping sound that we didn't want to lose. We developed techniques, little editing tricks, to make it work, but it meant lots of splices that could break at any time.

When we were done cutting the reels, they were shipped to the Academy, and a few weeks later all the companies nominated would go down for a big screening at the Academy theater that we called "the bake-off." All the competing studios were there with their reels. The lights went down, and as the editor, you prayed that your splices didn't break and spoil the whole presentation, possibly costing your team an Oscar. When the lights came up, we went home and waited for the five

1. *Star Wars*, *E.T.*, *The Empire Strikes Back*, *Return of the Jedi*, *Raiders of the Lost Ark*, *Temple of Doom (Raiders 2)*, *Cocoon*, *Who Framed Roger Rabbit*, *The Abyss*, *Terminator 2*, *Jurassic Park*, *Forrest Gump*, *The Mask*, and *The Lost World (Jurassic 2)*.

best to be picked. After that it wasn't until Oscar night that we knew who had won.

We always kept copies of these reels to show potential clients our work and also to screen for visiting big shots who were getting a tour. My favorite to show people was the one from *The Empire Strikes Back.* That one always impressed people. It was exciting and contained great work. The funny thing is that almost no one has ever seen these reels and they are amazing because they were all of the "wow" scenes from major effects films cut into a nonstop reel of action.

Sometimes even a bad film could make a good reel. Besides *The Empire Strikes Back,* probably the best reel I ever saw was for *Pearl Harbor,* which we worked on in 2000. The effects work in that film was breathtaking when you saw it in one stand-alone reel, having left the lousy acting and the poor storyline on the cutting room floor. That re-creation of the Japanese attack on Pearl was unbelievably real, so much so that I once got complaints from some college history professors about the dangers they saw in what we were capable of doing.

The history professors descended on me at the University of Indiana, Bloomington. How I wound up lecturing a bunch of professors started at Phil's barber shop. I have been going to Phil for my haircuts for almost thirty years. Phil is one of those guys they call "connectors." That observation was made by Malcolm Gladwell in his book *The Tipping Point,* where he describes a type of person who knows large numbers of people and is in the habit of making introductions. That describes my barber Phil exactly. Phil knows everybody and loves to make introductions.

Needing a haircut, I set off for Phil's, pondering something I had just read about a famous paleoanthropological find of Mary Leakey's: early human footprints captured and preserved in volcanic ash from 3.6 million years ago. These prints revealed tremendous clues about how our ancestors walked, yet there was not enough money to properly house the find from the elements.

When I hit the chair at Phil's, I started to expound about what a shame it was that a mere radio preacher could easily raise millions of dollars, yet Mary Leaky was having trouble with funds to protect a hugely important find, one that revealed valuable information about ourselves.

Phil said, "Bill, Desmond Clark," gesturing to the gentleman directly across from the barber chair I was sitting in. Dr. Clark was an emeritus professor of anthropology at the University of California, Berkeley, having guided the world's foremost paleoanthropology program. He had taught most of the leading paleoanthropologists in the world.

This fellow was all class. A British gentleman educated at Christ's College, Cambridge, he had lived and studied in Berkeley for years. What he said to me was as foreign to an American ear as Swahili. He said, "I am having some people over to my home on Friday for cocktails. Won't you join us?" Desmond had never seen me before in his life.

That's the thing about Phil's barbershop: You never know who will be sitting there on your next visit. Someone once told me there are dozens of PhDs per square mile in my neighborhood. I don't know if that is true or not, but I can tell you that the person I bought my house from was one of the discoverers of Element 103 in the periodic table, and Daniel Ellsberg, of *Pentagon Papers* fame, is a neighbor. Not to mention the couple who founded and run MoveOn.org, possibly the most influential political organization in the country.

I wasn't going to miss this gathering, so my wife and I drove to a slightly different section of the Berkeley hills for cocktails. The affair was somewhat similar to some of my professors' hosting of graduate students at their homes during my college days, except this group also contained what I like to call famous people you've never heard of. For instance, I was introduced to Garniss Curtis, who invented potassium-argon dating to precisely date fossils. I also met Nick Toth and Kathy Schick, directors of the Stone Age Institute of Anthropology in Bloomington, Indiana.

Nick and I got to talking, and when he learned what I did for a living, he invited me to give a lecture on special effects at Indiana University, where Nick and Kathy are professors in addition to running their institute for the study of early man. The Stone Age Institute is largely, but not exclusively, funded by Gordon Getty, the oil billionaire from San Francisco. It would not be long before I was flying around on Gordon's private plane, all thanks to Phil the barber. I will say more about traveling with Gordon later, but just let me say here that his jet is no puny, multimillion-dollar Gulfstream. This is an airliner that Gordon had converted for his personal use.

For the lecture I brought some behind-the-scenes footage from the film *Saving Private Ryan,* which I had worked on. The scene I chose to illustrate what was possible to achieve with visual effects did not involve make-believe. There were no spaceships or monsters in what I showed, because I wanted to emphasize that things could be done to alter reality in ways that were not well known.

Spielberg had wanted a shot that depicted the scene at Omaha Beach a day or so after the ferocious D-Day assault. It would show an armada of ships, landing craft, German blockade and balloons still up, as well as hundreds of troops, tanks, jeeps, etc., swarming the newly taken beach. It would have the feel of a sort of mop-up operation still in progress.

What we were given to work with was a huge crane shot that slowly revealed a beach with absolutely nothing in the frame other than the ocean and the beach itself. We added everything else. I ran the before and after versions of the shot, which started with a couple of GIs in a passing jeep and then swooped slowly up for an aerial view from a height of maybe twenty-five feet. I didn't hear a gasp, but the audience I'm sure had never seen such a realistic scene created out of almost nothing. As I found out later, they were just not prepared to see such wholesale fakery in what otherwise appeared to be a straightforward period film.

At the cocktail get-together after the film, I was approached by a serious-looking group of history professors who were disturbed by the implications of what I had just shown them. They thought this was dangerous. It was some kind of a reassemblage of history that reminded them of such German propaganda films as Leni Riefenstahl's *Triumph of the Will.*

"It's a movie, fellows," I replied. But they would not be deterred. Why could I not see that the implications here were disturbing? I tried every way I could think of to say, "This is entertainment; we make stuff up for a living."

It's not like I hadn't thought about these things a lot, especially after we made the incredibly realistic-looking dinosaurs in *Jurassic Park.* I had even made a documentary on the making of that film in which I interviewed one of the principal creators of the effects, Dennis Muren, the man with nine Oscars. Dennis was an especially keen critic of anything visual. He had spent his entire career, as we all had, studying images we had recently faked, trying to make them look, even better, trying to make them look real. What was his reaction to these creatures we had created? He said, "I have studied them and studied them, and I cannot find a flaw."

Talk about powerful images. These were powerful enough to add creepy to them. These dinosaurs were creepy powerful. I even went out to a movie theater and filmed some of the very first patrons as they came out of the show. "What did you think? How do you think they were made?" Those were the questions I had been thinking about since I had seen what we were about to unleash on the moviegoing public, a year earlier. How will people react when they see something so realistic? Something that they simultaneously know is fake? Something that cannot be real?

Well, they didn't care. They just didn't know or care how it was done. To them it was just a cool movie. "I liked it when the dinosaur ate that guy." That was the most articulate response I ever got.

So no, I wasn't concerned that our techniques would be used for evil purposes. I did, however, always think we could have made the most incredible UFO film ever captured by an amateur. We would fake it so it looked like some home-movie geek had shot footage of an alien spaceship landing or something, and leave it in an old 8mm camera at a flea market for someone to find. I never could get anyone to go along with me on that, but we did have fun debunking a book of supposed UFO still photos that some conspiracy guy brought in one time.

Film School

In the generations before mine, ambitious young men wanted to be famous novelists. For many in my generation, they wanted to be famous filmmakers. To write you need a pencil and a piece of paper. To make a movie no clear path seemed to exist except for film school, and almost all of my contemporaries went. Lucas, Coppola, Spielberg, Scorsese, etc., all went to film school in either New York or Los Angeles. I went to San Francisco State, starting in 1968.

Here I could have access to a lot of expensive movie cameras and editing equipment that was otherwise unavailable to me. It wasn't so much the instruction that mattered, it was getting my hands on the tools by which I could make movies. Also, the environment was important. Just being around other filmmakers who shared the same interest was stimulating because that gave us all an audience to critique our work.

The Hollywood film schools were designed around the theatrical studio films that had been made for years, while State had become a haven for independent films. We made art films, underground films, and protest films. Hollywood had disdain for us. One studio mogul remarked, "Independent? Independent of what?" Yet, some of the techniques we developed out of poverty and ignorance were starting to have an effect, like rapid editing, abrupt jump cutting around a scene, snap zooming in on a face, and swooshing a handheld camera around a set. Many of these things slowly began to creep into major feature films.

At State I had several interesting teachers. One was the screenwriter Lester Cole, who was one of the Hollywood Ten that were blacklisted as communist sympathizers in the 1950s in the witch hunt set off by Joseph McCarthy's House Un-American Activities Committee. Cole had written more than forty screenplays that were made into motion pictures, an incredible record. After the blacklisting he wrote under cover names and only had a few reach the screen, but one was *Born Free,* which was a big success. Lester introduced me to his agent to help me sell my Jack Johnson film.

Lester was the real thing, a guy who had actually been a major player in Hollywood. Most of the rest of the instructors were artist types or mostly had worked in television, but I learned something from all of them. James Broughton was a well-known poet and independent filmmaker, and his lectures inspired creativity. He used to live with the film critic Pauline Kael, so it was a cultured group. One guy had been a crowd arranger in Westerns, and another worked sound on *The Lone Ranger*.

Some students were only interested in film theory; they watched movies and wrote papers. The rest of us took production courses. We had instruction in filming, sound recording, and screenwriting. But the real divide was whether you could make a movie that would work for an audience. One guy made a very artsy porn film and tried to sell it to one of the grind houses on Market Street. They told him if he "cut out all the artsy crap" he had a deal.

I was born in San Francisco, but was only able to move back to the city in the late 1960s, for school, amid the cultural revolution that was exploding among my age group all across the country, but especially here. All of a sudden, fresh off the Summer of Love, in the middle of the Vietnam War and the Sexual Revolution, San Francisco was the place to be. The flight to the suburbs was officially over for the young people who were coming to town in droves, and I was comfortable with the whole thing except that I wasn't a joiner. I would find my own way to contribute.

There has been a lot written about this youth revolution that I was in the middle of here, but with the exception of Abbie Hoffman, most have failed to get it right. In his last speech he said, "In the 1960s, apartheid was driven out of America. Legal segregation—Jim Crow—ended . . . We ended the idea that women are second-class citizens. Now it doesn't matter who sits in the Oval Office . . . We were young, we were reckless, arrogant, silly, headstrong . . . and we were right! I regret nothing!"

Looking at the job listings in the *San Francisco Chronicle* back then, I used to see a whole column labeled "Colored." When my girlfriend took the mathematics test for a job at IBM, hers was the highest score they had ever tested, yet she was simply told at the placement interview that "we don't hire women." You can't do that anymore.

I was in my third month of film school when the Black Student Union shut down San Francisco State University over access to higher public education. Our film group started making films about the strike itself, and I continued to work on my documentary on the black boxing champion Jack Johnson and his struggles with racism in America. I supported the strike but thought it foolish to give up access to the movie tools that were needed to make a consciousness-raising documentary on the very topic the strike was about.

Governor—later president—Ronald Reagan used an age-old tactic to end the strike: overwhelming force. He flooded the campus with police in riot gear, and it worked. They brought in a whole squadron of mounted police, their horses equipped with rubber caps over their metal horseshoes so they wouldn't slip on the pavement while running down students. Cops were stationed everywhere, even in the main library.

In the end, however, the students got what they wanted out of it, which was a Black Studies Department and a revised entry policy for minorities. Both sides had been radicalized by now. The anger over the Vietnam War put young people in the streets and also brought the right wing back to prominence fighting "communists" and leading directly to Nixon's anti-crime/anti-black Southern strategy that would give the Solid South to the Republicans, who own it today.

One member of my film class decided to shoot himself in the foot as a protest and exit strategy to the Vietnam War and the draft. A friend of mine at the time, Warren Haack, filmed the guy shooting himself, stuck the printed version of the Selective Service Act on a title card at the head of the film, and won the National Student Film Award that year. George Lucas had also won the same award but for a very different kind of film. His was called *THX 1138* and was about a time in the future where technology was used to dehumanize people. This was the difference between my film school and Hollywood's. Our films were about hard-core reality and theirs were fables. Fables are successful.

George expanded his student film into a feature motion picture released by a major studio. My student film was developed as well, just not by me (*The Great White Hope*). I had the right topic, just not the pathway to get it there. I didn't understand the game yet, or how powerful fables are.

I was like most people who have no idea about how movies are made or the fantasy world movies spin for them. If they did, they wouldn't show up in Atlanta, Georgia, looking for the Tara mansion from the movie *Gone with the Wind,* which was actually shot on a back lot in Hollywood. Even people in my own family were not immune.

By 1973 I was living in a two-bedroom flat in a 1912 building in the Cow Hollow section of San Francisco. An older Italian couple named Agnese owned the building and a couple of others around town. This couple became my model in later years for how to retire and live comfortably. The husband puttered around the apartment buildings, and they lived well off the rent roll. When asked about his credit rating, he would reply, "What do you care? I pay cash."

One of my girlfriend's cousins had been a police detective in Detroit for many years. He was a really cool guy, very worldly-wise, and he loved living the good life of fancy vacations and fine restaurants. When David first came to San Francisco to stay with us, he was such a Humphrey Bogart fan that he wanted us to show him where Brigid O'Shaughnessy had shot Sam Spade's partner, Miles Archer, in *The Maltese Falcon*. David was quite disappointed when we had to tell him that it was all filmed on a sound stage in Hollywood. Once again I was struck by the power of the spinning fable. Here was a tough Detroit cop in a swoon over a movie.

We made it up to David by taking him to Ernie's, which had been featured in Alfred Hitchcock's film *Vertigo* and was probably the fanciest restaurant in the city at the time. David loved movies and wanted to see any place where they had been made. Hitchcock himself was often at Ernie's when he was in the city. In fact, he had some of his favorite wines stored in the restaurant's wine cellar.

But David's fantasies didn't end with movies. Like all film fans he also had heroes, and there was someone else David wanted to see in San Francisco. So the detective in him went to work.

Cow Hollow, where we lived, was just one block from the Marina District, which runs right down to San Francisco Bay. This was the neighborhood where detective David struck gold. For many years after David made his Marina District find, I would drive visitors to this nearby area and stop in front of a modest house saying, "Two of the most famous people in the world lived in that house at the same time. Can you guess who they were?"

No one ever guessed it, and though I haven't asked anyone in years, I still don't think anyone could guess. It was Joe DiMaggio and Marilyn Monroe. They were married at San Francisco City Hall in 1954 and had lived there in Joe's family home. The receptionist at the recording studio where I worked said that when she was in high school, she remembered seeing Marilyn shopping on Chestnut Street in the Marina several times. David had been a seasoned police detective and he knew how to find stuff out. "Just talk to the mailmen," he used to say. "They know everything." So David tracked down the mail carrier for that route and bluffed his way to the address. I had been steeped in the reality filmmaking of San Francisco State documentaries, but I was starting to appreciate this even more powerful form of heroes and our journeys to find them.

DiMaggio was still alive then. I knew that because this was in the 1970s and Joe had come into our sound recording studio one day to do a voiceover commercial for Mr. Coffee, the widely sold and nationally advertised coffee machine. Joe was the spokesman for the company, and he was in all their ads at the time. One could say that at that time, Joe *was* "Mr. Coffee." Since we knew that he was a pretty private guy, we had him come in on a Saturday when we were closed. As he was settling in at the microphone, my friend George, who was doing the recording, asked him if he would like a cup of coffee. Joe looked at him, and in a slightly gruff manner said, "*I hate coffee.*"

"Francis Coppola Wishes to Speak with You"

I WAS ALWAYS TRYING TO LEARN MORE ABOUT HOW TO MAKE MOVIES back then, but in the late 1960s there were no movies available to study except in theaters, no old movies to see except in revival houses. I had to go to the UCLA film library in Los Angeles to find original screenplays. The ones that I could find that had been published were invariably the finished movie in print—which is not something you can really learn much from, because if it was a really good film, the finished product looks impossibly perfect. That published screenplay is not what they started with, and it will just discourage you into thinking that you could never write something as great as that.

I found it best to look for the earlier versions of the screenplays that I wanted to study and discovered they are not at all like the film that went through months of shooting and editing. They are not always blueprints for great films—they became great films while they were being made. If you look at the original screenplay for *Annie Hall* (if you can find it), you will see that the screenplay is not even about the character Annie. That story was crafted in the cutting room and by rewriting the commentary. The original screenplay versions of *Star Wars* were so long and shaggy that they had to be made into three films. I take nothing away from screenwriters saying this—their writing is the genesis of movies—just don't beat yourself up in thinking the published screenplays are so perfect, you could never do that. Most people can't do it, even great writers can't necessarily do it, but you can learn a lot by studying the originals.

Since there was no way to watch older films, even classics, unless you could catch them at a revival house, I sought out the movies I wanted to study and made sound recordings of them by sneaking a tape recorder into the theaters. It worked surprisingly well. The audio quality was excellent, and I got the bonus of the audience's reaction. This was a distraction until I realized how carefully the writers and directors plotted those reactions. Richard Zanuck told the story of his hearing the audience during a preview screening of *Jaws*. "We didn't know what we had until we took it to Texas. I was out in the lobby while the film was being screened, getting a cup of coffee. I'll tell you when that shark first jumps out of the water, the audience screamed so loud it shook the building. That's when I knew we had a monster on our hands."

I only had these tapes and what original screenplays I could find (I would buy bootlegged ones in Hollywood) to learn from—that and watching new movies and revival-house classics—but there were some surprise benefits. I learned how important the quality of an actor's voice is to the performance. My God, in some of these old classic black-and-white movies the voices have so much authority and nuance. Yet, when watching the same film in its entirety, not just a soundtrack, there is so much going on visually that the voice quality can escape your notice, as well as how the music works to undergrid the filmmaker's direction or misdirection of the audience's attention.

Another thing I learned from these old movies concerned the mystique of a movie character and the mysterious power that a movie star can have over the audiences. There is a story that Clark Gable took Carol Lombard on a date while he was courting her. Both were already famous and they later married, but this was an earlier time. When he got her home, he parked his car in front of her apartment and said, "Can I come up?" To which she replied, "Who do you think you are, *Clark Gable*?"

There is actually a little more Hollywood to this story than might first appear. Many in show business are famous by their professional names, which are quite unlike their real names or real personalities. Woody Allen's real name is Allen Konigsberg; Michael Caine, Maurice Micklewhite; Judy Garland, Frances Gumm; Natalie Portman, Natalie

Hershlag. It is very hard for the public to separate the actor from the real person. Humphrey Bogart was often challenged by tough guys simply because he became famous for playing tough guys. He was far from a hoodlum, having come from a wealthy East Coast family. His father was a surgeon and his mother a wealthy heiress. In fact, his mother's illustration of him was used for the original Gerber baby food ads. The point is that he was the opposite of the characters he played.

My first encounter with anything to do with Hollywood feature films as an adult occurred when the two most successful film school graduates, Francis Coppola and George Lucas, decided they were going to locate in Northern California, not Los Angeles.

It was 1970, and I was fresh out of film school myself. I had been lucky enough to get a job at a small film company in San Francisco owned by a distinguished inventor and audio engineer named Bill Palmer.

During World War II, American intelligence suspected that Germany had developed some new kind of recording device because though they sent bombers to every city where Hitler appeared to be giving a live broadcast, they were having no luck in killing him. Intelligence thought that they could tell "live" from "recorded" broadcasts because all known recording methods had a lot of background hiss. No loud hiss, must be a live Hitler broadcast, send in the bombers. But they never got him, so this made army intelligence suspicious.

Immediately upon Germany's defeat, the military sent in specialists and found a new type of recorder, a tape recorder. Not wax, not vinyl, not wire, but magnetic tape. Bill Palmer and a partner, Jack Mullin, got their hands on the German machine and developed an American version. Soon, through the Ampex company of Palo Alto, all major studios and broadcast networks were using tape recorders. These engineers' work also led to the early video recorders.

I started as a sound technician, but the company did every motion picture service there was, from script to screen. It was here that I learned how to make movies. If I wanted to know something, I went to Bill and asked. I quickly learned that when Bill explained it, it was so easy to understand, because he actually knew what he was talking about. You get the confusing answers from people who don't.

Since film school I had been trying to finish my documentary historical film on boxing champion Jack Johnson, who was the inspiration for the Broadway play *The Great White Hope,* by Howard Sackler. If I had not been a poor film student, I might have been able to beat Sackler to the punch, but I could only afford to work on it nights and weekends, and then only when I had some extra money. But then something happened to change all that.

I had been away from my apartment for a couple of days, and as I opened the door upon my return, the phone was ringing. Picking up, I heard, "I have been trying to reach you for days. Francis Coppola saw your film and wants to talk to you." This was the phone call all young filmmakers wait for, and I was no exception.

Coppola and several of his filmmaking buddies, including George Lucas, had founded a movie production company in San Francisco called American Zoetrope. The Zoetrope was an early moving image parlor device. You spun it, and while looking through a slit, you saw still drawings come to life and move in much the same way as a child's flip book animates sequences of stick drawings.

Coppola had a policy of screening student and local filmmakers' work at the end of the day every Friday. People were encouraged to drop their film off for these after-hours screenings. My film was not done yet, but I had a silent work print that I could show, so I had left it at Zoetrope Studios.

My film was made up of rare black-and-white still photos and even scarcer motion picture footage of Johnson, all of which I had located through painstaking research and contacting film and photo collections all over the world. The story centered on Johnson's winning the Heavyweight Championship of the World and then going on to defeat the much-admired white ex-champion, Jim Jeffries. The Jeffries loss to a black man caused race riots across the country, and the movie footage of the fight itself was declared illegal. Also, Johnson was later arrested. So my film had rare and powerful stuff, and it made an impression.

Soon I was meeting with Francis and getting a tour of his studio. George was somewhere there finishing his film. This was before *The Godfather* and before the release of George's first feature, *THX 1138,* which was also to be the first release of a multiple-studio film deal that had financed the Zoetrope studio. Coppola had also directed, but his claim to fame was winning the Oscar in 1970 for coauthoring the movie *Patton* with Edwin North, though no one ever remembers North, just Coppola. North had written *The Day the Earth Stood Still* and *Young Man with a Horn,* among many other films. According to the producer of *Patton,* John McCarthy, "Coppola's script was effulgent, imaginative, airy, really awful good, but in need of some restructuring. We lined up North . . . He took the Coppola script and worked it to the point where it had more cohesion and hung together better, and had a much more workable dramatic structure." Just for the record, dramatic structure is everything in movie stories.

Francis told me he liked my project and asked how he could help me. I said I needed a place to edit. His studio had all the latest in movie technology, and young filmmakers were drooling to get their hands on it; so was I. "Why don't you come and work for us?" he said. Now, that was a bombshell I hadn't expected. It was all very vague, but essentially I could work for them and finish my film as well. There were guys I knew who would have walked from Los Angeles on a bed of nails for this opportunity, but I turned him down.

I explained that I had just started a new job with another company, and I just couldn't walk out on them so soon. He was taken aback, but what could he say? I was just some naive kid who hadn't wised up yet. So he said that was very admirable of me.

Then he explained why he had originally called me in. He said his friend Martin Ritt was directing the motion picture version of *The Great White Hope* and my film would be a perfect short to run before the picture. He would call Martin and see what could be worked out. "Oh, and by the way," he said, "you can still edit your film here." And I did, but Ritt told Coppola he was too far along to include my movie.

I brought in my film and went to work. I still had a full-time job, but nights and weekends I was working away at Zoetrope Studios. Soon I started to notice something strange. They had all this fancy stuff, a trendy old brick warehouse with all the latest flatbed editing machines imported from Europe. They had huge black-and-white blowups of famous movie scenes and film directors (that would later find their way to ILM). They had the best carpet and office furniture that money could buy, and a huge old-fashioned espresso machine topped by a gold eagle. It was designed to impress and it did. Except there was one problem: All the little stuff you need to edit a movie, they didn't have. No tape at all, no splicers for cutting film, no supplies of any kind. OK, I thought. I guess everyone just brings their own stuff. And that is what I did.

Within months, *THX 1138* was released and it dropped dead. The studio hated the film and all the other projects Coppola had lined up. They cut off all money and even made Francis repay what had been spent. Zoetrope vanished from the landscape (at least until *The Godfather*), but I still had a job and was able to finish my film, *Jeffries-Johnson 1910*. Now I knew why there were no supplies: They were broke and counting on the release of *THX* to save them.

I entered my Jack Johnson film in the San Francisco International Film Festival and won a minor award, but they refused to show it, even though the opening festival feature was *The Great White Hope*. So a bunch of us local filmmakers, tired of being rejected every year, formed our own alternative festival and rented Fugazi Hall in North Beach, and my film was the feature of the evening. Coppola attended the S.F. Festival but then snuck out and came to ours, playing the tuba on the stage there, to the entertainment of everyone. We made Herb Caen's column in the *San Francisco Chronicle* and embarrassed the stuffed shirts at the high-society festival that had ignored us.

I picked up a good review from the *Chronicle*'s movie critic, Judy Stone, and got a distribution deal from McGraw-Hill Films. When I got my royalty advance check, I walked into a downtown bank and approached a pretty young teller. She looked at it and said in a breathless movie starlet's voice, "Are you an author?" That's when I knew I had made the right career choice. I was twenty-four years old.

After my Jack Johnson movie, I tried to find grant money for the next documentary I wanted to make. The subject was Ulysses S. Grant, the famous Civil War general and president. I had read everything I could get my hands on about him, including his personal memoirs that had been published by Mark Twain. It was these memoirs that Gertrude

Stein had instructed Ernest Hemingway to study if he wanted to learn how to write. Edmund Wilson compared them to Thoreau's *Walden* and Whitman's *Leaves of Grass*. It was these little-known aspects of this great man's life that I wanted to bring to an audience's attention by extracting them from the past. This project got me the chance at an internship with the American Film Institute, but I was unable to obtain the money to make the film, so it became an article called "Me and General Grant."

Hanging out at Zoetrope the little bit that I did had by now caused my thinking to change. Out of college I had thought that if I could just work somewhere in the movie business and still make films on the side, I would be perfectly happy. Now that I had seen what the really aggressive young filmmakers were doing, it made me wonder if I should change tactics. I could continue to beg for filmmaking grants or do what producers did, get control of a property and leverage that to get a movie made. I could still use my historical material, just in a larger crapshoot.

Mike Medavoy

BY ABOUT 1974, I HAD BECOME FASCINATED BY THE LIFE OF WILLIE Sutton, the notorious bank robber, the guy who when asked why he had robbed banks famously replied, "Because that's where the money was." I had read his autobiography and was determined to get a movie made about his life.

Sutton was a very interesting guy. He was a bank robber but he was known as "The Actor" because he never used violence and the gun he carried was only what he called "a necessary prop." He would use disguises such as police uniforms to gain entry to a bank before it opened. Once inside he would reveal something scary, like a machine gun, to make the employees freeze. It was safer that way. Willie knew any lesser gun might make people do something foolish, something off script.

He would then go to the bank's manager and introduce what he called "the psychological bribe." Knowing that the manager would bravely refuse to open the safe when the time lock went off, Willie explained that the manager had a greater responsibility to protect his employees than the money. He was giving the man the excuse he needed to save face, but still open the safe. Willie was a brilliant man. What actor, I thought, wouldn't want to play a character who used disguises, costumes, and acting skills to successfully rob banks?

While I was trying to negotiate the rights to the book, I wrote a treatment called *Willie: The Actor* and I was also trying to interest Paul Newman, but with no luck. His agent told me Paul didn't want to play any criminal types, which was pretty funny to me because he starred in *Butch Cassidy and the Sundance Kid.*

Desperate to find someone that would listen to me, I went to a talk at the San Francisco International Film Festival given by Mike Medavoy. Medavoy had been a Hollywood agent and later producer. At the time he was a big shot at United Artists.

During his talk he answered several questions by local filmmakers about how to get an agent or break into movies. It was in response to these questions that he finally summed up by saying, "Look, your job as young filmmakers is to get in to see me. But of course, you can't get in to see me."

He was presenting a sort of catch-22. It was like he was saying, "In order to get a job, you already have to have a job." Well, I said to myself, I can get in to see him if that's what it takes, and I set out with a plan.

I flew down to Los Angeles and got a room at the Highland Gardens Motel, an old apartment house on Franklin. A lot of young actors and film people hung out there, and it was always a surprise to find that your "motel" room had a large kitchen and sometimes a couple of bedrooms. There was a pool, palm trees, the whole bit. Also, it was cheap and close to everything in Hollywood. This was where Janis Joplin OD'd on heroin in 1970. Room 105.

My plan was to get onto the studio lot where Medavoy had an office, walk around until I found it, and try to either drop off my treatment or maybe even get in to see him, which I thought was unlikely.

My first obstacle was getting onto the lot. There were security guards and a gatehouse. You had to have an appointment to enter, unless of course you worked there. I reasoned that the most important status symbol in Los Angles after your car was a parking space at an L.A. studio. I didn't even want to attempt driving onto the lot. That was too bold; I would never make it. So I upped the ante and tried something even bolder.

I figured all the studio hotshots—the young ones anyway, the ones with neither gray hair nor manners—were probably pretty rude to lowly folk like security guards. Plus, these guys might not have enough status yet for a private parking spot on the studio lot near the main offices. I had seen some of them walking on and off with their secretaries, probably going to and from lunch. They had suits and briefcases and their secretaries wore skirts. Security just watched them walk past.

So I put on a suit, carried an empty briefcase, and had my girlfriend walk two steps behind me. When I got to the guardhouse, the guy started to ask me something and I gave him some arrogant bullshit and he just backed away. We were now inside the palace gates.

We decided I should explore alone so as to arouse less suspicion. This was like a spy mission. When I finally found Medavoy's office, I went in and talked to the secretary. Here was the lucky part. His regular secretary was off sick that day and this was a substitute, a fill-in that didn't really know the protocol. I gave her my name and said I was here to see Mr. Medavoy. "I don't see your name on this list," she said. "There must be some mistake," I answered back. She got flustered and decided she'd better do as I asked.

She called Medavoy and said, "Mr. Kimberlin is here to see you." He soon opened his office door and invited me in. He actually had his arm around my shoulders as we crossed into his lavish office with its oriental rugs and fine furniture. "How can I help you, Bill?" he asked. I went into my Willie Sutton movie pitch and handed him my script treatment. At this point Medavoy was acting a little confused. He didn't know quite what was happening or who the hell I was, but he took my treatment and thanked me as he said good-bye at his door.

I had been trying to snag an agent so I wouldn't have to go through stuff like this anymore, so when I spotted a phone booth while crossing the studio lot, I popped inside, ready to call the agent one of my film professors had introduced me to. When I looked at the phone in the booth, it was just an empty shell, and I suddenly realized this was a studio prop, not a real phone booth. Hoping no one was watching my idiot move, I exited the fake booth and left the lot. The guards don't care who leaves, so I disappeared back onto the Hollywood streets, looking for a real phone booth.

I had always heard that while it was tough to get an agent, if you already had a sale, or at least a hot lead, most agents would gladly sign you to pick up an easy 10 percent. So I called an agent I had spoken to before. When I got him on the phone, I stupidly said, "I'm calling from Mike Medavoy's office." Just at that point my toll money dropped into the pay phone cash box with a clash and the agent said something like,

"Does Mr. Medavoy use pay phones now?" "Well, I'm just outside on the street," I replied. I don't remember what he said next, but I think he said, "OK, I will check it out."

What a great day this had been, I thought. So my girlfriend and I headed off to the Polo Lounge at the Beverly Hills Hotel for a celebratory drink. One thing I should mention is that in those days when I was trying not to look so young and poor, I always left my callback number as the Beverly Hills Hotel. I used it like an office and messenger service. We ate at the lounge, hung out in the lobby, and made phone calls from there, but slept in the Highland Gardens on the cheap.

While we were having dinner in the Polo Lounge, I noticed that someone at another table, who I couldn't quite see, had asked that a phone be brought to his table. Of course, this was a time way before any kind of personal phone or cellphone.

The Polo Lounge was not like other restaurants; it catered to Hollywood people making deals over meals. So each table was wired with a phone jack, and if you got a call or needed to make one, your waiter would just bring you a phone and plug it in for you.

This was all new to me, and I was anxious to see who the important person was that had ordered the phone. When the man finally left his table, I saw who it was, even though I didn't recognize him at first because he looked so different. It was Don King, the fight promoter, the guy with the wild hair who produced many a Muhammad Ali fight. Except there was no wild hair and he was dressed in a conservative suit. He looked like any other businessman. So, it was all hype and the press ate it up, making Don a very wealthy man. That's show business.

When I returned to my lobby office at the Beverly Hills Hotel the next day, there was a message for me to call Mike Medavoy's office. Great, I thought, now we're getting somewhere.

When I called the office, you'd think I had snatched the Lindbergh baby, as Truman Capote once said. They chewed me up one side and down the other. "We will never do business with you again, your script will be returned unread," etc. It was the classic "you'll never eat lunch in this town again" threat. But it scared the hell out of me. Here I was, a young film student type trying to hustle a deal, but I didn't know what

I was doing. There are no rules in that game, just what works, and this clearly hadn't worked.

Much later, I read that Steven Spielberg had bragged about doing much the same thing when he was coming up, except he had even moved into an empty studio office before he was found out.

Panicked, I called my friend Don, who lived in Hollywood and had seen it all. What he said calmed me down a little. He asked, "Did you punch him?" "Are you crazy?" I said. "Of course not." "You can't be too aggressive in Hollywood, Bill," he said. "Forget about it." And I eventually did, but it took a while.

I flew back to San Francisco with my tail between my legs, but I wasn't done yet. My Jack Johnson documentary had gotten me an invitation to the American Film Institute (AFI). The institute was holed up in the old Greystone Mansion in Beverly Hills. Oilman Edward Doheny built the place for $3 million in 1928 for his son, who promptly shot himself. By the early 1970s the city owned it and leased it to the AFI for a dollar a year or something. A lot of young filmmakers hung out there at the time, either taking part in their film classes or attending talks by famous film directors from Harold Lloyd to John Huston. I never met him, but somewhere on the estate David Lynch, later the director of *The Elephant Man, Blue Velvet,* and the television drama *Twin Peaks,* was living in one of the old garages, trying to finish *Eraserhead,* his first feature.

My goal was to get an internship with a Hollywood director. I didn't need any more film courses—I wanted to start working with real film industry people. During my interview with the staff that placed interns with directors, I explained that I didn't really need to be with some celebrated director, just give me an old pro, someone who could take a few hundred pounds of film and in three months give you a movie. I'm sure they had no idea what I was talking about, but they sent me to interview with Richard Fleischer, who was a solid old-time studio director whose father was the creator of the *Betty Boop* and *Popeye the Sailor* comedy shorts.

Richard was probably best known for having directed *20,000 Leagues Under the Sea,* which was a huge hit for Disney, and *Tora! Tora! Tora!,* which got a lot of publicity but dropped dead at the box office. He had also made *Compulsion* about the famous Leopold and Loeb murder case, starring Orson Welles as their defense attorney, Clarence Darrow. In 1971 Fleischer was slated to direct *The New Centurions,* which was based on the best-selling police novel by Joseph Wambaugh, and I was to be his intern on that picture. I had read the book and it was very good, and better still the screenplay had been written by Sterling Silliphant, who had written one of my favorite movies, *In the Heat of the Night.*

Wambaugh was an ex-cop whose first novel on police procedures became a *New York Times* bestseller, introducing a new kind of literature. This was a raw depiction of a cop's life on the streets of Los Angeles before and during the Watts riots of 1965. It was to star George C. Scott, Stacy Keach, and Jane Alexander.

I was instructed to meet Fleischer for lunch at the executive dining room on the Columbia Studios lot in Hollywood. This time I had an appointment and the guard at the gate had my name. Columbia was originally part of a group of studios that were called "poverty row" because they made low-budget pictures, mostly Westerns. It was run by the legendary Harry Cohn, probably the most hated man in Hollywood, who in thirty years managed to never have a negative return on his slate of films. It was also the home of Frank Capra, who directed *It Happened One Night* with Clark Gable and Claudette Colbert, which catapulted Columbia into major studio status. At Cohn's funeral, one fellow when asked why he had attended said, "I wanted to make sure the bastard was dead."

Fleischer was in his mid-fifties and very cordial, but wary. He explained that these internships could be tricky politically because I would be seen to have jumped ahead of everyone else on the crew, so I had to be very diplomatic. I tried to convince him that while I had only made documentaries, I wanted to learn how to make feature films with actors.

Every once in a while people would drop by our table and ask Fleischer when his current film, *The New Centurions,* would start production. This whole ritual reminds me now of the opening scenes of *The Godfather,* when the wedding guests were coming by to show their respect and to ask for favors. These were studio production people whose jobs depended largely on directors like Fleischer getting their projects greenlit, with an approved budget, and put on the studio production schedule.

Fleischer had a reputation as a studio director, someone the studio could trust. He struck me as a gentleman—in charge, but without the braggadocio of many Hollywood studio directors. He told me I could stay through the entire process, right up to the final sound mix and premiere. This was a golden opportunity. Then he asked me how I was going to live for a year without a salary. I just wasn't prepared for this question. Everything had happened so fast that I couldn't give a convincing answer.

Flying home, I reviewed my performance and I realized I had blown it. The next day I sent him a telegram explaining my reluctance to be specific and assuring him I would do whatever it took to make this internship happen. When I called the AFI, they said they didn't know what happened but Fleischer had asked to interview someone else. It seems a little dramatic now, but back then I thought I was running out of chances.

Opportunities like this just didn't come along all that often and here I had been afraid to pull the trigger, afraid to just wing it and see how far I could get. Why hadn't I been able to communicate, "I'm all in, I have no reservations"? It was the money. I just couldn't afford to quit my job and do this, and I guess it showed. Normally a person could go to their parents, but I just didn't have that option. So maybe I *was* a little screwed up. Was it this "orphan" thing? Perhaps you have to know more about who you are before you can go jumping off cliffs. Then something kind of strange happened.

Back when I was talking with Francis Coppola at American Zoetrope, there had been a photographer there who took a picture of Francis and me talking under one of those huge black-and-white pictures of Hollywood directors he had in the hallways, one of the ones that would later wind up in my office at ILM. This photo was published in a flashy new magazine called *Show,* and when my buddies saw it, they thought I must have hit the big time because here I was hanging out with Coppola.

When they checked in with me, we got to talking, and I learned they weren't doing any better than I was, maybe worse. One of my friends at the time was Jim O'Fallon. He was trained as a chemist but had caught the film bug in college and had tried for a year to get a film job with no luck. When he finally had to find work just to pay the rent, he went looking for a job as a chemist and had one the next day at a soft drink company. This demonstrated how difficult it was to try to get into the movie business.

Don Sanders, the guy I had called after getting in trouble with Medavoy, was trying to make it as a movie sound recordist. He had struggled forever and couldn't catch a break. It took years, but he finally got hired at the very last minute when a company producing a new television pilot was leaving for location in Texas the next day and was desperate. Don told me the producer said, "I'm going to hire you, but just remember, I can fire you just as easily." About a year later they aired the pilot and it was called *Dallas*. This show ran for fourteen years. A job like that is one in a million. When I finally caught up with Don again, I asked about his big break. "Oh, they fired me and everyone else when the pilot was picked up by the network. Brought in all their own people." Hollywood is a tough town.

So, I'd had it. In 1973, when my brother and I came into a little money from leasing a small piece of property our parents had left us, I decided that if I couldn't get a start in Hollywood movies, I'd make my own damn movie. But before that could happen, before I made the film that finally got me into big-time moviemaking, I had to bump along the underground of independent filmmaking, trying to stay alive as a creative person.

Chan Is Missing

My days were now spent working at Palmer's and trying to make some headway in the larger filmmaking world. I kept myself busy with making small movies wherever I could.

I directed a public service television spot starring Slim Pickins, who had famously played Major "King" Kong in Stanley Kubrick's *Dr. Strangelove*. Pickens had been a rodeo cowboy and bit player in movies until *Strangelove* made him famous. He told me Kubrick was a genius who could carry on a complex conversation with you while at the same time playing chess with someone else, but he would often make you do a scene a hundred times. Slim kept forgetting his lines with me and I had to learn ways around that, real fast. It was all about experimenting, taking whatever opportunity presented itself and seeing if you could make something out of it. The writer Hunter S. Thompson had summed it up in advice to a friend by telling him to "beware of goals," because while you may achieve them, that won't give you a happy life. Instead, Thompson said, "decide how you want to live and then see what you can do to make a living within that way of life." I had decided how I was going to live: I was going to make films however I could.

My friend Rick Schmidt, who would later write the influential book *Feature Film Making at Used Car Prices,* which outlines how a person could make their own films at a moderate cost, was working as an editor on an early film of Wayne Wang's (who later directed *The Joy Luck Club*) called *Chan Is Missing*. This movie cost about $20,000 to make and was largely financed with grants.

Around 1980 *Chan Is Missing,* like almost all locally made independent films, was rejected by the San Francisco International Film

Festival. We were all very much used to this, but this time things went a little differently. Wayne Wang was a Chinese American living in San Francisco, which has a large Asian community, and his entry film cans had been set up to reveal if they had been opened. They had not. It was an embarrassing development for a film that came to represent a new look at the Asian-American experience, through San Francisco's Chinatown. Festivals often view only several minutes of an entry if all the judges agree to not go on, but to not even open the film cans of a local Chinese filmmaker?

Wayne didn't give up and his film got in the New Directors program at the Museum of Modern Art in New York, and that basically launched his career. Roger Ebert wrote, "*Chan Is Missing* is a small, whimsical treasure of a film that gives us a real feeling for the people of San Francisco's Chinatown . . . Charlie Chan is missing from this film, and what replaces him is a warm, low-key, affectionate and funny look at some real Chinese-Americans." The *New York Times*'s Vincent Canby called it "a matchless delight."

This was just more evidence to me that the "art film" game was somewhat rigged and I had to find another way. What about Hollywood? Ever since *Easy Rider* had upended the movie business with a cheap road picture that seemed to come out of nowhere and make a fortune at the box office, the commercial movie business had changed. It was guerilla filmmaking at best, but if you could get a movie finished or almost finished, Hollywood could not afford to not take a look at it.

American Nitro

Working at Palmer's I had seen a lot of different kinds of small films come through that were fairly straightforward documentaries, industrials, commercials, or sales films. But a few were quite different. These were films that were made for a specific audience, like ski films or aviation films.

One day Bob Cummings came into our studio to do some voiceover work on a record called "The Sounds of Aviation." Cummings was an actor who had been in Alfred Hitchcock's *Saboteur* and *Dial M for Murder,* but he was perhaps most well-known for his long-running television program, *The Bob Cummings Show.* Bob's passion was airplanes, and for good reason: He was the godson of Orville Wright who, along with his brother Wilbur, were the aviation pioneers known as the Wright Brothers. It turns out that there was, and is, a passionate audience for anything aviation, even just the classic sounds.

Many similar projects came through, from the hugely popular ski films to one called *The Alaska Wilderness Adventure* by a man named Fred Meader. These filmmakers rented auditoriums or movie theaters for "one night only" showings and just raked in the cash from wildly enthusiastic fans of the subjects. The films were in fact smaller versions of Hollywood's so-called exploitation films. These guys deliberately targeted an audience and made "special interest" films just for them. Hollywood did rock 'n' roll and beach blanket movies, and these fellows did aviation, back to the earth, or sports films. Both were popular and made money. Hollywood did the drive-in circuit, and our guys did auditoriums or what was then called "four-walling," where you rented a movie theater on a slow night for a flat fee, ran your own show, and kept all the cash from the box office.

My friend George, who had done the DiMaggio recording, went to one of the screenings of *The Alaska Wilderness Adventure* and came back to report that the filmmaker, Fred, had come out of the auditorium with pockets stuffed full of cash. So, I began to think, why couldn't I do that? All I needed was a suitable topic to exploit.

The whole subject of "exploitation films" has been vastly misinterpreted. Mel Gibson's *The Passion of the Christ* is an exploitation film. Michael Moore's *Fahrenheit 9/11* is an exploitation film. It's a category, not a scarlet letter. These are genre films. They used to be called "B" movies and they occupied the bottom half of a double feature. They often had subjects like science fiction or horror; others were Westerns. Jack Nicholson went on to stardom from one of them, *Easy Rider*.

The distinction between "A" pictures and exploitation films ends when the bottom half of a double bill breaks out, as *Bonnie and Clyde* did in 1967. It was based on a little-known book that I happened to have read called *Dillinger Days,* by John Toland. When I first read the book, the chapter on Bonnie Parker and Clyde Barrow intrigued me. What a great movie idea, I thought.

When I finally saw that someone had indeed made the movie, it was at a drive-in as the bottom half of a double bill. In those days, drive-ins were called "ozoners" and walk-ins were called "hardtops" by the movie industry trade magazines. *Bonnie and Clyde* was the first movie that so impressed me that I went back the next day—this time to a hardtop—to see it again. I saw it as a brilliant breakthrough movie, and it was. But it didn't survive a horrendous Bosley Crowther review in the *New York Times,* and the distributor pulled the film from release. Crowther had called it "a cheap piece of bald-faced slapstick comedy that treats the hideous depredations of that sleazy, moronic pair as though they were as full of fun and frolic as the jazz-age cut-ups in *Thoroughly Modern Millie*."

But then, in an unprecedented event, the critical consensus reversed. *Time* magazine wrote a favorable review and apologized for its first negative one. The prominent film critic Pauline Kael wrote a rave review in the *New Yorker,* with the film going on to be a smash hit across the country. The movie's impact was so strong, it even influenced fashion styles for a time.

This event was a marker for me. A single bad review could destroy all your efforts in one day. Like a Broadway show with millions of dollars invested, your small effort could die at the box office before you even had a chance. In the movie business no one is immune to the prospect of an empty theater, not Steven Spielberg, not George Lucas, not anyone. No one cares that you have put your heart, soul, and all your money into a film that just dropped dead. Nor should they. It is one of the last great gambles that a person with no credentials can make, and if it pays off, there is no limit to the profits that are possible. When a film hits big, it is the fastest return of investment capital in the history of capitalism. Invest $200 million in a big-city skyscraper and you might see a return on your original investment in ten years. In a blockbuster film, you could see it in six months or less.

Years later, on *Jedi,* I was sitting next to George Lucas during an ILM lunch break and was able to engage him in a movie conversation. I mentioned that I thought that Arthur Penn's *Bonnie and Clyde* was a great film. George said, "Arthur called my office the other day, looking for work. His problem is that he is an 'A' director and an 'A' director commands an 'A' salary, and there aren't that many 'A' projects around these days." He also suggested that Penn was more of a "theatrical" director than a filmmaker, implying that that was a little passé. I felt like I was hearing Irving Thalberg explain why the legendary filmmaker Erich von Stroheim could no longer be a director and had to find work as an actor. It is not that I doubted anything George said, it was that this dose of reality just made me sad. It also reminds me now of something George said years later, when I was nearing the end of my Lucasfilm/ILM career. He was quoted as saying, "I am at a point financially where no one can tell me I am too old or too un-cool to make movies." That was to become my goal as well.

In my lifetime effort to remain independent enough to always be able to be "uncool" and still make movies, I found a project that I thought might fit the bill. What if I made a film that had a built-in audience?

My brother Jim and I were going to be partners in this project, and somewhat later we invited a friend of mine, Tim, to join us. We explored various topics but I really wanted to make something that was the exact opposite of my Johnson documentary, which had been a classic historical piece made with tons of research and the rare still photos and antique movie clips I had collected. I wanted to make something full of color and sound with as much action as was possible to record.

One weekend as Jim and I were driving around, we came upon what appeared to be an abandoned drag strip where they raced hopped-up cars. Neither of us knew anything about this sport, but as we peered through the chain-link fence, we could see large grandstands that held the spectators. My brother felt strongly that there was something here, something in this subject matter that could have, as he described it, "energy."

We later learned that this huge tract of land was owned by the Southern Pacific Railroad and it was currently leased to something called International Raceway Parks. There was perhaps a half-mile of asphalt strip with a carefully measured-off quarter-mile, equipped with a sophisticated array of timing lights that could measure speeds into the thousandths of a second. Overlooking the strip was a tall observation tower with large glass windows, which housed the race announcer as well as track officialdom. There was little else besides a snack bar and a tall white fence covered with billboard ads for cigarettes and motor oil. This security fence surrounded the racetrack in such a way that only paying customers could see anything or enter. Somehow we had slipped through an unlocked gate.

When I thought about it, I did have a connection to this place. All my summers as a child had been spent at my aunt's summer resort located in the Anderson Valley, which is about a hundred miles north of San Francisco. It was an idyllic place for childhood explorations and fun: sixty acres of farmland, a mile of riverfront for swimming and fishing, and the wonders of resort living, with its soda and ice cream fountain, recreation hall, croquet and tennis courts, and interesting guests from all over California. The guests got a cabin and three home-cooked meals a day in the large dining room for $65 a week. It was a real vacation for all the mothers—no cooking, just playing with the kids all day at the river and taking strolls down our country road after dinner. I loved it there.

After my parents died, I had petitioned my uncle in Marin to let me stay on at summer's end, and both he and my Anderson Valley aunt agreed it would be a good idea. The local high school was so small that at orientation day in the gymnasium, I asked the fellow next to me if our bleacher held the freshman class. "No," he said, "this is the entire school." Ours was the largest freshman class in the school's history, twenty-eight pupils. Now, when I hear someone say that they came from a small town, I just laugh.

I call this time my *American Graffiti* years. Drinking beer, driving hot rod cars, and chasing girls was my primary occupation back then. We even marked off the local highway and drag-raced our cars. Midway through high school, a rumor flooded our gossip channels. Someone had mounted an old jet engine from a WWII fighter plane on wheels and launched it down the Fremont drag strip. When they first fired it up, in front of a howling mob that filled the grandstands, the story went, the jet engine's force blew the fence down. Stories like this galvanized us; it seemed preposterous, but also funny and cool.

It was all coming back to me now. This track we were looking at—same track. This could be a movie, I thought: huge fan base, crazy antics, and potential drama by the boatload. It wasn't Woodstock, but it would have to do.

We went out for a look-see at the announcement of the next big race. If you lived in California back in the seventies, you will remember the radio ads for these race events. There were always two announcers screaming at the radio audience about dragsters, jet cars, and funny cars and ending with, "Sunday! Sunday! Sunday!" These ads blanketed the airwaves before every big race and would build crowds in the thousands.

I had seen surfing films and films on boxing, wrestling, and roller derby, but nothing like this. With nicknames like "The Snake" or "*The* Mongoose" or "Jungle Jim," these drivers piloted 2,000-horsepower dragsters with fiberglass bodies on them that just barely resembled the fans' street cars. They hauled their race cars from track to track around the country, sleeping in local motels and racing against each other for cash prizes, or if their name alone could guarantee a crowd, there would be a bonus payment for just showing up. It was a subculture, and I wanted to explore it.

My idea was to go out there and just turn on the camera and film what happened. The film theorists called it cinema verité (truthful cinema) or direct cinema. I just wanted to try to represent the subject as objectively as possible. I didn't want any narrator telling you what to make of all this—I had worked on too many documentaries like that. I wanted to capture this crazy subculture, and to document it right down to the last nut and bolt. This was Americana in the raw.

It wasn't easy. We had a little money from a real estate deal I had pulled off, but we had to learn how to capture what was going on in this wild, blue-collar sport that we really knew nothing about. We were all working full-time jobs, using holidays and weekends to film and vacation time for me to start editing it. My brother and I purchased a professional Eclair (a 16mm movie camera) and a Nagra tape recorder, along with editing equipment and a dual-system projection setup that would let us project our work, with sound, while we were still in progress.

For big races I would hire other cameramen and soundmen so we could cover each race from both ends of the track. We got real close to these cars so it would be authentic—closer than was wise, and closer than anyone would let you get today. Right on top of these nitromethane-burning cars it was so loud you could hardly stand it, and breathing, with the raw nitro fuel belching out of these monsters, was painful. Even with the huge ear protectors we used, the vibrations the sound waves set off in the air were so powerful, they once literally drove me to the ground. It rattled the marrow in my bones. Standing next to a jet plane taking off was nothing compared to this.

Every shot we took had live sync sound. Nothing was laid in afterwards as sound design. This caused huge problems when we tried to record people working on their cars in what they called the "pit" area of the track. Every driver and every car was spread out across this race-car prep area, into which the spectators and fans were allowed to wander for an extra fee. With the area studded with loudspeakers and huge engines that might erupt at any time, it was a nightmare to try to record the human voice. But through trial and error and a lot of wasted takes, we were finally able to master it.

What were we making here? My friends were puzzled. One told me that "you can't make a film that makes light of these people and also attract them as a paying audience." The screenwriter Terry Southern had warned, "You cannot have both joke and art." Yet, he went on to make *Dr.*

Strangelove with Stanley Kubrick, and that was exactly what I intended to do. I wanted that very balance, and since we had no sponsors, we could do whatever we wanted. The races were outrageous spectacles, and the personalities were outsized. The crew members had great nicknames. There was the pinstriper whose hands were so incredibly steady that he was tagged "Shaky Jake." Then there was "Waterbed Fred," who was known for his accomplishments with the ladies. This was a cornucopia of Americana, and I wanted in.

Part of making *American Nitro* was to just try and upset some stuffed shirts in the art world, and I knew it could be done. I had worked with the namesake nephew of the writer John Fante at Palmer's. His uncle had written a famous book called *Ask the Dust,* and his work has been described as "dirty realism." The painters of the so-called Ashcan school were also committed to a populist realism, so I knew I could invade a low-grade exploitation genre to reveal something that had not been explored before in the conventional art world. There were dangers that we would be misinterpreted, but I was willing to risk them.

In 1978 I saw a film by the celebrated documentary filmmaker Errol Morris called *Gates of Heaven,* a near-comedic account about people, their pets, and those that exploit them. It was a fine and sophisticated art film, much praised. I saw it in Berkeley near the UC campus and the audience roared with laughter at the people depicted in the film. If anyone featured in that film had been in the audience, they would have been mortified. He made fools of them. I vowed that I would never make a film that I couldn't show to the people in it. It is so easy to set someone up in a documentary like this that I think the filmmaker has a duty to fairness. If someone makes a fool out of himself, that is one thing; you don't have to egg him on and then celebrate it.

After we filmed enough races, we went on to document the guy in the jet car that I had heard about so many years ago in high school. It turned out that the driver had by now lost both his legs in a horrendous jet-car crash, yet having survived it, he continued to race with artificial legs. There were also many other so-called exhibition vehicles, like wheel-standing cars that ran down the track on their rear tires only, a motorcycle fitted with a hang glider that could jump huge distances over semitrucks parked end to end, and—the wildest of them all—mock military vehicles designed to look like tanks and howitzer transports that raced each other sporting blown nitro engines under the sponsorship of the United States Army. Part circus, part dangerous sport, we recorded it all.

We interviewed one major driver, Tom "The Mongoose" McEwen, at his home in Fountain Valley, California, where he kept his race cars in his suburban backyard. When we asked him if his neighbors ever complained about him tuning up his race cars there, he said, "If they did, every kid in the neighborhood would run away from home." Tom was the mastermind in bringing big-time sponsors, like toymaker Mattel, to the sport. Kids loved the model cars with their colorful names like *The Mongoose* and *The Snake,* and Tom was also behind the Mongoose bicycles that are still found in stores. But more than this, when other sports impresarios saw what Tom had accomplished—attracting sponsors other than sport-specific ones, like motor oil, to racing—they started to pile in, eventually redefining what sponsorship could be for all sports. It started with Tom.

We went to the engine builders and body and paint shops that fabricated the race cars and documented it all. This racing game was getting expensive, as the nitromethane fuel that both powered and exploded these engines at every race cost $340 per drum, and Tom had used thirty drums in 1978. This was at the height of the first American gas crisis, and the cars were burning six gallons of nitro fuel on a single quarter-mile run. It was all craziness, but I thought if we could just get this down on film, something could be made out of it. It was going to be our version of an art film disguised as a drive-in movie exploitation film, which I thought the hard-core fans would pay to see.

My only shot at art film status for this film came from the author Tom Wolfe. In 1965 Wolfe published his first book, which was a collection of essays. One of the essays, originally published in *Esquire* magazine in 1963, commented on L.A. car culture and was titled "The Kandy-Kolored Tangerine-Flake Streamline Baby." This article is noted for having changed American writing, introducing what was called "the new journalism." What Wolfe wrote was in response to what he saw:

> *The educated classes in this country, as in every country, the people who grow up to control visual and printed communication media, are all plugged into what is, when one gets down to it, an ancient, aristocratic aesthetic. Stock-car racing, custom cars—and, for that matter, the Jerk, the Monkey, rock music—still seem beneath serious consideration, still the preserve of ratty people with ratty hair and dermatitis and corroded thoracic boxes and so forth. Yet all these rancid people are creating new styles all the time and changing the life of the whole country in ways that nobody even seems to bother to record, much less analyze.*

Well, we were recording it in our movie, which we decided to call *American Nitro*. When we thought we had a good rough cut of the movie, we took it to some high school auto shop classes to screen it before our intended audience of adolescent males who were interested in cars. Boy, they did not want to watch a movie, and I didn't blame them, having seen so many bad instructional films in high school. But we convinced them that nothing like this had ever been shown in a school before and would never be again. They watched it. We had them fill out preview cards listing what they liked or didn't like. What did they like? "The fiery wrecks and crashes." We had plenty of those. What didn't they like? "The fat chick." We had a girls sequence as well as a crash sequence and we showed all the girls, not just the beauties, although there were plenty of those.

Our good or excellent scores were quite high, so we thought it was working. But my gut told me the movie was peaking too early. Rather than asking questions, sometimes your best clues to whether a movie is working or not is to just watch it with a fresh audience. If it drags you will sense it and soon start looking for a scissors to fix it. Because I was still running it on my interlock projector with separate picture and sound, I was able take it apart and fix it. I moved the high point as close as I could to the end of the movie. Following that climax, I showed the final race and brought up the music as we headed into the tail titles.

We were not going directly to film festivals—we were going to try our luck with Hollywood distributors. We set up screenings for several major studios and they all passed. It was too late, they had already done *Endless Summer,* the hit surfing movie, and now wanted to place their "A" pictures in the drive-ins. They had realized how much more money they could make going very wide and not discriminating between upscale and downscale theater venues.

But I had another idea: Why not go to the theater owners themselves? These guys were the real showmen—they knew what would work and what wouldn't. But the distributors had them over a barrel. The distributors controlled all the product and made the theater chains bid for the new pictures without ever getting a chance to see them. It was called "blind bidding." All they knew was that they were bidding against other large chains for the new James Bond film, for instance, sight unseen. And for this privilege they would have to return 90 percent of the first month's box office to the studios. They got the candy sales and the hope of reaching a 50 percent split if the film stuck around long enough. And there were some theaters that refused to replace films like *Star Wars* even after a year because they had reached the 50 percent split and were making so much money.

So I took our film and screened it for one of the largest theater chains in the western United States, Syufy, which later became Century Theatres. At the same time I was talking to sub-distributors that represented the local interests of many smaller national film distributors. The buyer for Syufy took one look at our movie and said, "I'll take it." This started the subs angling for it, and we chose one that represented a New York company called Cannon Releasing. They had one major hit, a picture starring Peter Boyle titled *Joe,* which made them a lot of money. The minute I stepped into their New York office, I knew they were crooks, but crooks with a distribution pipeline that would get our movie into at least one theater in almost every city in the United States, and following that, most of the rest of the world. It was a tradeoff: Either accept this bad deal now, while someone wanted to invest money in it and release it, or risk it sitting on a shelf like every other filmmaker's homemade movie.

Departing from the normal sequence of festivals to distribution, we did the opposite. Now that the film had distribution, we went to a couple of festivals. The first, in France, was the Deauville American

Film Festival. France has a history of celebrating American cinema. We sent our film but we were too poor to fly over and attend, so I have no idea how they reacted. I did get a few letters from foreign distributors, but Cannon had foreign.

The other festival was the huge Filmex festival in Los Angeles. For this screening, against the wishes of the L.A. fire department, we put a AA top fuel dragster in the lobby of the Dorothy Chandler Pavilion theater. I don't know what Dorothy would have made of it, but we got reviews in all the L.A. papers, including the trade magazines *Variety*, the bible of show business, and the *Hollywood Reporter*. But it was the description of the film in the Filmex catalog that we liked the best. It read: "It is an exercise in asphalt anthropology, capturing the rowdiness and violence of a Roman spectacle: high-speed crack-ups, men afire, semi-nude maidens in attendance, and the legions of racers and fans who have pledged their lives to timing records—and intangibles harder to define." Finally, someone got it.

One of the high points for me was walking down Madison Avenue in New York in 1979 and reading the *Variety* review of *Nitro*. I was thirty-two years old and had somehow gotten my movie into national distribution. It had been seven years since I got my Jack Johnson movie into distribution and I now had another one, but on a much larger scale. Exploitation film or not, I did it. There are many fine screenwriters in Hollywood that make lots of money selling screenplays for movies that never actually get made.

By now Cannon Distributing had been sold to some real shysters named Golan and Globus. They took our film and several others (one was called *Gas Pump Girls*) and bundled them like sub-prime mortgages, raising millions of dollars on the potential of the bundled films to generate cash flow. This was a neat trick and it propelled Cannon to great heights. What we got out of it was a full-page ad displaying our movie poster in *Variety* and a worldwide release.

The Cannon distribution strategy was to go into an area like Sacramento or the San Francisco Bay Area and blanket the radio and television media with the movie trailer and radio spots and hope to fill theaters. We sold out the theaters in some places and usually lasted a week, sometimes two weeks. But it was a new world. We were opening against major studio pictures like *The Deer Hunter* and *Escape from Alcatraz.* It was like walking amongst elephants. One wrong step and you would be crushed.

It was actually quite a rush. We ran around to every city we could reach, from San Francisco to Los Angeles, peeking over drive-in movie theater fences to see our movie playing on the huge screens. We even had the local distributor call an indoor "hardtop" and the manager came down to his theater on a Sunday to let us into a screening there. No filmmakers had ever shown up at his movie house in all the years he had been in business, and he was intrigued. So were we.

Friends sent me photos of movie marquees displaying *American Nitro* in towns all across the country. The movie generated about $1.2 million in ticket sales, which was pretty good for a kind of outsider art film posing as an exploitation picture. Our end of this should have been about 40 percent since we had financed it. Getting paid was another matter.

When I first started looking for a distributor, I called a guy I knew that had directed some low-budget films. I told him I was thinking of writing letters to distributors about my film. He said, "That would be like sending a postcard to Stalin." I had no idea how rough the movie business could be. When Cannon was bought out by two Israeli cousins named Golan and Globus, they raised enough money to launch a renewed Cannon Films and eventually built the company to near-major-studio status. That is, until they were brought down by a Securities and Exchange Commission investigation that torpedoed their stock price. I hope we had some small hand in that because we amply supplied the commission with reams of paperwork. Subsequently we got a rather large check and the rights to our movie were returned to us. The last time I saw either Golan or Globus was in a photo not long after our settlement—they were being introduced to the Queen of England.

I learned that if anyone ever does get paid on one of these percentage-of-profit deals, it is because the studio wants his next project. We didn't have another project yet, so it took several years and a lot of legal expenses to become whole again, but we did it just in time for the home video revolution.

By 1987 home video sales were the major profit generator for the studios. I first noticed this when all of our ILM clients from Steven Spielberg on suddenly changed their movie release standard from wide-screen Panavision back to the historic almost square, television-screen-friendly format of the past. What was going on?

I found out when we decided to rerelease our movie on VHS tape, now that we had gotten the rights back. We signed up for a booth at the Las Vegas Convention Center during a big home-video dealers convention. It was a madhouse. The "booth" alone for the video release of the movie *Platoon* reportedly cost $1 million to build. We had a card table. People were placing huge orders for video titles to rent in video stores all over the world. Even the porn distributors where there, having left their Learjets at the Las Vegas airport. They were selling porn tapes for $100 each, cash only, and the line of buyers stretched across the auditorium.

This convention demonstrated why major movies were now released in standard format. Widescreen was too expensive and difficult to transfer to home video, and the distribution money was now largely in renting and selling tapes. We took orders like everyone else and sold some tapes, but we didn't have a national ad campaign to help sell our movie and we would never again sign up with a distributor—it's too hard to get paid. We were a little early for what I wanted to do, but that would come with the rise of the Internet, YouTube, Facebook, and PayPal.

Right now my job was still at Lucasland, but I didn't want to see myself totally swallowed up in it any more. My goal had always been to work somewhere in the movie business to make a living, but to also have my own outside projects. Getting the distribution rights for *Nitro* back helped me retain and expand my own creative interests once again.

The Screamer

At ILM we studied images all day, sitting in darkened screening rooms watching special effects shots over and over looking for flaws, looking for more ways to fool the eye into seeing what we wanted people to see. Our movie projectors had been modified so we could run our film at any speed and also run in reverse. The projection booths could be filled with racks of film rollers so we could loop any shot we wanted to study. And study we did, endlessly. Beyond this we would have the shots flopped left–right and watch them from this new perspective, trying to refresh our brains to see things anew, always seeking clues as to what we could add that might sell the shot as real.

When I first started working at ILM, I just sat there and listened to the others' comments, but over time I began to see things myself. It was all about perspective: light and shadow, balance and redirection. We wanted to take temporary control of the viewer's brain and convince him or her that we were telling the truth, when we obviously were lying. We were offering visual proof to support our lies and we almost always won because we had a coconspirator—the audience. They always want to suspend their disbelief; they love being fooled and scared, being pushed to the edge and then surprised and relieved when we pull them back. So we got really good at that. Soon my eye doctor was asking, "What the hell do you do for a living? Your eye tests are off the charts!"

But we couldn't fool everyone. George had moved his company away from Hollywood, but we still had to work with them. The idea was to work on other directors' movies in between movies that George wanted to make. In this way a large staff of talented people could be kept together until another Lucas production came along. Otherwise, all the talent would have to be laid off and it would disperse back to Los Angeles, where the majority of the movie industry was located. So we went to work for Hollywood.

I used to say that working for Lucasfilm was like a Boy Scout camp compared to Hollywood or New York filmmaking, and I didn't know how our people were going to mix with them. We were soon to find out.

On *Die Hard 2* (1990), we were supposed to do some plane crash shots. We got to bid on the job through the wooing of the producer, Joel Silver, by our sales staff. Now, the first thing you have to know about Silver is that he is one of the most important producers in Hollywood. He produced the *Die Hard* pictures and the *Lethal Weapon* pictures, as well as *48 Hrs.*, *The Matrix,* and scores of others. His pictures have made the studios billions of dollars in ticket sales. The *Hollywood Reporter* devoted an entire issue to saluting him, and practically the whole industry took out vanity ads saying how much they all liked and admired him. The second thing you have to know is that Joel is a screamer. If he doesn't get his way, he will throw a red-faced, vein-bulging tantrum.

I discovered that Joel was a lot younger than I anticipated when he came by Industrial Light and Magic, where our general manager and publicity people had arranged a special screening for him. He was actually an interesting character who collected major artworks and Frank Lloyd Wright houses. He would buy and restore the Wright houses at great expense and then keep them as residences for himself.

On this day we were going to show Joel the forest fire footage that we had shot for Steven Spielberg's film *Always,* which starred Richard Dreyfuss (who for some reason people occasionally mistake me for), John Goodman, and Holly Hunter. We had just finished our work on this picture and we had an impressive reel of major fire effects to show him. Our crews had rented a giant old car-assembly plant near Point Richmond, not far from our studio. Tons of live trees that looked real but were actually about one-quarter scale in size were brought into this massive industrial building and set ablaze.

The setup had a giant firefighting-type aircraft that our model shop had built on a gantry simulating flight over a raging forest fire. When edited together into a sequence with close-ups of the actors in simulated—but full-size—cockpits, this footage made a very exciting and realistic forest fire fight.

Just as we were about to roll the film for Mr. Silver to demonstrate what great work we could do for him, he turned around in his seat and said to the group, "The fire sequence in my film is being done by a friend of mine, who happens to be in the effects business. I will look at your reel, but just to be clear, I don't fuck my friends."

I am not sure, but I don't think many people in that room had ever seen this reel. They had seen the movie, of course, but this was different. It wasn't just the short, quick cuts that had been selected to cut into the movie—this was an all-out, nonstop, traveling shot of a large plane set against a wildly exploding backdrop of a massive forest in full blaze. It was impressive.

When the lights came up, Joel was excited. He told us that this was the greatest fire effects reel he had ever seen and we were soon awarded the work. So much for friendship in Hollywood. Joel, however, was not done with us yet. When you sign on with this guy, you are along for a wild ride.

We went down to the 20th Century Fox studio to meet with Joel and his director for *Die Hard 2,* Renny Harlin. We went to the air terminal set and then to Joel's office, which was in one of those old-style bungalows that only the biggest of Hollywood stars used to rate. Here we showed the director and producer some actual FAA airplane crash tests. These were a reference for discussing our special effects shots for the movie. Everyone was impressed with the video, and the rate of speed for shooting our miniatures was discussed.

There was a problem. The director, after learning that we planned to cover the shots with only three high-speed cameras, suggested we use more. At that point our visual effects supervisor, Mike McAlister, who was responsible for shooting all of this, explained that this would not only increase costs, but there were not that many of this special type of camera available.

Joel walked in and out of our meeting room taking phone calls all through the discussion. We were in a white, wood-frame building that had originally been built for Frank Sinatra. This fact alone attested to Joel's importance to the studio. The bungalow was paneled in wood but very sparsely furnished. His modern art was displayed. Big ceramic cars, classic movie posters, and toys with movie themes were scattered about. It was all very informal, more like an artist's studio than a production office. Joel was famous for saying, "I'm not in this business to make art; I'm in it to make money to buy art."

The budget came up. Joel said he had just talked to the studio and they wouldn't approve more than a certain figure. The ILM producer for this project was Chrissie England. She had started at Lucasfilm in 1977 as a receptionist, and by 1978 was George Lucas's secretary. She was one of the oldest employees, and it was rumored that George had granted her a job for life. Whatever the case, she was quite attractive and knew how to deal with powerful men. Chrissie mentioned that additional shots would cost about $300,000 more.

Joel started to talk, but I could see that something very strange was happening to him right before our eyes. It was as if we were seeing Dr. Jekyll slowly transforming into the monster, Mr. Hyde. He was working up a ferocious anger. First he talked loud. Then he swore a little bit. He used this to feed adrenaline into his system. He built up this yelling until he was screaming. When he screamed, he would look up at the ceiling and his neck was bulging like the Hulk. He kept saying not to bring up "MORE COSTS." He did not want to hear that there would be "MORE COSTS." This tirade built to a crescendo that instructed us to "NEVER MENTION IT TO HIM AGAIN." We were no longer in Marin County.

During this screaming tirade I was dying to stand up and say, "I have to go to the toilet." But I couldn't do it. It might have cost me my job, and this guy wasn't worth it. I knew how to deal with him; I had seen this before in New York when confronted with a similar situation. If you start to laugh at this type of guy, the air escapes them and they fold like a punctured ball. But it wasn't my choice; I was part of a team.

Chrissie said that some things could be cut. Mike said that he would never add anything unnecessarily. Joel, point made, became normal and left the room. But he only stopped just outside the door and sent for Renny, the director, who had said nothing during the outburst but must have been in shock to find that his requests were in jeopardy.

Safely outside, the director undoubtedly received assurances that this was just business and not to worry, you will have everything you need. In Hollywood, directors, writers, actors, and some others are universally referred to as "talent." They are a special class, a special breed, and they are given the widest latitude possible, especially when they are in the middle of a costly production.

When we left, Mike stopped the director and said, "What do you want me to do? I work for you. But after this, I'm not going to add anything." After a long pause, the director said, "This is a process we have to go through [meaning the screaming fits about money]. It will eventually work itself all out."

Chrissie and I walked back to the car together and I said, "I wouldn't take this too seriously. I'm sure this guy pulls this crap at his Mercedes dealer when he doesn't like the price."

Die Hard 2 had been budgeted at a cost of $42 million (a big number at the time), but it ballooned to $67 million. It was reported that when a Fox executive admonished Silver, the producer would reply, "Fuck you, slimeball."

Die Hard 2 grossed $240 million worldwide.

The Players

Dealing with Joel Silver was not the first time we had had problems with studio clients. It goes with the territory. With the 1986 film *The Golden Child,* staring Eddie Murphy, ILM started out on a good footing with the director, Michael Ritchie, and with the production company. At this point we were on a roll as the hottest effects company in the world. Although Hollywood resented anyone outside of Los Angeles, we were too important to ignore, so we had their grudging respect. That didn't last long on this production.

At first, they accepted everything we suggested with a "you're the experts" attitude. But because the work was so difficult to pull off and was so slow in coming, the director gradually became unhappy with my supervisor, Ken Ralston, and ILM in general. In addition, it didn't help that the other big movie we were working on at the time, *Star Trek III: The Search for Spock,* was in trouble and Ken had been enlisted to helm both pictures at the same time. When Michael Ritchie found out, he became furious.

Basically, for *Golden Child* we were to create a monster that the bad guy in the movie could turn into, and who Eddie Murphy could face in battle. Murphy had picked this project to try to expand the range of characters he could play.

For one of our first production meetings, the *Golden Child* team flew up to ILM to confer with us. Here, we were to go over the storyboards and discuss how many expensive visual effects shots would be necessary to tell the story, how each would be shot, and in which shots we would need to see both the monster and Eddie. Sometimes we could suggest ways to eliminate shots, which was important because losing just one shot might save the production studio $200,000. This whole process was full of landmines for us, however, because while we wanted to please the director and give him what he wanted, the studio was the one paying the bills, so we had an obligation to them as well.

We had to start the meeting without one major player, the producer, Edward S. Feldman. When he finally did arrive, he turned out to be an older gentleman who walked with a cane. He reminded me of the college professor I had in speech class, but he had a good story about why he was late. It seems that it was Feldman's job to see that Eddie Murphy, who was at a high point in his career, had a house near the studio in Los Angeles that was suitable for a star.

There are a lot of houses for rent in Hollywood or, more precisely, Beverly Hills, Brentwood, and Holmby Hills. Some have been purchased by investors and are rented out between sales, and some are owned by people who move about the world and between houses as they work in the entertainment industry. These houses are listed in the back pages of industry trade publications like the *Hollywood Reporter*, especially the Friday edition. The rents on these places were astounding. Many mansions would go for $75,000 a month or more, and were the type that studios would rent for their stars, recording artists, or executives as temporary residences.

Now, the house that Eddie wanted was the mansion that the musician Prince had recently been living in. But there was a problem. It seems that Eddie believed that Prince was a devil worshiper or into Satanism or something that looked like it, and Eddie, being a Catholic, refused to move into the mansion until the place could be cleansed.

The only person qualified to do this kind of work was a Catholic priest so, Feldman says, "That's why I was late. I was trying to find a priest that could do an exorcism on the house." Welcome to Hollywood.

When Murphy finally came up to ILM for his blue-screen shoot, he had a small black entourage with him and they all pretty much kept to themselves. He had a limo and his buddies had one as well. He had also brought a motor home for relaxing in between takes. None of this is unusual, of course, it was just that Eddie was very stiff and ill at ease. Even the director, Michael Ritchie, couldn't seem to loosen him up, and

Murphy had specifically chosen Ritchie as the director. I certainly didn't expect Murphy to be funny.

This reminded me of an account I had read of someone who was at Groucho Marx's house while Groucho and all his comedian friends watched a new comic on television. The writer observed that while the TV comic was very funny, neither Groucho nor his buddies laughed. They would simply remark, "Now that, that was funny." They were in total analyst mode. Not that all comedians are like that—there are exceptions. Jim Carrey and the late Robin Williams, for example, could be so "on" that you worried about them.

Perhaps because ILM and Marin County are so lily-white, Eddie never really relaxed, let alone joked around. He did do some crew photos with some of our production assistants, but that was about all.

But there is something else that is related to this standoffishness that has always surprised me about the movie business, and that is in what low esteem actors are sometimes held by the crew. Perhaps it is because the actors come in and do their bit and then leave their images and multiple takes with the directors, editors, and post-production crews who will have to work with this material, reviewing and re-reviewing it for months and months. Perhaps this causes an insensitivity to set in. The actors wear on you as you see the same scenes and hear the same lines over and over again. Hundreds of times. Thousands of times. You spend so much time in screening rooms wading through miles of these performances, oftentimes without the benefit of sound, that I suppose it is only natural for the subjects to become the butt of flip remarks. This is especially true if the crew senses what, in their minds, is phoniness or pretentiousness. Oddly, it is often the director who will either start it or egg it on.

During *Memoirs of an Invisible Man* in 1992, another vehicle for a star—this time Chevy Chase—trying to break his stereotype, the actor was being insulted by the director, John Carpenter (at least behind his back). John kept saying that Chevy was a pussy. To me, Chase was good on camera, relaxed and funny. I thought he did a good job and his movie wasn't half bad. But off-camera he was treated like a ditz for his posing and small tantrums. His wearing a toupee didn't help either. Few actors escape this. Perhaps we in the movie trenches know too much. We know that actors are just people, with publicity agents. Only the true professionals seem to entirely escape these negative critiques from the crew.

For example, when Hume Cronyn and Jessica Tandy were working on *Cocoon* in 1986 at ILM for the director and former child star Ron Howard, they commanded great respect. Certainly for their talent, but also for their unassuming naturalness that must have come from working in the theater—which is more of an actor's medium than film and where the crew is more part of a team—for so many years. Also, I think we were all impressed to see these two relaxing and talking to bystanders and then instantly transforming themselves into their characters the moment the director said, "OK, let's try one." It was as if they just turned slightly and began performing exactly where they had left off, without missing a beat. It appeared so effortless and casual that it was hard to not be impressed.

Also on *Cocoon* the atmosphere on the set was completely different. For starters, the director, Ron Howard, had been an actor for most of his life. Of course, he had been a child star, perhaps most well-known for his role as Opie on the old Andy Griffith television show, but he had survived the ending of his childhood acting career and resumed it as a young adult in, interestingly enough, *American Graffiti,* where he first worked with Lucas. His recollections on working with George on *Graffiti* are instructive. Apparently, George's direction of actors was limited to instructions like "faster," "slower," or "that was great." Ron went up to him and said, "Just tell us what you want. We're actors, we can do it." No small part of an actor's success is working with a director who understands actors.

When Ron showed up at ILM to work on *Cocoon,* he had already directed two hits, *Grand Theft Auto* (classic exploitation film) and *Splash.* I remember him bursting into my editorial department saying, "Where's George?" He must have been proud to return as a successful director, and he was about to get a lot more successful with *Cocoon.*

One evening Ron asked to book our small screening room so he could show his current *Cocoon* rough cut to his producers, Lily and Richard Zanuck. Richard had produced *Jaws*, *The Sting,* and *The Sound of Music* among many other major films and would next produce *Driving Miss Daisy*. In addition, his father was Daryl Zanuck, the legendary studio boss who ran 20th Century Fox for nearly 40 years. Richard's wife,

Artist's apology drawing left on my desk.
AUTHOR'S COLLECTION

Building D screening room with me just to the right behind George Lucas. AUTHOR'S COLLECTION

My childhood next-door neighbor, Bessie Barriscale (Mrs. Hickman). AUTHOR'S COLLECTION

Me with E.T., the subject of a small film that surprised us all except for our receptionist. AUTHOR'S COLLECTION

Posing with famous actors in the ILM model shop. AUTHOR'S COLLECTION

At my ILM editing bench beneath one of those Zoetrope photos that seemed to follow me around the movie business. AUTHOR'S COLLECTION

Me filming entirely too close to nitro-burning dragsters. AUTHOR'S COLLECTION

Squishing Bob Hoskins for *Roger Rabbit* was easy. Making it look funny was the hard part. AUTHOR'S COLLECTION

Directing the great Slim Pickens in a TV spot. AUTHOR'S COLLECTION

Our family home in San Francisco as it looked in 1916 before my father bought it.
AUTHOR'S COLLECTION

Our ILM front office display sometime in the 1990s.
AUTHOR'S COLLECTION

Snapshot of George's office at the Ranch. AUTHOR'S COLLECTION

ILM lobby mannequin of Darth Maul. AUTHOR'S COLLECTION

My favorite spot at ILM, the model shop. AUTHOR'S COLLECTION

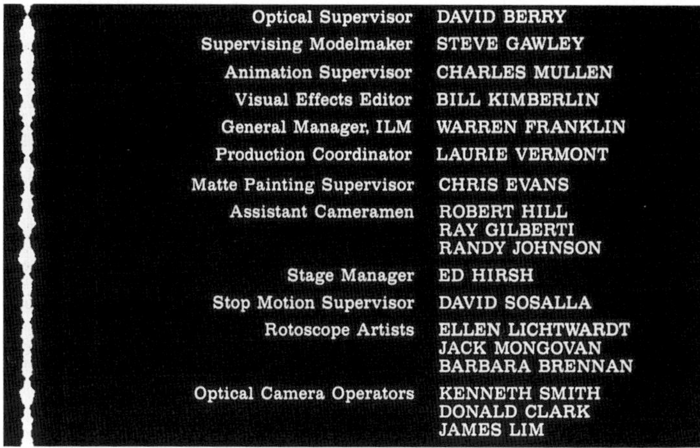

Jedi film credits. My name in that endless list. AUTHOR'S COLLECTION

"Jungle Jim" car and fan from *American Nitro*. PHOTO CREDIT: BEVERLY CONNOR; AUTHOR'S COLLECTION

Original ILM door disguised as The Kerner Company. It now hangs on the wall of the new ILM in the San Francisco Presidio. PHOTO CREDIT: JEFF DORAN; AUTHOR'S COLLECTION

Reminder to cameramen posted on the wall in our VistaVision line-up room at ILM. Note graffiti by camera assistants. AUTHOR'S COLLECTION

I'm lining up space ships for a shot in *Jedi*. Note the black-and-white strips I'm bipacking together. These were quick camera tests identical to the color film shot for the movie. Just easier to work with on many element shots. AUTHOR'S COLLECTION

The Ranch main house as seen from Lake Ewok. My first year, only part of the foundation had been built and we asked George what it was going to be. He responded, "That will be my office." AUTHOR'S COLLECTION

My meeting with Francis Coppola at the Zoetrope Studios in San Francisco. This was pre-*Godfather* and he is offering his help. AUTHOR'S COLLECTION

Better Hurry
Up Bill.

A note from my boss Ken Ralston. This is how we dealt with the pressure, we joked about it. AUTHOR'S COLLECTION

Our film *American Nitro* opened against some stiff competition, but we survived. AUTHOR'S COLLECTION

We showed our movie to artist Larry Duke and this is what he came up with. Just the outrageous tone we wanted and the hint there might be something more to this movie. AUTHOR'S COLLECTION

PROJECT: Jedi | SHOT: SB-19 | DATE: 2-15-83 | EDITOR: Bill K.

KEY NUMBER	↓ THIS CROSSES OVER →	1	2 Falcon	3 X-Wing	4 A-Wing #1	5 A-Wing #2	6 Y-Wing	7 Deathstar	8 DS 1F	9 DS IN	10 Endor tk-3	11 Endor 3M	12 Acbars Cruiser	13 Acbar Cr. 1L	14 Reb Fleet	15 Reb F
36X 60124-138	1) Fakon (SB-55 tk2)		X	X	X	X	X	X	X	X	X			X	X	X
62X 16990-7002	2) X-Wing (SB-55#1-1)			X	X	X	X	X	X	X	X			X	X	X
62X 81908-923	3) A-Wing (SB-55#1-1)					X				X	X			X	X	X
362X 17052-067	4) A-Wing (SB-55#2-1)						X	X	X	X	X	X	X	X	X	X
362X 17019-034	5) Y-Wing (SB-55#1-1)									X	X			X	X	X
562X 67607-623	6) Deathstar tk1 Mirror									X	X					X
R62X 67624-640	7) Deathstar 1F Mirror									X	X					X
B62X 67655-672	8) Deathstar IN Mirror									X	X					X
362X 86886-904	9) Endor tk3															X
B62X 86905-921	10) Endor 3M															X
62X 38317-333	11) Acbars Cruiser tk1						X	X	X	X	X			X	X	X
62X 38334-353	12) Acbars Cruiser 1L						X	X	X	X	X			X	X	X
362X 99567-582	13) Reb Fleet 1A						X	X	X	X	X					X
62X 99595-609	14) Reb Fleel 1M						X	X	X	X	X					X
62X 23078-091	15) Stars tk1															

My instruction sheet for building *Jedi* Space Battle shot #19 (SB19). Note that the first five ships I used were from another shot. AUTHOR'S COLLECTION

One of my many employee gifts from Lucasfilm, this one showing the original name of *Return of the Jedi*. AUTHOR'S COLLECTION

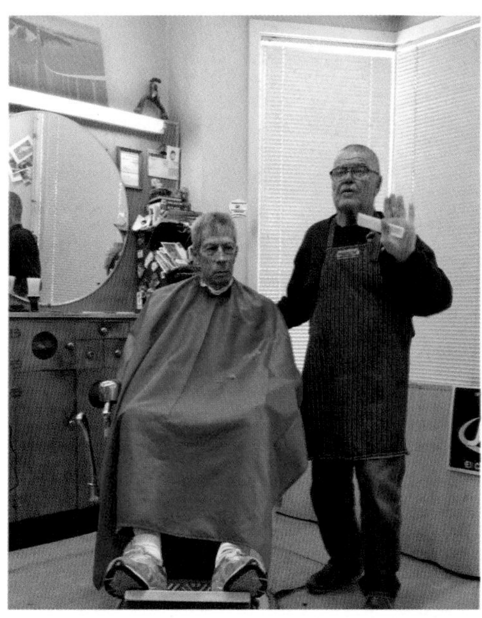

My friend Phil the barber. You never know who will walk into Phil's shop. I spent a week flying around on Gordon Getty's private airliner because of Phil. AUTHOR'S COLLECTION

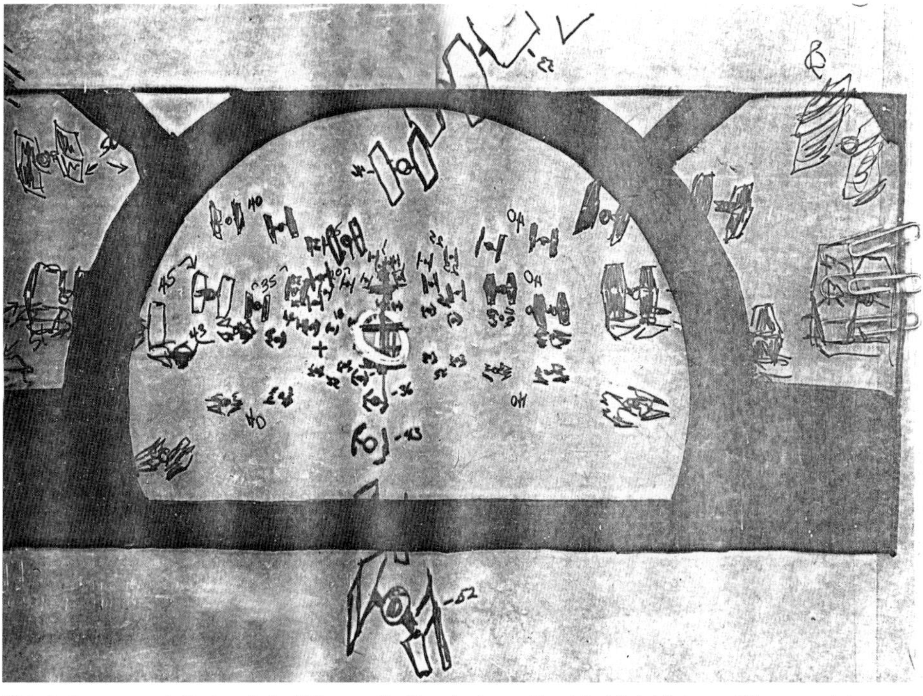

This is how we plotted out *Jedi* Space Battle shots on the big VistaVision editing machines. We made a mask representing the Panavision cutoff and piled cells with outlines of every ship in the shot at every frame where they moved significantly. It could get confusing especially when you were in a hurry, which was always. AUTHOR'S COLLECTION

This is in the C theater. We had a kind of totem tower listing the films we had worked on and any Oscars won. R2 stood guard. AUTHOR'S COLLECTION

Saved *Newsweek* cover story from our pre–Radio City Music Hall screening dinner where the producers grabbed it out of my hands in a frenzy. Notice the sweaty hand smears over Roger's head and the "Who is . . ." title. That's producer flop-sweat fears. AUTHOR'S COLLECTION

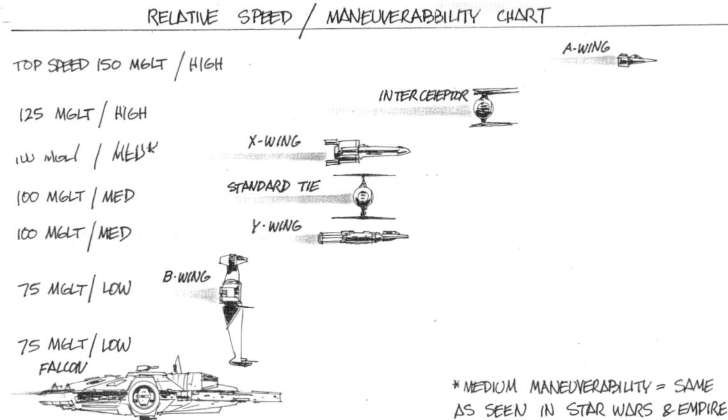

This hung in the ILM line-up room where we built up shots for *Jedi*. This is how we maintained consistency between Star Wars films. Primitive, but effective. AUTHOR'S COLLECTION

We all got to pick an original hand-painted cell from *Roger Rabbit*. I chose the scene where Eddie Valiant tells Roger how his brother was killed by a Toon. Shows how painted animation synced with live action. AUTHOR'S COLLECTION

When the movie first came out I bought this Roger doll in its original box. AUTHOR'S COLLECTION

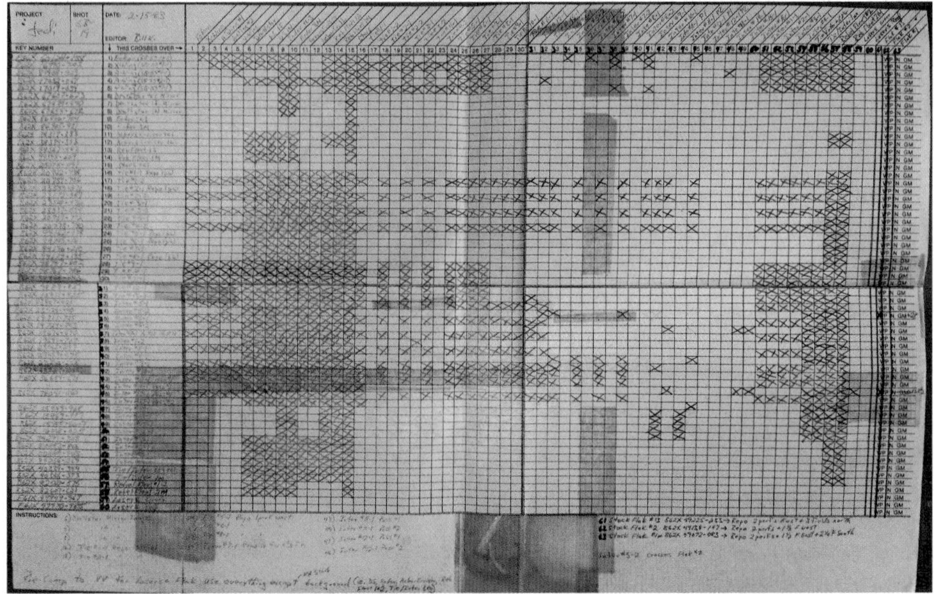

What we called a crossover sheet, my instructions for optically printing ships in front of the Death Star in *Jedi* Space Battle Shot #19 (cover photo). SB19 had so many elements that I had to tape four regular ones together. The small X's represent to the printer where I want one ship to pass in front of another. AUTHOR'S COLLECTION

Working camera on my friend Rick Schmidt's film in Death Valley. The actress holding an Oscar in extreme close-up says, "I would like to thank the Academy . . ." and we pull out to reveal where she came from. AUTHOR'S COLLECTION

We had this relative size chart posted on our wall in *Roger Rabbit* effects editorial. I'm smiling just looking at it. AUTHOR'S COLLECTION

The rest of a long, long chart. AUTHOR'S COLLECTION

Caught some stage crew moving a Storm Trooper across the studio lot. One seemed to think I was the Paparazzi. AUTHOR'S COLLECTION

Technical building, Skywalker Ranch. George designed the Ranch along a storyline. What if an old farmer suddenly got rich and converted a winery building to another purpose? It has bricked-up windows, as if it had been repurposed and not built new. AUTHOR'S COLLECTION

Titanic model we built for *Ghostbusters*. AUTHOR'S COLLECTION

The Pit. Spaz's ILM lair deep under C theater. L to R Mark Dippe, Dennis Muren, Eric Armstrong, Steve "Spaz" Williams. Note foreground T-Rex model. PHOTO CREDIT: © INDUSTRIAL LIGHT & MAGIC. ALL RIGHTS RESERVED.

Lily, was a lot younger than Richard, but far from a trophy wife. She was an aggressive and talented producer in her own right. During breaks in shooting the effects for *Cocoon* on the main stage, we all ate a catered lunch together and I got a kick out of Lily's encouraging Richard to tell stories about Hollywood in the old days. "He's got a million of them," she said with the glee of a kid wanting to hear the same bedtime stories over and over. I didn't doubt that this man, whose famous father had once fired him and had him thrown off the studio lot, had great stories to tell but it was his unerring eye for the projects to pursue that impressed me. In the fast-buck world of Hollywood, what kind of producer decides to make a movie about old people (*Cocoon*) and then another movie about a black chauffer and an even older woman (*Driving Miss Daisy*)? A great producer, that's what kind. Richard and Lily picked up the Best Picture Oscar for *Daisy*.

Usually directors are a little nervous about showing their films before they are done, but in this case Ron was happy for anyone to take a peek. I sat in on the screening for Richard and Lily, and it was easy to tell this was a good movie. The acting was great, and the story just flowed.

You can learn a lot by watching a film that doesn't have all the final polish yet. With most really good films you start to watch and learn, but pretty soon you are pulled in and you get caught up in it, and the next thing you know, it's over. With an unfinished film or sometimes even a bad film, there is less chance it will mesmerize you and you've got a chance to examine it and see how the machinery is working. The few times I have taught a class in filmmaking (at San Francisco State University and S.F. City College), I had the students watch the famous scene in the original *Godfather* where Michael, the war hero, explains how the family can kill McCluskey, the corrupt police captain. I had them watch that scene silent so they could see how the director, Francis Coppola, uses a long, slow dolly shot all the way across the room to end with a big close-up of Michael's face just as he finishes his speech with "then I'll kill them both." The dialogue is great, but the big dramatic punch is all the more effective when it is set up just right. Watching that scene without sound and then listening to it without the picture is one way to get just enough detachment to learn something.

Watching this rough cut of *Cocoon,* I couldn't tell that Ron Howard was going to go on to be a major director, but I could see he was a bright kid with an infectious sense of how much fun this all was, making movies. I also knew that Richard Zanuck, his producer, had mentored and protected Steven Spielberg on *Jaws* when the going got rough and the mechanical shark they were using in the water off Martha's Vineyard wouldn't work half the time. Richard called the studio and said, "If I see one studio Learjet set down in Martha's Vineyard, I will shut the production down." That is how a good producer protects his director and the project. Richard knew just how to deal with the powerful at the studio: threaten their profits.

What Do You Do?

My fellow editors and I used to joke about people coming to work for Lucasfilm as being "rescued." You could make good money there as opposed to almost any other outside job. You could get promoted and move higher on the salary scale. You could buy a house and many did, especially when it became apparent that if you were asked back on new pictures, this job wasn't going to end anytime soon. Directors were lining up to get our "secret sauce" of visual effects that would set their movies apart from the rest.

Yet, what was I involved in here? It was an exciting place to work, at least in the early days, because for the first time I was in a situation where there seemed to be no limits as to where I could go. There was a time when just mentioning that you worked at Lucasfilm would get you a job interview. Yet I wasn't in command of the ship anymore. When I worked at Palmer's, there was time to pursue other things. I had made two films while working there, and both got distribution. My Grandfather Mason had admonished his sons, "Don't ever work for anybody. Work for yourself."

There is a line in the movie *The Misfits* (written by Arthur Miller) that is bantered about by several characters regarding roping wild horses that will become dog food: "It's better than wages. Anything is better than wages." You could lose your soul taking a job. I had seen it many times. It was a dangerous thing, especially if the money was good. You could get caught as a waiter, say, making $300 a night in tips and get used to the easy money and not be able to give it up. Then you wake up one day and that is what you are, a waiter. I kept asking myself, am I doing that? Am I just a glorified waiter?

I had known guys that had it even worse. Their job became their identity. It was the first question asked when meeting someone at a social gathering: "What do you do for a living?" It was epidemic. Once you took that job, you were an employee. America had become an entire nation of employees. I used to think, what's going to happen to these people if they lose their jobs? They think they are safe, but they are not. They've got a house and a car and a family. Everything depends on that job now.

But of course there was a downside to any artistic lifestyle that was perfectly expressed in the old joke, "What do you call an artist without a girlfriend? Homeless." When I was hustling to make my own films after college, my friends all talked about it. How long can we go on doing this before we can't anymore? How many years are we going to give ourselves to "make it" before we have to admit that it's never going to happen? And then what? It was scary to contemplate being forty years old with no career and a thin résumé. I remember the words of Mario Puzo who, after a life of failure as a minor novelist, became a best-selling author with his book and movie deal for *The Godfather.* A reporter asked him how it felt and he said, "It's like finding out you don't have to die."

As a guy trying to be a filmmaker, I was neither the first nor the last to waddle through this dilemma. Everyone has to find their own path. I had taken what little I knew about my family and used it as a model. As a doctor, my father worked for himself. My aunt and uncle owned and ran a summer resort. They were not employees, they could not be laid off. They could go bankrupt, but you couldn't fire them. Was even a part of this still possible?

I thought back to my old landlords the Agneses, who owned apartment buildings. If a person could get their name on some California real estate deeds, that might just do it. So I started working on this as a backup plan while I was still hustling to make films and write. William Faulkner had said that the best job he was ever offered was to become a manager in a brothel. In his opinion, it was the perfect milieu for an artist to work in.

Then I got "rescued." I was pulled into a world that was moving so fast that there was little time for such niceties as your own life. This was more like a battlefield environment. There were generals to encourage advancing, nurses to comfort the wounded, and a firing squad for deserters. Veterans guided the new troops and recounted their past victories under George, the supreme commander and benevolent dictator. Success was our narcotic; box office and Oscars our goal. We also tried to make the coolest-looking stuff we could come up with.

Yet I was always looking for a side business or backup plan as insurance against the fickle nature of filmmaking, where you are essentially fired every Friday. Ever since 1973 when I did my first land lease deal, I had started becoming obsessed with real estate. I drove around with real estate option contracts in my glove box, just in case I saw the right property. I bought all the books and studied the tax advantages. Double declining depreciation schedules, expenses to offset income taxes from salary income, investment leverage ratios, property tax caps—I learned it all.

Real estate investing has many stories of missed opportunities. The best advice I ever got was this admonition: "The profit is made in the purchase, not the sale." That may sound counterintuitive but it's just another way of saying, "Buy low, sell high." I did a few deals but I ultimately decided I would rather make a movie than repair broken plumbing, at least for the moment. Still, there was one property that got away that annoys me yet. It was on Washington street in San Francisco's Pacific Heights district. Three four-bedroom flats for $119,000. That building today is worth at least $7 million.

The Oracle

At the center of everything was Oracle. It was the Lucasfilm database system, and in 1982 Oracle was my introduction to computers. It was a Unix-based system that was probably mounted on Sun Microsystems servers that linked the entire company, from the Los Angeles offices such as the Egg Company (George naming things again) to all the divisions in Marin County, where the bulk of the company was located. Oracle was clunky and occasionally went down, temporarily paralyzing us, but it was also powerful. You could ask it for all of the X-wing fighter aircraft shots with pilots looking left, for instance, and it would immediately produce a list. Wow.

We also had e-mail that connected everyone, something the general population wouldn't be familiar with for another decade. Added to that was a companywide electronic billboard we called allmessages. It was our personal internet before there was an Internet. Working here was sometimes like seeing into the future. One could extrapolate these things to their logical conclusions.

We already had computer-controlled camera systems that allowed our spaceship models, for instance, to be filmed multiple times, each time producing a separate strip of film that highlighted a different detail of the ship. Since all of these strips of film were identical, they could be composited together, yet with each part being individually controllable in terms of exposure or color. There would be the ship itself as one element, then its running lights, engine glow, laser cannon fire, whatever you wanted, all as easily manipulable parts. Want the engines brighter but not the spaceship? Done.

By 1984 someone in the optical department had brought in a Macintosh personal computer to keep track of his work, and over in the computer division the guys were producing the first entirely computer-generated shot for the film *Young Sherlock*. It was an effect that could not be achieved using traditional methods. A stained glass window depicting a knight in armor comes to life, with the knight leaping out of the window to threaten a passing priest.

Sometime after this shot was produced, I projected John Lasseter's *Luxo Jr.* for the Pixar team in the Building D screening room. It had more than technology going for it. John had created a character with which the audience could empathize. This was a Luxo lamp that had feelings. There was no sound yet with these computer-generated images, and perhaps that is why they brought to mind for me the pathos that Charlie Chaplin's silent films could evoke. This was a marker for me—something had just happened.

It was at about this time I went home and said to my wife that the world had changed and now "the code was king." She always reminds me that I had that insight early on. Computer code and programming languages were the new "means of production." The San Francisco Bay Area, where I lived, was about to explode with a new kind of intellectual property, written in code. I felt like a bystander, but at least I saw it coming. My wife eventually became a computer programmer and built me a number of websites for my various interests, some of which actually make money.

I've always had lots of interests. Movies, real estate, writing, photography, collecting books, Hollywood history—it's a long list but the core of it finds me trying to learn and make a commentary record of the world I live in. It's not a new or uncommon act; man's earliest known efforts of recording the times in which he lived were cave paintings about 30,000 years ago.

There are libraries full of information, but it always seemed to me that documents about how things really were are scarce—at least unfiltered ones. However insightful, novels are fiction, filtered through the writers' biases. History books are distillations from research, and most of the rest are sponsored works shaded by politics or commercial interests. This leaves journals, diaries, realistic paintings, photographs, audio recordings, artifacts, and documentary movies as some of the few sources of reality-based accounts, as reasonably reliable records of civilization.

Three of these have always fascinated me: photographs, documentary films, and travel journals from Charles Dickens's to John Steinbeck's. Of course, none of these are unbiased, but your expectation is that the author is recounting the truth as he sees it, and you are free to accept or reject it—not a choice one can ordinarily make with a work of art. With art, the whole point is to accept its message as artistic truth. That's why we talk about and accept "artistic license." I appreciate art mostly because it can give us insight into ourselves, not because it is a record.

Faulkner wrote, "The aim of every artist is to arrest motion . . . so that a hundred years later, when a stranger looks at it, it moves again." I take photographs, make documentaries, and write in the hope of freezing just one tiny moment in the river of time that continues to wash over us all. What other choice is there besides painting on the cave wall, just as our ancestors did? Paint in the hope that what we paint will help those that come after us to better understand us and themselves.

The Smell of Napalm

In the early days, the Building D screening room was the real workhorse of the company because it was where we held most dailies. After the Ranch was built, we inherited the Building C screening room as well, which had been originally designed as a sound mixing theater. Because C was the elegant one, I wanted to call it "Graceland" and D, the lowly workroom, "Jonestown." That was never approved, partially because it was a dig at our obsessive postproduction supervisor who was named Jones and also because his female assistant was an Elvis fan who considered it an insult to his memory or something. I was never sure how calling it "Graceland" insulted a rock star who died of an overdose, but in any case I did have the projectionist play the Paul Simon song "Graceland" occasionally as people were being seated there.

Both of these screening rooms were "hot miked" so the projectionists could hear instructions from the directors and supervisors as to what they wanted projected. By this I mean that they had "live" microphones in the theaters so that anything said in the room could be heard in the projection booth. This gave the potential of conversations being inadvertently overheard, either because we all forgot that we were on an open mike (which was easy to do) or because clients hadn't been in the rooms before and didn't know they were being heard. One time I inadvertently overheard a married couple, who were two of the biggest producers in Hollywood, talking alone in the D theater. They were eating sandwiches and waiting for us to screen their dailies, when she said to him, "Do you remember when we were poor?"

In addition to the mikes, I thought it would save a lot of time if I installed a video camera that looked directly at the projection screen so

I could watch on a monitor in my office as the various dailies occurred throughout the day. In this way I could also continue working until my shots came up in dailies and were starting to be discussed. Once I had this installed, various members of management insisted that they have monitors in their offices as well. There was no reason for them to have monitors, but it became a power thing.

Now I had a tricky political problem on my hands. This idea could save the company hundreds, perhaps thousands, of work hours lost to employees sitting in dailies waiting for their shots to come up for discussion, if we could give them all monitors like I had. Yet coincidently at the same time, the screening rooms started to be used by our artists to draw live nude models. All of a sudden, the models were being broadcast. I don't think anyone else ever knew that this happened, but soon I was able to show the artists how to shut off the system while they were working and all was well again, at least for a while.

About this time I realized that these projection rooms had become more than places to study our work—they had become gathering places for union meetings, drama clubs, and lectures, as well as the artists. Occasionally I would find someone sleeping there after having worked all night. Then once we started using video projection as well as film projection, the rooms were where we all watched special presentations like the Oscars broadcasts that almost always included some of our colleagues. Both rooms were jammed to watch the verdict in the O. J. Simpson murder trial. In a way it was our commons, our public space. Even George got involved.

A few of us were film buffs and occasionally we would use the theaters to run a classic film after work and invite either the director or cinematographer to talk about the film with us. We screened *Easy Rider* and asked László Kovács, its cinematographer, to speak about shooting it. He said he almost turned down the film because he had already shot so many motorcycle pictures, but Dennis Hopper talked him into it by just telling him the story, which László said sounded like a Greek tragedy. We could only get people who were up from Los Angeles, or out from New York, and happened to be working with us on some project. I always wanted to get a writer but never ran into one.

George came down for our *American Graffiti* screening, and I asked him if he had any nostalgia for the great low-light cinematography of his movie. It had been shot in what was called Techniscope, which divides each frame into two horizontal frames, saving money on film stock but adding some grain. Essentially it was an innovative way to shoot a wide-screen movie on a small budget and get a great look. This screening was at a time when George was pushing the Hollywood film world to go digital. His answer was that he wasn't primarily known for his cinematography and he was fine with the look he could get with digital. It was a disappointing answer for me. It did make sense, but did it make art? George had famously turned down Vilmos Zsigmond as the cinematographer of one of his *Star Wars* movies because "the guy wants a million bucks."

Eventually management asked me to shut the video cameras down and I did. It must be some kind of law of human nature that when things are being recorded, whether by White House taping systems or bystander police videos, things are revealed. I saw it early and now we are apparently all going to see it for quite a while with the current police actions caught on digital video.

I did, however, finally get to have a writer come speak to us, just in a more roundabout way. We were working on some shots for the movie *Red Dawn* (1984) and I met a character with an even wider a range of interests than my own. We were scheduled to screen dailies for director John Milius after lunch. John is a legend in the movie business as a screenwriter, director, and notable character. He had written *Apocalypse Now* for Francis Coppola, including the classic line "I love the smell of napalm in the morning," not to mention having inspired the character John Milner in *American Graffiti*. Steven Spielberg had called him "the greatest hood-of-a-car screenwriter I ever met." He rode with the fastest guns in Hollywood. At one point all the top directors were his friends and admirers and, as far as I know, they still are. John was the kind of personality that could build strong bonds with people. He was about friendship, loyalty, and talent.

Not that everyone agreed with him or his right-leaning politics—it was just that he was such a genuine person, his flamboyant statements could be understood as simply his passion for the reality of history. He understood the Roman warrior and the Japanese samurai better than anyone else in movies. He collected and reveled in shotguns and other weaponry. In some ways, he was a man out of time. In liberal Hollywood, to be on the national board of directors of the NRA could make for difficult cocktail party conversations in Beverly Hills mansions, but he managed it and I saw why when he suddenly and unexpectedly appeared in our editorial department. Directors didn't usually travel around a studio without an entourage, but Milius did.

The huge black-and-white photos that I used to see hanging from the brick walls in the old warehouse location of American Zoetrope had migrated to our facility in Marin. The optical department had the best two. One was a great still from *Flash Gordon* and the other was from *Citizen Kane.* The lobby of Building C had the giant ape busting through the gates in *King Kong.* In editorial, we had Akira Kurosawa holding a samurai sword and, behind my editing bench, Sergei Eisenstein holding film up to the light during editing.

Milius was the kind of guy who could have expounded on any of the topics suggested by these photos, from *King Kong* to Eisenstein. In other words, he could give you three or four minutes, even a half-hour lecture, right on the spot about something suggested in the photos.

I have only known one other person that could do that, and he was a land surveyor I had met while looking for country property. He could give you an overview of almost any subject. One time he went over the Peloponnesian Wars with me while we were having coffee.

Milius reminded me of the surveyor. John was just brimming with information, and the topic he chose was the samurai sword that Kurosawa held in the large photo on our wall. As an expert on weaponry, he was careful to note that he was not speaking about real samurai swords, which he could have easily done, but how replicas were made for the movies. How they faked them to look real and yet not endanger the actors. Since fakery was our business, we of course listened.

In making movies there are practical effects, like breakaway bottles for hitting barroom cowboys over the head in Westerns, and special visual effects, used in making movie dinosaurs. There is sometimes crossover between the two, but John was telling us about a unique type of movie prop used to pull off practical effects that could be used on set without additional help from us. He knew a lot about these swords and could make it interesting.

The part that impressed me was that here was a famous screenwriter and sometime movie director that was both a colleague and personal friend to Clint Eastwood, Steven Spielberg, Francis Coppola, George Lucas, and all of the rest of the top people in Hollywood, and we were, the goofballs at the bottom of the movie food chain. Yet for some reason he is hanging out with us for the afternoon. Milius seemed to me the very embodiment of the creative character. Like Eugene O'Neill or Ernest Hemingway, he was all about artistic emphasis. He magnified the fine details of life into art.

We finally got him into the Building D screening room by enticing him with a take-out hamburger from Foodles, a poor imitation of a restaurant near us that I avoided whenever possible. I was hoping that while the hamburger might be bad, it was not likely to injure him. So we brought the lights down and projected the shots we had been working on. After about ten minutes of sitting in the dark watching the film, we heard John's voice from the back of the theater, "This may be the greatest hamburger I ever ate in my life."

I didn't learn any screenwriting secrets from him, but just talking to John was inspiration enough to confirm that I was in an exciting business where anyone might walk in the door. Some that did were Michael Jackson (wearing a surgical mask), Sylvester Stallone (who is surprisingly short, maybe five foot eight or so), Tom Cruise (who may be a little nuts, but is also a savvy producer), Susan Sarandon (who threw a fit during her FX makeup session for *Witches of Eastwick*), Akira Kurosawa (dignified), Mick Jagger's daughter (who wanted to try out film editing), and many others I've forgotten.

Roger Rabbit

By the time *Who Framed Roger Rabbit* (1988) came along, I had been head of ILM editorial for a while. I supervised the other effects editors, their assistants, negative cutters, projectionists, screening rooms, and our film archives as well as our commercial editorial department. We were the nerve center of the company. Everything passed through us.

Disney had brought us the *Roger Rabbit* project to be directed by Bob Zemeckis, and it was a monster. Every shot in the movie was either full animation or live action with animated characters interacting with the actors in an otherwise conventional movie. The scope of this project was so large that it was scheduled to take a full two years to complete. It was grueling but was also probably the most fun project I ever worked on.

Zemeckis had been all set to direct *Cocoon* until a disastrous screening of his first major directing effort, *Romancing the Stone.* Making a movie is an ongoing creative process, and you don't really know what you have until you are done. Apparently the *Romancing* screening for the studio didn't go all that well. However, when his movie was finally released to audiences, it was a big hit and this success allowed him to direct *Back to the Future,* which was so successful that it spawned sequels, some of which I worked on. Now he could do anything he wanted and he chose *Roger Rabbit.*

There was precedent for a movie of this type from both Disney and MGM but not at this scale. An entire feature film was unprecedented. The earlier films just had a short sequence of, for instance, Jerry from the *Tom and Jerry* cartoons dancing with Gene Kelly in *Anchors Aweigh* or Julie Andrews dancing with cartoon penguins in *Mary Poppins*. Both of these had used dance numbers and locked-down cameras that could be meticulously timed so that animators could draw the cartoon characters to seemingly interact with the live action. *Roger* was going to require shooting an entire movie with every scene plotted for the actor to be moving and looking in the exact right way so that months later the animators could hand-draw their characters to completely integrate with the movie story. No one had ever tried to do anything with this complexity, and to top it off, this was going to be a major studio investment in an animated character that no one had ever heard of before.

Considering all of these unknowns, the producers, both Disney and Steven Spielberg's Amblin Entertainment, elected to pay ILM to do some tests to prove that this concept could actually work. Again, Ken Ralston and I worked together on this project, Ken as the director of special effects and I as his editor.

Ken designed two tests with the idea of making the animators' tasks so hard that if they could pull it off, the movie could be made. We called the two scenes RR1 and RR2.

In RR1 Ken played Roger's neighbor, and when the goofy rabbit comes by to mooch a cup of coffee, Ken becomes so angry he stuffs Roger into the coffee cup. RR2 was much more elaborate. It involved Jessica Rabbit's live-action car, Roger, and a dark alleyway. This created all kinds of animation challenges. Roger would have to be animated walking through the headlight beams of a real car, going behind glass, being reflected in mirrors, and appearing in a dark shadowy alley under the illumination of a *swinging lamp*, all the while interacting with Jessica and a stand-in actor representing Bob Hoskins, who was to be the human star. Just to make the animation job even more difficult, Ken had the camera moving as if this were a conventional movie.

We shot the scenes on VistaVision film, made eight-by-ten B&W still enlargements of the hundreds of frames where Roger or Jessica appeared, pin-registered them so they would conform to animation tables, and shipped the whole batch off to Disney to see if they could animated it.

Months later the full-color animation came back, which we composited with our live-action background using a bunch of optical tricks to make it all look seamless. I then synced up the soundtrack, and sent it off to Spielberg and Zemeckis.

Spielberg called the next day. Everything worked, it was beautiful and funny as hell, so please reserve the next two years of your lives for us. That was more or less the message.

When Bob Zemeckis came around, he was like a big college kid with a slight, side-of-the-mouth, Chicago South Side accent. He was a writer/director and had pulled off some amazingly complicated movie stories, like the masterly complex *Back to the Future* present/past comedies and much later the hugely popular *Forrest Gump*. He had energy. He was funny, and smart. He and my boss, Ken Ralston, got along famously, especially because Bob trusted Ken, and I was along for the ride.

Zemeckis really wasn't a Hollywood guy in a lot of ways, but he knew how to play the game. One time he and Ken were riding around Los Angeles when the news on the radio reported that Steven Spielberg had given new cars to the stars of his latest film. Bob reacted quickly to this news and immediately used his car phone to call his agent. "Get me a car" was all he needed to say. Did he need someone to give him anything, much less a car? No, that was not the point. The point was that *not getting a car* could be a sign. Maybe Bob was slipping. Why would his producer start handing out cars and he not receive one? Would Hollywood be saying, "I hear he's making a movie about some rabbit nobody's ever heard of. Remember *Howard the Duck*? Some of the same guys are working on this rabbit movie." It is always best to stomp out these potential little fires right away.

Roger Rabbit was so complicated that the production actually put out a small book of about thirty pages explaining everything about what we called "the pipeline." This detailed the exact route that the production product would take from the sound stages at Elstree Studios in London and location shoots, to Amblin Studios, to ILM, to director of animation Richard Williams in England, to Disney Animation in Hollywood and Florida, then back to ILM, and finally back to Bob's cutting room at Amblin.

The entire movie had to be shot and edited before the animation could be drawn. This meant that the director could not change anything once the cut was locked. Find an actor's take that you now like better? Can't use it or otherwise the whole scene would have to be re-animated.

The movie had something like 185,000 frames of hand-drawn animation, having been done before computer graphics existed, and a lot of it was very tricky.

For instance, there is a shot where Bob Hoskins is hiding Roger from the weasels who have come looking for him. Bob is doing the dishes at the time, so he hides Roger in the dishwater and pretends to keep washing as the weasels look around the apartment. Of course, when Roger runs out of air, he pops his head up and spits water in Bob's face. The sink was rigged with a mechanical sprayer that popped up in sync with Bob's actions, and the animators drew Roger over the water sprayer and hid it behind their drawings. All of this effort was required so the interaction between the animated characters and the live-action actors would look real. Real—not animated—water hits Bob in the face when Roger spits it out.

One of the stages the movie went through, before the final OK was given to start the full-color inking and painting of thousands of cells, was called the pencil test. The animators would draw just the outlines of the characters' actions over the thousands of large B&W still frames of the movie we had sent them. ILM would then composite these drawings over the actual film of the scenes and send these temporary comps to Bob's cutting room, where they would replace their cartoon-less shots with these roughly animated ones. The eye lines of the animated characters had to match those of the actors and every action had to integrate perfectly before the order went out to go for full-color animation. We would then repeat the compositing, only this time with the beautiful final product of the animators. We used every trick in our armada of optical printing devices to add shadows, sparkles, and mattes to make each shot a perfect amalgamation of actors and the crazy antics of Roger and his cartoon cohorts.

There were two parts of this movie that were breakthroughs. It was one thing to have Roger zipping around the real world, but the script called for Bob Hoskins to enter Roger's world of Toontown. We used traditional special effects to allow Bob to experience the logic (or illogic) of this cartoon world, as well as what we thought of as "toon physics." Walking off a cartoon skyscraper, Hoskins had to hang momentarily in the air before dropping a thousand feet to the street below, just like a cartoon character would. We squished him flat in an out-of-control cartoon elevator ride (see photo), and then had him escape Toontown in a cartoon taxi cab.

The other breakthrough was the opening of the movie. Before the movie appears to start, the audience is treated to a classic Warner Brothers / Tex Avery–style cartoon starring Roger Rabbit. When I first saw this cartoon, I thought it was great, but that was only the beginning. The gag was that the camera would pull back out of the cartoon and into the real world, revealing the cartoon's human director, who angrily invades the cartoon to admonish Roger for a dialog flub, only to have Roger chase after the director, who stomps out of the cartoon onto his live-action film studio world of cameramen, script girls, and director's chairs.

The backstory on this scene, which would introduce the audience to the concept of the film's mixing the cartoon world with the real world, was who would play the part of the cartoon director. The scene would open a movie about an unknown cartoon character that was costing Disney $45 million to make. Disney was being run at this time by Michael Eisner. Eisner had been hired by Roy Disney to turn the studio around, as it had fallen on hard times. He had been at Paramount Studios before Disney and at ABC television before that, so he had a long history in the entertainment industry. Part of that history included a long-running feud with none other than Joel Silver, the screamer. They hated each other.

Zemeckis thought it would be funny to hire Joel to play the director of the Roger cartoon that opens the movie. As mentioned earlier, Joel is a major figure in Hollywood, so he and Zemeckis had to collude to hide what they were planning. Somehow they kept his hiring out of all the paperwork that Eisner would ever see, so that the studio head would never know anything about it until Bob showed him the finished movie.

The story I got was that Eisner, on seeing the opening to his $45 million gamble, turned to Zemeckis and remarked, "That guy looks a lot like Joel Silver." To which Bob replied, "It is. Isn't he great?" And Eisner's only comment was, "He is pretty good." He was good. Very good. I guess he really can play angry, as well as be angry. In Hollywood, talent is golden. It a rare and beautiful thing, even if sometimes it gets a little ugly.

With the movie finished, Disney decided to do some previews in Pasadena, California, not far from Hollywood. The studios have been testing movies in Pasadena for decades. The Marx brothers had previewed *A Night at the Opera* there and no one laughed. Groucho said, "Maybe they're sad. Did you know that the mayor died today?" To this day no one has figured out why they didn't laugh at one of the funniest movies ever made—one that went on to not only be successful, but also a national movie comedy treasure. We hoped for better luck.

There were several screenings, each to a different age group. The one I attended was something like ages eighteen to thirty-four. Several of the younger ones walked out halfway through the cartoon open. That was a shock, but the rest of the audience stayed and watched the whole movie. All the studios use companies that specialize in doing this kind of work and they claim to be experts. When we previewed *The Golden Child* in Sacramento, I remember the audience rated it at something like a 69 on the "how did you like the movie" scale of 0 to 100. The preview company in that case basically told the director, "Make these specific changes and we can all but guarantee you a 74 next time." Believe me, I'd much rather hear what Marcia Lucas had to say.

I never saw the numbers, but the audience seemed to like the movie. Except for one guy. When the preview company asked for comments, this fellow stood up and said, "I liked the movie but I would never take my children to see it." I thought the Disney executives would keel over dead. He had a problem with what he considered some of the salty language the Baby Herman character uses when he gets angry. Stuff like, "The problem is I got a fifty-year-old lust and a three-year-old dinky" and "Whatta you know, you dumb broad? You got the IQ of a rattle." I thought it was going to be curtains for some of the language, but to Disney's credit, they didn't change a thing from what I could tell. At the risk of losing a major part of their audience, they pulled the trigger and released the movie.

The company flew us to New York for the premiere at Radio City Music Hall. Before the screening there was a dinner where the producers, director, and some of my colleagues were starting to gather. As I walked down the street towards the restaurant, I stopped by a newsstand. There was our movie on the cover of everything from *Newsweek* to the *New York Times*. I glanced at the reviews and they were all raves. Roger Ebert seemed to sum them all up writing, "They had to make a good movie while inventing new technology at the same time . . . I've never seen anything like it before. Roger Rabbit and his cartoon comrades cast real shadows. They shake the hands and grab the coats and rattle the teeth of real actors . . . *Who Framed Roger Rabbit* is sheer, enchanted entertainment from the first frame to the last—a joyous, giddy, goofy celebration of the kind of fun you can have with a movie camera."

I bought a few of the major magazines with Roger on their covers and plopped myself down at the pre-movie dinner. "Look, fellows, your movie is all over the newsstands." For some crazy reason, it was like no one had seen any of this yet—not the studio executives, the director, or the producers. They practically tore them out of my hands, admonishing me because I hadn't brought dozens of copies. Who me? I thought. I'm only here because Ken Ralston invited me; you are the biggest big shots in Hollywood. Where the hell is publicity, isn't that their job? It was all quickly forgotten as everyone started reading aloud many of the choicest quotes of praise for the movie.

Who Framed Roger Rabbit went on to gross about $330 million worldwide, beginning a turnaround for Disney that continues to this day.

Back to the Future

In *Back to the Future III* (1990) there was a gag about having to get an old steam engine to help push their time-traveling, but out of gas, DeLorean up to 88 mph before car and train both fly off the tracks and crash into a canyon below. With their DeLorean out of gas, it was the only way for the characters, Marty and Doc, to escape the Old West past, which they had traveled to in their time machine. Got it? The scripts were well-written, and most people did get it.

My boss, Ken Ralston, was searching for a location to shoot this scene. I thought I knew of a place that would be perfect: an old rock quarry up in the hills of northern Marin County. The quarry had been defunct for years, but my stepfather used to work there in the 1950s and he even lived there for a time after it closed. The owners preferred having someone on the property, so he lived there for free—quite an accomplishment in such a high-priced area as Marin.

As a kid, I would go up there on weekends with a friend and we would hike out into the hills behind the quarry to go camping, often taking rifles for squirrel hunting. There were acres of land to explore, so I knew it fairly well. We used to find huge stone bowls there that the local Indian tribe, the Miwoks, used for grinding corn eons ago. George named the Ewoks in *Star Wars* after these early Marin County Miwoks, so it seemed fitting that this place be used to shoot a movie. I had even shot one of my student films there; it was a horror movie before that genre exploded at the box office with films like *Night of the Living Dead.*

It seemed like wherever I went in Marin, some of my family history was there, and not all of it was pleasant. But my attitude was to wade right in and confront whatever ghosts of childhood I might encounter.

Not everyone feels that way. My brother went to school with a guy in Marin that belonged to a family of the biggest political figures in the state. Governors, judges, and high officials were threaded closely through it. He grew up under intense pressure to succeed and he did succeed, but a haunted childhood home life of alcoholism and God knows what else controls him to this day, making any thought of ever returning to Marin abhorrent. My view is to revisit whatever demons you might have had in the past and take back the control you lacked as a child. I'm for metaphorically driving your Mercedes up on the lawn of your old self and announcing your return. Now, here I was back at the rock quarry.

After my father died, my mother moved to Marin and bought a 1951 baby blue Cadillac that had belonged to Bill Harrah, the Reno gambling magnate. Apparently Harrah had bought it for a girlfriend who didn't work out. My father had told momma to get a good car, and in those days a good car for a widow meant a Cadillac.

By now an old suitor had shown up, a family friend during the good old days in Sausalito when she was the daughter of a rich man. His name was Yates, and he was a poor Southern boy from South Carolina who had run away from an abusive home. He had traveled a lot, first as what they called a "peanut butcher," selling candy and nuts on the railroads, then as a "wiper," the lowest engine room position on freight ships that went all over the world. But in my mother's teenage years he delivered for a drugstore on a motorcycle, drove a cab, and hung out at the fire department. My grandmother liked him and he was always welcome at the big Sausalito house where my grandfather brought all kinds of people home for Sunday dinner.

Yates had taught himself to read and write and had the classic Southern manners of a gentleman, but a working-class one. He had dated all the "Mason Girls" (my mother and her sisters) at one time or another, but he was a poor boy and they were the daughters of a millionaire.

After my father died, Yates was back in full pursuit. His job record was sketchy, he was too heavy, he wasn't from her class at all, and he had a problem with alcohol. By rights, my mother should have married another doctor or someone—anyone—else. She was still quite attractive, and only forty years old. But that didn't happen, and when most of my father's family met a man who couldn't hold his liquor, they disappeared from our lives. On my mother's side, they all sent ice buckets as wedding gifts.

The irony here is that by the time my mother got really sick, and was in and out of hospitals, and the bills were piling up, Yates had become a highly paid heavy-equipment and tall-crane operator. He had worked his way up in the Operating Engineers Union and was in demand, having brought his drinking under control. He would still go on benders, but not while working on projects. His union paid all the hospital bills. As I grew older, Yates became a more and more complicated figure. As he slowly gained in wealth, he became a gift-giver who offered short and hilarious vacations from our increasingly humble lives. These were the benders. We would stay at the best hotels and eat at the finest restaurants, all on Yates.

Having slowly awakened from a childhood where everyone's parents were business executives, judges, law partners, doctors, or just wealthy, we began to notice that some people drove cabs or waited tables for a living, at a dollar or two an hour, while our stepfather was a laborer yet made $17 an hour. Many heavy-equipment operators where drinkers and unreliable; Yates was a drinker but completely reliable, a rare commodity. As my mother's marriage to Yates failed, he was exiled, first to the maids' quarters and eventually out of the house altogether. He still took my brother and me on trips, but he had moved to the rock quarry.

Slowly things changed. My uncle sold the house, and I went to live with my Aunt Leonore in Boonville. My brother and I were split up, and we only saw our stepfather Yates occasionally now. He bought me a car when I turned sixteen, and we had one more wild excursion with him, where he closed for a day a bowling alley he had invested in so I could drink at the bar as an underage college kid.

I never saw the quarry again until my boss Ken rode up there with his wife on horseback one weekend and pronounced it perfect for the set. Our model shop had built a ¼th-scale period steam engine to match the full-size one they had commandeered at the production's location, in the old gold-mining city of Jamestown in the foothills of the Sierra Nevada.

At the quarry they constructed twenty yards or so of track and a partially destroyed railroad trestle, all to scale. The story involved the characters escaping the past as their DeLorean blasted them back to the future, but with the steam engine that propelled their car shooting off the broken trestle bridge and diving into the quarry canyon. Of course, the engine appeared to explode as it hit the bottom. We never failed to explode something if we could possibly help it. Buster Keaton ran a real steam engine off a trestle in his masterpiece *The General* and guess what? It didn't explode. That's because there was nothing to explode except steam from the boiler perhaps. Ours did explode—it's a movie cliché. A car goes off a cliff, it explodes. Especially if there is a bad guy in it. It should only explode on a good guy if he has made a last-second escape.

In movie parlance, the girl screams when she sees a monster or the killer. She also falls down in trying to escape either one. That is usually caused by the presence of stylish footwear, but it can even happen in sneakers. Men don't scream at either monsters or killers, but they do forget to bring their gun. You can shout advice at the screen all you like, but for a time he is going to be unarmed and vulnerable. I think this is one of the reasons the NRA has been so successful in arming America—movie guns. I left a preview screening of a new movie once and heard one studio executive ask the other, "What did you think?" and the other executive said, "No guns." This meant he thought it was going to fail at the box office, and it did. You break movie logic at your peril.

Still, the *Back to the Future* scripts were beautiful things. Just to pull off the complex time-travel story lines alone was a feat, but to additionally still have good character development, action, and humor, all in a satisfying movie story—*that* makes both sense and fun of itself. It is a rare thing.

I drove up to the Western town sets in both Jamestown, where the full-size steam locomotive was a famous local attraction, and the nearby town of Sonora, where additional sets were built. Other movies had been shot in Jamestown using the loco, including the depot sequence in perhaps my favorite movie, *High Noon.* (Somewhere I read that Bill Clinton ran *High Noon* something like eleven times while he was in the White House.)

My aunt Dru Barner lived in this same gold country area and had once dated the man who wrote the book *The Tin Star,* on which *High Noon* was based. The family called her Druie and she was a true horseman, gender aside. She was the first woman to win the Tevis Cup, riding her horse on a grueling trek over an old Pony Express route. It was a hundred-mile trail ride that had to be completed in twenty-four hours. She started at 5:15 a.m. near Truckee, California, went across the crest of the Sierra Nevada, and ended at 5:15 a.m. in Auburn, California, the town where she lived. She carried a Pony Express mail sack with a letter to me, which I still have. I was fourteen, and this was an endurance ride for horses and people that I didn't fully understand, but I have subsequently met horse people who, when they learn that Dru Barner was my aunt, look a little astonished. My aunt was almost fifty years old when she finally won this race, and she neither screamed nor fell down on this ride . . . ever.

Pixar

I PULLED UP TO ILM ONE MORNING AROUND 1986 AND THERE WAS A new Porsche parked on the street in front of Building C. Unlike the modified tilt-up warehouse where I worked, George and Marcia had designed C from the ground up. At its heart was a magnificent Art Deco screening room that was primarily used as a sound mixing theater for movies. Directors spend months sitting in these kinds of rooms, guiding the process of the final sound design of their films. Feature films are essentially shot silent, with just the best temporary voice track of the actors that can be grabbed on location. Every other sound you hear is laid in—footsteps, car engines, growling dogs, all of it. What can't be found in the huge studio sound libraries is created, on the spot or in the field, in a process called Foley, after Jack Foley, who brought to film his techniques from the old "live" radio programs where sound effects had to be created during the broadcasts.

The rough dialogue captured on location is often replaced using a technique called ADR, or automatic dialogue replacement. The actor watches and listens to himself speaking his original lines and mimics himself in a new "clean" recording. Then all of these elements, and especially the musical score, written specifically for the movie, is finalized in the sound mixing theater under the supervision of the director.

Since filmmakers spend their lives on location, in editing rooms, or in mixing theaters like this one, George and Marcia decided to build the most beautiful and comfortable one they could imagine. I never toured anyone into that room whose first reaction upon my opening the door wasn't to say "Wow." But that wasn't all this building had to offer. Marcia was primarily an editor, so there was also a suite of film editing rooms across the front of the building. Most editing rooms are dingy holes buried somewhere on a big movie studio lot. Not these. These had the thick beige carpets normally found only in an executive's office. They had a bank of windows that were shaded by an overhanging balcony that hid a long patio garden, which could be reached by French doors off each room.

Behind the theater was a huge shooting stage that was connected by a well-insulated door and an air lock which, the theater having been built in such a way that it floated independently inside the larger building, made it nearly soundproof. The stage was three stories high and equipped for shooting special effects against a large blue-screen backdrop.

On the top floor was the Lucasfilm computer division. Since the license plate on that fancy Porsche I had seen parked out front said NEXT, it wasn't too hard to figure out that Steve Jobs was visiting the computer guys (contrary to what others have written, Jobs's car did indeed have a license plate). Steve had famously been forced out of Apple, the company he cofounded, and had started a new venture called Next.

We called the computer guys "propeller heads" because they were all brainiacs to us, working on money-losing projects. They took our teasing well, though, and once showed up at a company meeting wearing beanie hats with little plastic propellers on top that spun when they walked. The ones I knew, and them barely, were John Lasseter, Ed Catmull, David DiFrancesco, Ralph Guggenheim, and Don Conway.

The propeller heads were working on several important things here. One was a laser scanner that could convert motion picture film to digital data. Moviemaking had broken down to image capture and image processing. Digital capture didn't exist yet. It could be pulled off, but it wasn't practical. So most directors shot on film, scanned it to digital, manipulated it, and then scanned it back to film again for release to theaters.

Once you have motion pictures in a digital format inside a computer, anything is possible. You can manipulate the image, composite it with other elements, and essentially do anything you want with it. When you are done, you scan it back to film and cut it into your movie, and nobody is the wiser. This simple technical feat would soon revolutionize moviemaking. We had pioneered the scanner with Eastman Kodak.

The other thing they were working on was the Pixar, a software system for manipulating computer images, images that were solely the product of ones and zeros—digital data that could have full photo realism, indistinguishable from images captured by a motion picture camera, yet flexible enough to allow any image an artist might imagine to be produced. Much of this was years away from practical reality and would still require millions of dollars of additional investment. That is where Steve Jobs came in. Much like his legendary visit to Xerox PARC in Palo Alto, where he was shown the graphical user interface, the pointing device, an advanced version of the mouse, etc.—all of which he would walk back to Apple and incorporate into his future personal computers—this Lucasfilm fishing expedition would also prove fruitful.

In 1983 the part of the Lucasfilm computer division working on producing images hired a young animator who had been fired from Disney named John Lasseter to help them spiff up the demonstration films they were producing. Up to that point they had shown off the power of their software by producing fairly boring examples on film.

John and his team would often call me up and ask for some screening room time so they could see their work projected on the big screen. This is where I first saw a computer-generated film Lasseter had animated called *Luxo Jr.* If you've ever seen the company logo at the head of a Pixar production, you will recognize the little lamp character animated there—that's Luxo.

This screening was amazing to me. Up until now all these guys had ever brought for screenings were technical demonstrations of the fine points of computer animation problems they had solved. This had Luxo lamps as fully realized cartoon characters. In its own way, it was brilliant. I remember thinking, if this guy can get that much emotion out of a desk lamp, we are looking at a real talent here.

John continued to make several wonderful animated films for Lucasfilm, but what his team really wanted to make was a feature animated film. At some point one of the lead computer people had a meeting with George, outlining what they proposed to do. George listened carefully, said good-bye, and drove back to the Ranch. The next day the president of Lucasfilm came down to the computer division and said, "Don't ever mention this idea to George again." This was a very costly decision for George to make, because Pixar was to go on to become by far the most successful animation studio in the world. When it was sold to Disney, the return to Steve Jobs dwarfed the money he had made from Apple.

Money was the reason for the decision to sell what would become Pixar to Jobs—that and the fact that George had stated many times, "There is only one filmmaker at this company, and that is George Lucas." He didn't want things going out, essentially under his name, that could bomb and tarnish Lucasfilm's reputation. If he was going to put something on the line, then he wanted to control it. But the money was the biggest factor.

After the successful release of *Jedi,* George and Marcia announced that they were divorcing. Divorces are expensive and this one was no different, except for the fact that Marcia was a full partner in building the film empire that was now to be split. The sad thing was that her contributions were no longer going to be felt. It is not easy to find someone who is not only capable of pointing out flaws in dramatic film structure, but also able to tell you how to fix them.

There is a story about Steven Spielberg running the original *Raiders of the Lost Ark* for his friends before it was released. Whatever you think of these "popcorn" movies, you have to admit that George and Steven came up with a hell of an entertaining thrill ride with this one. No matter. At the end of the screening, Marcia said, "There is no emotional resolution to the story. You need a scene where we find out what happens to Indy and the girl." She pinpointed the problem and offered a solution. Priceless advice. Steven shot an additional scene, released the movie, and the rest is history.

A team was hired to inventory the entire company, top to bottom. Every item was identified, tagged, and appraised. When they came through my department, they counted and tagged everything on my editing bench: "one splicer, one 35mm synchronizer, two rewinds," etc. When it was all added up, they split it right down the middle and George bought back the half of the company he didn't already own for $50 million. In hindsight, this is one of the greatest investments in motion picture history when one considers the fairly recent sale to Disney for $4.05 billion, not including the Ranch. To give you some perspective on big numbers like these, that ".05" after the "$4"—that's $50 million right there.

Steve Jobs purchased what was to become Pixar from Lucasfilm for $10 million, $5 million in cash and $5 million in other guarantees, with Lucas retaining the use of certain software that would be important to the company in the future.

One of the telling things about these kinds of deals is what was being sold, especially in light of the fact that we now know that there was collusion among many of the Bay Area technology companies, including Apple and Lucasfilm, in employee compensation. The companies had agreed among themselves to not compete with each other by offering salaries that the market would otherwise determine in competition for the best of the talent pool. They didn't want to have a market value placed on the talents of their most-valuable employees, so they forbade competition among high-tech companies for the best workers.

Yet many purchase contracts for entire companies include a crucial "key man" clause, meaning that the deal that they are making is largely for the talent and services of key employees. Without these individuals, there is no deal, as the rest of the assets are not worth the money being offered. Adam Smith's "invisible hand of the market place" had become merely a robotic arm controlled by the owners of high-tech companies. Employees were being paid by one set of valuations but then sold off by another.

Of course, I didn't know anything about this at the time. It seemed like the best employees were being compensated fairly for the skills they possessed—at least until a lot of movie companies went digital and things changed for everyone as computer graphics began to dominate our production world. In this new world, George Lucas would have never been hired by his own company, and neither would I.

After Pixar's huge successes at making feature animation movies, the same ones that they wanted to make for George, I heard George comment on his having sold it. "The only thing I regret," he said, "is having let this successful model out into the world where others could copy it." What an interesting comment. His greatest concern was the revealing of how we did things. The process. The secret sauce we used. And it was true, we had a very sophisticated system. Steven Spielberg later remarked in a

Wired magazine article, "I always thought that if ILM had run the space agency, we'd have colonized Mars by now."

Even though we groused about it all the time, the system we had was pretty damn good. Part of it was that we were extremely well organized. Everything was tracked—every shot, every element, every sequence, and every dollar. We always knew where we were and what the forecasts were for completing our work on time. Someone was watching every cog and wheel in the whole machine, with an oilcan ready should there be any squeaks. That was the logical stuff. Then there was the illogical stuff, the creative stuff.

We hired artist's models to come by for drawing classes open to everyone. We had what we called a "free speech" board hung just outside the door to editorial for people to post whatever they thought was of interest. It was like a mirror into what everyone was thinking, and it was often George's first stop after leaving dailies each morning. It was funny, informative, newsworthy, and outrageous, and it changed every day. As the keepers of the company film archives, editorial also kept track of this board and saved everything that was ever posted, storing large cardboard boxes of the clippings, artwork, signs, reviews, articles—whatever was posted—until we had a couple of decades' worth.

There was an artist's drawing of what the then-thirty-three-year-old Muhammad Ali might look like when he was in his seventies. There was a prediction that houses in the future might cost as much as $250,000 (something we all thought was impossible). But one of the most controversial things ever posted was an interview where George had stated that "what you are by age thirty is what you will be in life." That was too scary for most people to accept.

I'm sure someone has thrown all this out by now, but when I came to run editorial, I continued the tradition of my predecessors for at least another decade. This was all silly stuff, but it had its purpose. People gathered around this bulletin board just like they did the nearby coffee bar and water cooler, people who didn't normally interact because they didn't work together. I organized after-work poker parties and invited different people from around the company for similar reasons—just to get them to know each other better.

All these little things helped support a creative environment. It may not seem like much, but when I was touring a group of Japanese executives from Matsushita, the giant electronics company that goes by the name Panasonic in this country, around editorial one day (Lucasfilm had a deal to help them learn how to foster a more creative environment in their company), one of the executives called me aside and asked who decided which station to play on the radio that was blaring near someone's editing bench. I was a little taken aback by what the question implied. "Each employee decides for himself what he wants to listen to," I answered. It was apparent that this answer surprised them. It made me think that we would not be seeing a surge in Japanese creativity anytime soon.

I wish I could have shown them some of the many drawings that various artists I worked with over the years had left on my desk. Some were jokes from my supervisor Ken, suggesting that we were all doomed with a drawing of a *Titanic*-like ocean liner with ILM signage, sinking. Or Ken himself being eaten by a shark, or perhaps a drawing of a cartoon clock face urging me to "Hurry up, Bill."

Then there was the elaborate apology drawing from someone in the art department, lamenting that he had interrupted me the prior evening looking for something that he now realized he already had. The image was of him passed out among a bevy of pretty girls, with a caption suggesting that had he not been out-of-his-mind drunk, he never would have done such a thing.

It was this kind of silliness and camaraderie that helped us break the tension and bond with our comrades as if we were all in the same boat, which we were.

A Jolt of Money

Recently, I made an arrangement with the Motion Picture Academy Film Archive to permanently store the negatives from my films there. It is a wonderful program and archive dedicated to Mary Pickford, who was a founding member of the Academy. It is fitting that my modest contributions to movie history should wind up in the archive of my old neighbor Bessie Barriscale's buddy Mary. I drove the many cases of film to Los Angles myself.

I always preferred to drive from San Francisco rather than fly, whether it was for film business or for pleasure. I would go as far as Santa Barbara and stay there overnight. It is a beautiful town and is the second home to many Hollywood luminaries. The town is a sort of off-site Beverly Hills, for the *really* rich. It is one of those places where the vast worldwide flow of money finally lands. In a way it is the prize for making it big—this is the endgame. George recently purchased a $19 million teardown here just to get the beachfront.

The elite would stay in their hillside mansions and I would stay at the Motel 6, as I did again this trip. That was my beachfront. This motel is the *original* location of the national chain and is one block from the water. You can see the ocean from some of the rooms. It may be a dead-cheap motel, but it is in a beautiful neighborhood that is a mixture of expensive lodging and private homes. This was a perfect metaphor for what my life had become. I sometimes rubbed shoulders with the rich and famous, but I was just a visitor to their world.

In the morning I would walk over to the Shoreline Beach Cafe, which is right on the sand, where all the beautiful people are either having their morning coffee or plunked down after an early jog on a path that runs the several-mile length of the beach. For breakfast my wife and I would sometimes go to the Santa Barbara Biltmore, a luxury hotel that was built in a sort of Mediterranean / Spanish Revival style in 1927 and is now managed by the Four Seasons Hotel Group. It is outrageously expensive to actually stay there; however, brunch on the patio lets one see the whole glorious mix of rich gardens and the tastefully grand old hotel with unobstructed views of the ocean under an abundance of California sunshine, relatively cheaply.

Knowing that the hotel had recently undergone a $240 million restoration, we joked about who could possibly afford such an extravagance as to own a place like this. I was soon to find out.

I had been struggling for some time with what the definition of success was for me. Surely, having a trophy hotel such as this in your portfolio was the epitome of success in America. Yet, there was a flaw here. F. Scott Fitzgerald called it "the consoling proximity of millionaires." Now they were *billionaires* and I was working for them, but my question was, could I consort and not be tainted? Could I maintain my own goals and not adopt theirs? Or, on the contrary, should I adopt theirs—with enough money you could do what you wanted, couldn't you? Marcia Lucas once said, "When you get a big jolt of money, it's very easy to be in awe of it and lose touch with reality." I was in no danger of getting such a jolt, but still I think we all wonder what it would be like.

We walked along the narrow oceanfront road that separates the hotel from the water until we reached some of the private homes that also face the ocean. Because these large houses were few in number, they were obviously expensive. But it was the last one on the block that intrigued me. It was on a massive lot maybe three to five acres in size and looked as if Jay Gatsby might have lived there once. It was old but restored to leave a magnificent period look, or so I thought. There were second-story terraces, a long loggia and reflecting pond, covered walkways leading to a huge swimming pool and pool house, and acres of lawns and palm trees all facing the ocean.

Rather than walk back to the Biltmore the same way we had come, we thought we might get a better look by walking down the street behind this magnificent house. The mansion's property ended at a side road and there was nothing else beyond, other than an old and somewhat creepy cemetery half hidden in the trees. Was this where Santa Barbarians buried their dead? It looked like it. As we turned down the road behind the old house, there was a substantial wall with a giant set of iron gates preventing entry; otherwise some latter-day William Holden / *Sunset Boulevard* type might have swung his car in for hiding on the ample property: "I had landed myself in the driveway of some big mansion . . . the kind crazy movie people built in the crazy twenties. A neglected house gets an unhappy look. This one had it in spades."

But the strangest thing was the gates themselves. They were a marvel of ironwork but there was no latch on them. A small space separated each gate from the other when closed, but nothing else. There was no mechanism for opening them, no rod or gear or mechanics of any kind that revealed how they could possibly open. There was no speaker box for stating your case for seeking entry, no push buttons to tap in a code. It was a puzzle. We discussed this curious matter as we walked along the high wall only to find yet another identical set of gates. Here I think I even got down on my knees to more closely examine them.

About this time a very polite man in a nice suit appeared on the other side of the gate. Was this the gateman? I had observed that there appeared to be some kind of smaller house back about fifty feet from the gates and almost hidden. I asked him how the gates worked, and perhaps because he was bored he told us. Buried beneath the ground of each gate was a machine that operating through gears, was powerful enough to pivot the gates open from the stanchion on which each side hung.

To the question I had been thinking about since our joking around on the Biltmore patio garden as to who could afford such a thing, I was unable to phrase it delicately enough for him to answer. All he said was "just another millionaire." He reminded me of Raymond, the butler in *Citizen Kane*: All he knew was that Kane died holding the snow globe. But there was one more thing he did say. When I asked about the old mansion on the property, he said, "It was built six years ago from the ground up." Just like the gates, it was all a deception. This was no restoration of a fine old Santa Barbara home. It was like one of our movie sets, a new house that only appeared old. We thanked him and walked back to the hotel to get the car and go to dinner, but I needed to find out whose house this was because it was awfully tempting to be in awe of it or afraid of it.

It turned out that there was a man wealthy enough to own both the estate with the fancy gates and the Biltmore Hotel. He also owned the Sand Piper Golf Club, among numerous other resorts and businesses in town. He owns the Four Seasons Hotel in New York City and, as expected, is a billionaire. And what great American fortune resides behind those mansion walls?

He was the inventor of Beanie Babies. Ty Warner had worked in the toy business and decided to invent his own toy based on something he had seen in Europe. Using a strategy of deliberate scarcity, he was able to build his fortune on the beanbag-like toy. So the mogul I had imaged was real enough. It *was* possible to own a fabulous hotel with your own private cottage on the grounds, and an oceanfront mansion within walking distance.

It had all been so wonderfully deceptive. The old mansion that wasn't old. The owner who had created a toy fad big enough to make him a billionaire. It was like a setting fit for a hard-boiled detective story, but what was the *moral*? Perhaps it was like the lesson I learned from a newspaper article I once saved just because it was so intriguing.

In the gravel driveway to an old mansion in the Oakland Hills, not far from San Francisco where I was living at the time, a neighbor had spotted an elegant ladies' high-heel shoe that appeared be discarded. Alarmed, she called the police, who found the elderly lady occupant of the mansion had been murdered by someone who ransacked the house and must have dropped the shoe from their loot as they escaped.

I followed up on the article and learned that the victim was the widow of the man who invented the mechanical rabbit found at dog tracks. The key to this invention was to keep the rabbit tantalizingly within reach, but moving just that much faster than the dogs could run. It was diabolical, except that if you were a dog, you didn't know. In life, of course, that makes all the difference, knowing. When I see people racing to work, I often ask myself, do they know? Do they know that there is no rabbit?

Had it all been in that 1960s song by Jefferson Airplane, "White Rabbit," about the dangers in chasing rabbits when you know you're going to fall?

Had I found the rabbit or just the hole? Santa Barbara, the Biltmore, the Beanie Babies mansion? This was the closest I had yet come to confronting the great American sorting process, which creates the haves and the have-nots. The mansion could have belonged to the owner of an aluminum siding empire or a plumbing supply magnate, or Gatsby. After all, this was America. But is it just our zip codes and birth certificates that control our destiny? Maybe I was reading too much Raymond Chandler, but it made me ask myself when I was going "to give the wasp's nest a wallop" instead of being sucked in by the worlds I was observing. I wasn't ready yet, but I had a plan. I would still work, but perhaps I could be less desperate about it all now that I had looked the rabbit in the eye.

The Mask

Jim Carrey starred in *Ace Ventura: Pet Detective, Dumb and Dumber,* and *The Mask*. But when he and his costar, an obscure actress, came to ILM to shoot their effects scenes for *The Mask* (1994), nothing had been released yet, so he was an unknown commodity in motion pictures. *Ace Ventura* was finished, but no one had seen it yet. In fact, the studio was squabbling about his salary for *The Mask*, and they weren't too happy about the film's budget at $18 million either.

I would wander out to the big blue-screen stage where they were shooting once in a while, and Carrey was just kind of hanging out between takes. My ILM producer for this show was a guy named Goldman and he was fairly obnoxious. I think even he would agree that he was obnoxious. After Jim got a load of this guy, he started to mimic him, and it was both funny and uncanny to see. We were getting a glimpse of a comedic star that would explode onto the world stage in just months.

Jim's costar was, it was rumored, a former model and director Chuck Russell's girlfriend. That didn't sound good. This is the kind of stuff that floats around movie sets. It doesn't have to be true, it's just something to pass the time while waiting for the crew to light the next shot. It turns out that this "model" was Cameron Diaz, who this movie would introduce to the world as a star, a position she holds to this day.

Somehow I was allowed a video copy of the film in rough cut, and I took it home and watched it. Carrey was goofy funny as a shy bank teller, and Diaz was mesmerizing as the love interest. Talent was just leaking out of this thing, and even with just storyboards cut in where our shots would go, it was a remarkable comedy, except for one thing. The story gimmick was that the milquetoast Carrey character had found a mask that gave him supernatural powers when he put it on. But the movie opened with a kind of prologue where pirates land on a sandy beach and bury a cursed mask they believe brings evil to its owner. We did a couple of shots for the director in the sequence, but in the end he simply chopped the whole opening off and released the movie without it. Wise decision. Here was a lesson in story: Don't start at the beginning, start in mid-story. Write an introduction if you must, but then lop if off. You will rarely miss it.

Probably the craziest character at ILM who worked on this picture, and there were many candidates, was Steve "Spaz" Williams. They called him "Spaz" because he was anything but—like that huge kid in high school that everyone called "Tiny." He was a fairly big guy that rode a Harley and had a tattoo, but the interesting thing was that he had something I had never seen before. He was a creative artist type who also had high math, science, and computer skills. Things are somewhat different now, but back in the early 1990s most artists and writers that you met were somewhat computer-phobic. Not Spaz—he would do the original animation test of a dinosaur running through a field that convinced Spielberg to do all of *Jurassic Park* in computer-generated images. Spaz was goofy, sincere, highly talented, mischievous, and naive all rolled into one Harley-riding package.

He hung out in what we called "The Pit," which was an old sound recording room in the sub-basement of the glorious Art Deco–like C theater. It had no windows and was soundproof and was now filled with computer screens, empty beer cans, cigar butts, and trash bins filled with empty Styrofoam take-out food containers. Somewhat of an insomniac, Spaz would goof around all day and then work all night building beautiful and sometimes breakthrough computer animations. He had done the water creature in *The Abyss* and the chrome villain in *Terminator 2,* both for the director Jim Cameron.

For *The Mask* Spaz did all of the crazy Chuck Jones / Tex Avery–like animations Jim Carrey goes through, with the bulging eyes that pop two feet out of Carrey's head as his animated jaw drops to a table top with a thud.

Wearing a "wife beater" T-shirt under a leather jacket, you were apt to find Spaz in his living room dismantling his Harley-Davidson motorcycle or at the gun range shooting rifles, shotguns, or pistols from his armory-like gun collection—all of this being in service of studying life from the inside out. Michelangelo dissected human corpses to find out how the body worked so he could draw it realistically. Spaz was dissecting life to find out what lay beneath so he could create the living, breathing computer-generated characters he was always building.

The bad boy came out one evening at the Ranch. Basically, employees from divisions other than the Ranch were free to come out for lunch during the daytime. There was a restaurant in the recreation building that was mostly hamburgers, sandwiches, and salads. The other restaurant was in the main house. It had an actual chef and was usually where George ate. It was very informal and relaxed, but it did have sit-down meals with waiter service, complete with a dessert menu. This whole main house floor was open to employees and their guests. Below this level were film editing rooms for whatever project George might be working on. This area was somewhat private, but I would visit fellow editors there all the time. This downstairs level had a small but elegant screening room with walls of gorgeous old-growth redwood reclaimed from early railroad bridges and such. The seats were plush dark-red velvet and the fixtures were brass. The whole building was threaded with fiber optics because we could see that coming.

The library was perhaps my favorite because I am a library hound, as I read a lot and I'm always doing research for something. It became especially interesting to me after George decided to purchase the Paramount research library. Want to know what the interior of a barbershop looked like in the 1920s? They had boxes of photos for just this kind of reference. If you are making a historical picture, this is just the kind of material you need access to. I love all that stuff and it was fun to go through it; no one else was much interested if they weren't on a production.

The second floor up from the living and dining room areas was off-limits to employees and guests. That is where George has his office and writing room, as well as whatever other staff he needed. I was almost never on the second floor.

Sometime in 1990 we were working on *Terminator 2* for director Jim Cameron, and Spaz was one of the lead guys creating breakthrough effects. We also had a new vice president in charge of several divisions, Scott Ross. Scott thought of himself as a hipster. He had a background in music, stereo sales, and video postproduction. He was a bright guy and very ambitious. He wanted to run Lucasfilm, which constantly put him at odds with his Harvard-educated, cardigan-sweater-wearing boss, Doug Norby, who *did* run Lucasfilm. Doug was square and conservative, like George, and Scott was cool and aggressive, like Hollywood.

Scott got the idea for a speaker series and, using a stay at the Ranch as bait, lured an aging Timothy Leary to give a talk at ILM one evening, with a hosted dinner for a few select employees at the Ranch's main house restaurant. I always thought that the company should have sponsored more talks, but not from "turn on, tune in" celebrants. We should have been hosting talks from Silicon Valley's wide array of smart people, but we had no intellectual leadership, just hustlers.

The Leary talk was standing room only at our C theater. What he brought to demonstrate was an erotic computer game called "Virtual Valerie." It was the computer equivalent of a "peep show." Besides that, Leary's mind seemed shot. My girlfriend had heard him give a talk at the University of Michigan, where she was a philosophy major. Her critiques could be devastating. Leary, she said, embarrassed himself, and she thought his brain was addled even back then.

When question-and-answer time came, I asked Leary why on the eve of the computer revolution's opening whole new worlds for us, was he using it to sell soap? Worse than soap, soft-core porn? He kept thanking me for the question and responded that "after all, ILM has a commercial division." To me he was a phony, but Scott was radiant and couldn't wait for the Ranch dinner so he could hear celebrity gossip from the guy. I would not be attending, but Spaz would be.

That night Spaz and his fellow computer hotshot, Mark Dippé, were among a select group at the first speaker series dinner at the Ranch main house. The details have always remained sketchy because neither the Ranch nor anyone else wanted to publicize what happened. During the dinner, Spaz and Mark wandered off, beers in hand, and decided to step over the velvet rope guarding the stairway to the second floor to have a look around upstairs. The building was virtually empty. Soon they discovered George's office and took up residence. Some say they lit cigars and took turns sitting in George's chair, Spaz with his Wellington motorcycle boots firmly planted on George's big desk. Whatever happened, it quickly became part of Lucasfilm employee lore. It was stupid, but at the same time it pricked some of the company pomposity.

Unfortunately for them, they had set off the infrared alarm system and Ranch security appeared. Lines like "Who are you?" and "No one is allowed up here" were heard. Spaz and Mark thought it might be funny to say that they were actually two managers at ILM, but they changed their story when told they were lying. Fabricating other names, they were allowed to leave.

The funny thing is that these two were actually more important to the company than the leaders they had claimed to be. The truth is, companies are bought and sold on the value of talent like this.

When the president of Lucasfilm, Doug Norby, heard that Scott had invited Timothy Leary to a fancy dinner without authorization, he chewed him out, especially because both he and George thought Leary was a druggie, but when he later learned about the party in George's office, he really blew his top.

When George learned of this, he initially wanted the office offenders fired, which is understandable. "Why are people like this working for my company?" he reportedly asked. When it was explained to him that there were certain "key" employees that ILM could not do without, he relented. But they were famously "banned" from the Ranch. For some, this expression came to mean "distinguished," and when a group of ILM employees later split off, forming their own visual effects company, they named it Banned From The Ranch.

After this event, Scott Ross was scheming to overthrow Doug Norby and Norby was looking for an excuse to fire Scott. I had inherited a huge office that held my editing gear, my desk, and some really comfortable chairs that Marcia Lucas had commissioned. People used to drop by my office once in a while just to hide out from the pressure-cooker demands of their jobs. Mine was a quiet refuge, with old black-and-white panoramic photos of World War I soldiers and movie books galore. I had a whole set of "Where Are They Now?" books about forgotten people that were once famous, especially old Hollywood stars. There was also a very large movie library of not only our films, but also every interesting film on tape I could get my hands on.

When Scott plopped down in one of my easy chairs one afternoon, I knew something was wrong. He only came by to borrow movies to entertain his kids at home. When he started reminiscing, I knew he had been given the cement shoes by Norby and was just waiting for the lawyers to finish with his settlement agreement and walking papers. This was one of those "keep your mouth shut and you will get a nice check to go away" deals.

The next to go was Norby. This was a lot messier and was preceded by a public humiliation where he was ordered to go before an audience of employees and be lambasted with questions about where Scott was, since there had been no announcement yet. Scott couldn't talk and wasn't coming into the office anymore, so his allies engineered the ruckus.

Making a movie is a lot like fighting a battle, so if your generals are fighting each other instead of the enemy, it is usually best to fire them both, and that is what George did.

Spaz and Mark Dippé survived, but they could never go back to the Ranch or work on any *Star Wars* films, *ever*.

Off the Ground

Paul McCartney came to ILM to do a music video with his wife Linda and his band members in black Mercedes sedans. He had been impressed with the visual effects we did for a British Petroleum commercial and wanted an effects-driven video for his new single, "Off the Ground" (1993). The video would be shot at the Ranch on the scoring stage, and ILM would do the shots of Paul flying, using our big bluescreen stage.

Wherever Paul goes, security is a major factor. His fame and continued success had kept him in the spotlight and had allowed him to buy valuable music libraries of 1960s rock 'n' roll classics as well as maintain a fortune in the hundreds of millions of dollars. But John Lennon's death by assassination and the vagaries of a wild and unpredictable public had made him and his group understandably fearful of traveling without protection. The Ranch, being a private fiefdom of sorts, was the perfect location for Paul to work without fear of interruption.

The Ranch complex is entirely fenced and surrounded by tall Marin County hills in a naturally secluded area, with its own security, fire, and maintenance staff. A large wooden gate keeps out anyone not employed or having business there. When you drive up to the gate it opens automatically, which for some reason seems to amaze people when you take them there. However, just a short distance up the road is a guard house where each visitor is closely but politely questioned.

Paul and Linda seemed jolly and in a kind of "away from home" mood when I passed them on the Ranch one day on a walk from the technical building to the main house. Employees had been given instructions not to approach them and certainly not to ask for autographs.

The autograph thing I had always thought to be very unprofessional. George would sign things for children, but when his executives brought a bunch of mementos into to a meeting one time, he set them straight: "This is a business, not a fan club." On the other hand, I saw him sit down after we finished *The Phantom Menace* and sign things for his employees for hours to thank them for all their hard work. I thought it odd to be asking colleagues, even if they were famous directors or stars, for autographs.

In any case, this rule was mentioned several times during the McCartneys' stay, especially when they came down to our company for the flying shots. Paul had to be hoisted way up into the air by a system of rigging operated by specialists who normally work in the San Francisco theaters and Opera House. This can be dangerous, so the real pros don't use any mechanical motors; they work the rigs all by hand so they can instantly tell if something goes wrong.

During this time, my friend and fellow visual effects editor, Mike Gleason, was working on a script that involved American Indians called *Wisdom of the Elders,* and he had a friend named Dickie Dova who was one of the guys on the set. Dickie had been an Ice Follies comedian/ skater, and his father had been a famous comedian in vaudeville. Both were showmen and acrobats, but the father was also noted for having survived the crash of the *Hindenburg,* the German airship that had exploded on landing at Lakehurst, New Jersey, in 1937. The elder Dova had used his acrobatic skills to jump from the huge burning dirigible and roll on impact, breaking his fall. Every major anniversary of the famous disaster found the father on the news recalling his feat.

The fact that so many people like Dickie worked for ILM was one of the fascinating things about the place. There was an ex–special forces guy who served in Vietnam who was now a brilliant model maker, a guy from Montana who had been with the Swiss Ski Patrol and did the opening ski stunts for a James Bond film, a guy whose grandfather invented the Yellow Pages, the kid who created Photoshop, the founders of the Pixar movie studio—the list was endless.

Some were showmen, some entertainers, but all were enthusiastic creative people of one kind or another, so the "talent"—the actors, directors, and musicians who came to us for our expertise, no matter how famous—seemed to mesh easily with them.

After days on the big stage, Dickie, a good storyteller, had struck up quite a small-talk relationship with both Paul and Linda. At some point Mike's American Indian script came up, and Linda was immediately intrigued and wanted to see it, so Mike came over to the stage. At the door he ran into the producer in charge of the music video, who reminded him that it was a closed set. With a quick "Linda invited me," he was soon standing talking to Linda, as Paul swung on wires high above.

Mike had made a video to introduce his Indian project, and Linda agreed to a screening on the weekend. She then said, "I'd like you to meet Paul." Here I must interject that Mike was, and is, a record collector, and he had brought his *Abbey Road* album down to his editing room that day, just in case. "Do you think Paul would mind signing my album?" he asked. And Linda said, "I'm sure he would love to." Mike ran to get his album. So much for closed sets.

When Mike returned, Linda introduced him, and Mike showed Paul his copy of *Abbey Road*. On the cover of this album, released in 1969, all of the Beatles are crossing the street, Abbey Road, in a single file but with Paul inexplicably in bare feet while the rest of the group is wearing shoes. This unusual cover photo had caused intense Beatle fan speculation at the time, which then exploded into rumors that Paul had died.

Paul looked at the album and said, "Ah, *Abbey Road,* lot of controversy about that picture. I'll tell you how it happened that I had no shoes in that shot. The photographer wanted us to just walk across the street in a single file. Well, when we got all ready, he said we had lost the sun and we would have to wait. So we all sat in chairs at the side of the road for quite some time. We thought it was never going to happen. Well, sitting there my feet got hot, so I took off my shoes. Then, all of a sudden the photographer starts yelling that the sun has come out and we have to get the shot right away. So that's why I'm in bare feet. That's all it was."

For the weekend screening Linda and Paul were both present and Mike had arranged to gather together some of the people helping him with the potential film. He brought his producer and some others involved in the project, the most impressive of which was an elderly Indian chief or shaman who everyone called "Grandfather." This man was one of those rare people who alter the atmosphere just by entering a room. Gray-haired and dressed in traditional Indian garb, he had a real presence without saying a word.

Linda McCartney was a vegetarian, but beyond that she was also a vocal activist for the vegetarian cause. Her feelings on the matter were so strong that she questioned nearly everyone she met and proselytized her views. Naturally, my friend Mike was nervous enough about this screening because if it went well, the support of the McCartneys could be invaluable to him. In fact, without them, or someone like them, it was unlikely that the film could be made. Linda had already mentioned the idea of Paul doing a benefit concert at an Indian reservation, so things were looking good.

Then—to Mike's horror—before the screening could begin, Linda insisted on interrogating everyone in the theater on the subject of meat, mostly the eating of. Well, Mike's producer claimed that her doctor had ordered her to eat some meat, but other than that, she was against it. The others made similar excuses or denied eating meat at all. However, as Mike started to sink lower into his seat at the thought of what the elderly chief might say, Linda worked her way down the aisle of seats toward the eighty-year-old American Indian.

No one said anything, but they were all thinking the same thing: What possible answer could he give? His tribe had sustained themselves on buffalo and deer meat for at least 10,000 years.

As Mike held his breath, Linda finally reached Grandfather and asked what his views were on this subject. I must say that the chief was no phony. Without rising from his seat or raising his voice, he took charge of the moment like a great actor, and when he spoke, it was impossible to not strain to hear.

"All the animals are gone," he said.

We all turned our heads back toward Linda. There was a great pause while she pondered what he said. It had been the perfect response. She had nothing to say, so she sat down while our confederates in the projection booth immediately dimmed the lights and started the video.

For the record, no film was ever made. The McCartneys finished up their work and left in a few days. It happens a lot in the movie business: You get very close, and then it all goes away in a puff. This is why I have always felt such a strong bond with anyone who is trying to make a movie. It is an incredibly difficult thing to pull off, and I know that because I've done it myself.

Back to the Future III (*BTTF III*) Shooting large miniatures from camera car. Pat Turner on camera. PHOTO CREDIT: © INDUSTRIAL LIGHT & MAGIC. ALL RIGHTS RESERVED.

BTTF III. Crash and burn at my stepfather's old rock quarry. PHOTO CREDIT: © INDUSTRIAL LIGHT & MAGIC. ALL RIGHTS RESERVED.

BTTF III. We rarely missed a chance to blow something up whether it needed it or not. We called it movie logic. PHOTO CREDIT: © INDUSTRIAL LIGHT & MAGIC. ALL RIGHTS RESERVED.

ILM model shop masters Steve Gawley and Bill Beck.

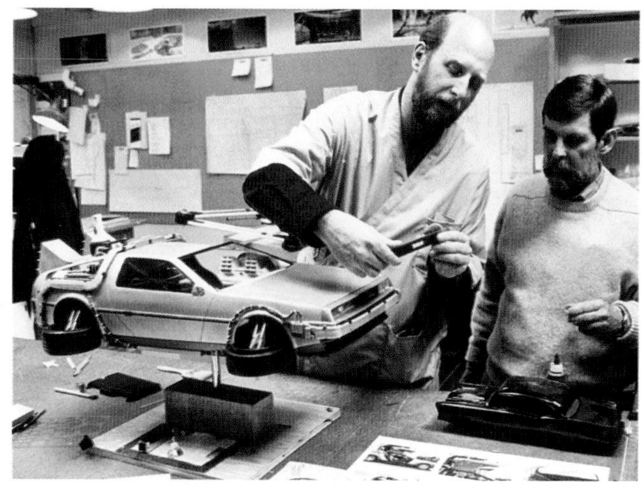

Setting up *BTTF III* shot. Visible from left: Chuck Ray, Scott Farrar, Pat Turner.

BTTF III. Mounted DeLorean for flying shot. Larry Tan.

Shooting *E.T.* space ship. Left to right: Marty Brenneis, Dennis Muren. PHOTO CREDIT: © INDUSTRIAL LIGHT & MAGIC. ALL RIGHTS RESERVED.

The Hunt for Red October (*HFRO*). Sub model on smoked set to simulate under sea. Pat Sweeney camera. PHOTO CREDIT: © INDUSTRIAL LIGHT & MAGIC. ALL RIGHTS RESERVED.

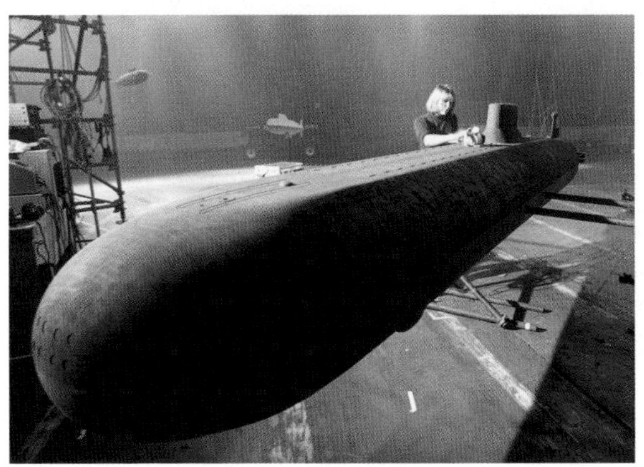

HFRO. ILM Main stage with large sub model. Kim Smith model maker. PHOTO CREDIT: © INDUSTRIAL LIGHT & MAGIC. ALL RIGHTS RESERVED.

Roger Rabbit. Pencil test to check action before painting cells.

Final painted animation cell.

Bob Hoskins working with water rig. Roger cells will lay over this live action film.

Final look of Roger and Hoskins. Real water. PHOTO CREDIT: © INDUSTRIAL LIGHT & MAGIC. ALL RIGHTS RESERVED.

Jedi Space Battle shot #19 (cover photo) was also used for this poster. AUTHOR'S COLLECTION

Bob Hoskins pleads for a parachute as he is falling in *Roger Rabbit*'s Toontown. PHOTO CREDIT: © INDUSTRIAL LIGHT & MAGIC. ALL RIGHTS RESERVED.

American Nitro artwork. AUTHOR'S COLLECTION

This *Roger Rabbit* storyboard image says it all, but note the poor fellow being launched. AUTHOR'S COLLECTION

Ken Ralston note left on my desk during *Roger Rabbit*. AUTHOR'S COLLECTION

Mike Gleason as Hitler. AUTHOR'S COLLECTION

My ILM 20 year distinguished service award. AUTHOR'S COLLECTION

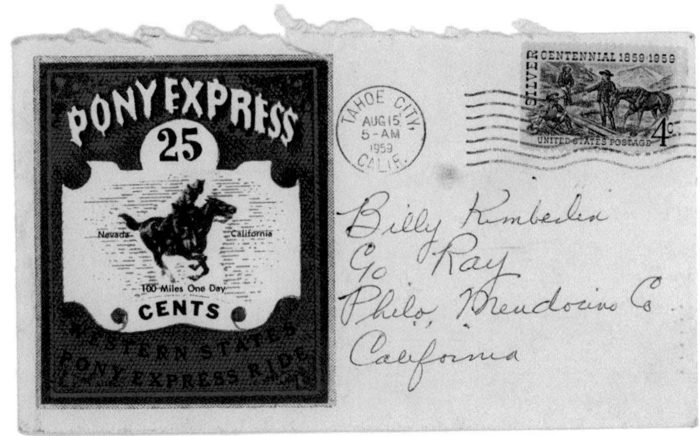

My aunt Druie carried this letter to me. First woman to win the 100 miles in 24 hours Tevis Cup Award. AUTHOR'S COLLECTION

Santa Barbara Beanie Babies Mansion. AUTHOR'S COLLECTION

Mysterious gate to the Ty Warner's Beanie Babies Mansion. AUTHOR'S COLLECTION

Undergoing a painful *Mars Attacks!* interrogation. AUTHOR'S COLLECTION

Dennis McKee, reformed bank robber, with my screenwriter. AUTHOR'S COLLECTION

Dennis McKee relaxing at home.
AUTHOR'S COLLECTION

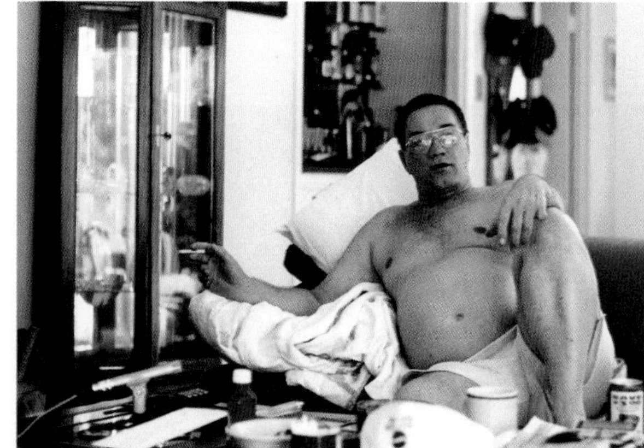

My grandfather Clint Mason's bootlegging truck as it looked when I discovered it in Anderson Valley. AUTHOR'S COLLECTION

Gordon Getty's jetliner as I approached the back entrance. Now I'm spoiled for any other way to travel. AUTHOR'S COLLECTION

So-called "Girl Head" attached to every roll of negative before printing. Yes, it is off color but this one I'm sentimental about. AUTHOR'S COLLECTION

My Harvey's Wagon Wheel slot machine. Sometimes I'm the sucker feeding in quarters and other times I'm the house emptying the cash box. AUTHOR'S COLLECTION

My great-grandfather, "The Seed King" J.M. Kimberlin. They say he was not a man to be trifled with. AUTHOR'S COLLECTION

Jim Carrey in makeup for *The Mask* but before the C.G. animation was added. An example of mixing practical makeup with C.G. AUTHOR'S COLLECTION

My great-grandfather's mansion in Santa Clara, California, 1909. Now Silicon Valley. AUTHOR'S COLLECTION

Large *Jurassic Park* ship model in front of the ILM shooting stage. This was crashed into a model shipping dock for the movie. Made a spectacular shot. AUTHOR'S COLLECTION

Kern River Oil Field near Kimberlina. They struck oil at 8 feet and I'm out billions of dollars. AUTHOR'S COLLECTION

This was a crew gift for working on *The Mask*. AUTHOR'S COLLECTION

SAN FRANCISCO CHRONICLE, FRIDAY, MAY 23, 1930

Gangster Killed Rum Informer, Shot Woman to Cheat Death Plot, He Charges

COUPLE LURED HIM TO BEACH, LUCICH SAYS

Mrs. Berri Fired Five Shots, Victim Used Gun as Club, He Declares

Slayer, Victim and Principals in Gang Murder, Rum Trial

Undersheriff Alex McCordy | Deputy Sheriff Leslie Tracy | M. S. Sturtevant | Mrs. Grace Berri | Vincent Lucich | Clinton Mason

The death car and the liquor and bullets found in it.

Charles Gruver Sr.

At left is Francis Yvonne Fantillo, an important witness in the case, and at right is Captain of Detectives Charles Dullea taking a statement from Vincent Lucich, admitted killer, center.

SLAYER HAS POLICE RECORD

Duel Charged in Rum Informer Killing

LIQUOR JURY DISCHARGED IN DEADLOCK

Unable to Agree After 14 Hours Deliberation; 45 Ballots Taken

My grandfather Clint Mason (top right photo) appears under a lurid headline to the horror of my family. AUTHOR'S COLLECTION

My mother and older brother on my first trip to Boonville, where I now have a small ranch. I was three months old. AUTHOR'S COLLECTION

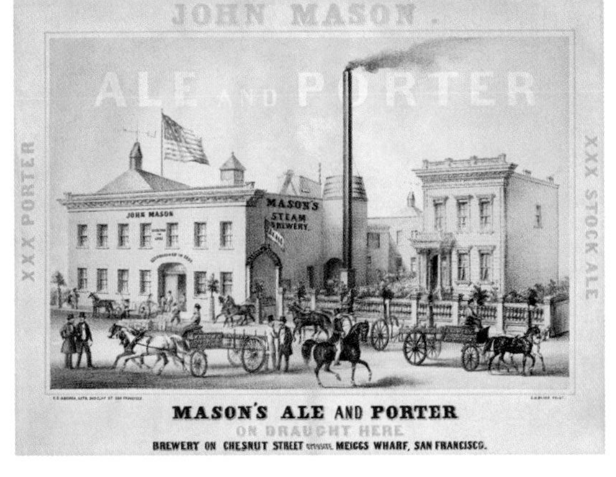

Original lithograph of my great-grandfather John Mason's early San Francisco Brewery. AUTHOR'S COLLECTION

Dennis McKee's Lexus with Pepsi 1 plates. Like a wild bird, once Dennis imprinted on the Pepsi brand he was a loyal fan for life. AUTHOR'S COLLECTION

We often made custom crew shirts for our films. This represented our challenge for *Schindler's List*. AUTHOR'S COLLECTION

Library of the Stone Age Institute with the skulls of our ancient ancestors on display, instead of the usual busts of the great men of history. AUTHOR'S COLLECTION

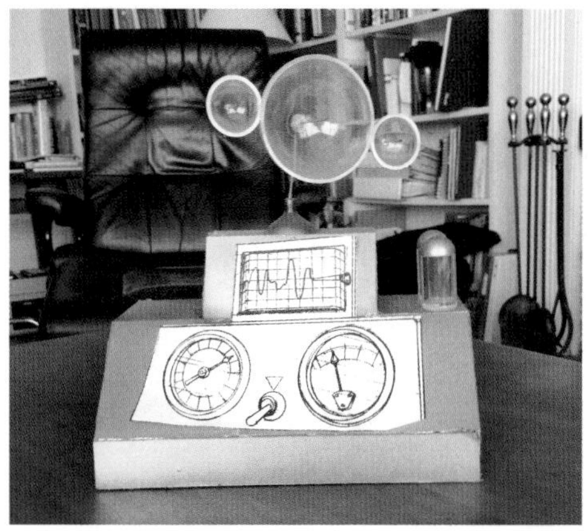

My UFO detector design. I am alien-free thanks to this baby. AUTHOR'S COLLECTION

View from my country house in Boonville. AUTHOR'S COLLECTION

Always a surprise when switching on the light and entering a room at ILM.
AUTHOR'S COLLECTION

Defining Myself

I ONCE READ A GREAT DESCRIPTION BY A SENIOR EXECUTIVE OUTLINING the Hollywood hierarchy. It went something like this: "There is the major motion picture from a big studio, then there's the independent successful film, then big television, then the good art film, then the bad one, then bad television, then schlock movies, and finally, celebrity boxing, the bottom rung." I overheard it put another way in an L.A. restaurant one time: "Spielberg and those guys are on top. I'm on the sleazebag level. Below me are the nobodies. At least I'm a sleazebag and not a nobody."

I fell somewhere between the art film and the schlock moviemaker. George used to say, "There are a lot of pencils and typewriters in the world but not a lot of novels. Why? Because it takes guts to write a book." My goal was to keep on working and make whatever creative projects I could. For me, it has always been, how can I support myself and still live a creative life? It is not, how far can I climb up some employment ladder?

The inevitable question at parties was, "What do you do?" I sometimes had trouble answering that one. If I said that I worked for Lucasfilm, that would end the chance that anything else would be discussed during the evening because everyone wanted to hear about what they thought of as a glamorous job. The next line would be, "Oh, you have a creative job?" These were people that worked for insurance companies or banks, and they had a different perspective than I did. I was certainly no big success, but it seemed like it to people who were outside our little world.

The movie jobs that I had had were certainly unusual by most standards. I had worked as a documentary filmmaker, making my own films, and as an editor on both my own projects and those of others. Now I was a visual effects editor on the largest films of my generation. I once calculated that when I started, there were probably only about ten visual effects editors in the world. Not that that meant anything. The biggest guy in visual effects at that time was probably Dennis Muren, a multiple Oscar winner, and even he was destined to be a mere footnote in movie history, if that.

So who was I really? Where did I come from? My father was a mystery to me because I was too young to remember him. I knew how to do research from my documentary training, so I started looking into my family. I needed to answer some questions that went all the way back to the movie director internship that I had sabotaged because I was alone in the world. If I could just place myself in the context of my family, whether they were alive or not, it might help.

I would get a letter once in a while from my Aunt Neva, who was in her nineties and my father's sister, so I went to see her in a nursing home and tape-recorded her memories almost like in an interview. This became immensely valuable to me as time went on. It was a reference that I would return to whenever I could find the time to look into things.

One thing Aunt Neva said when asked about my father's family history was, "It's all in the Bancroft." I had visited this library at the University of California, Berkeley, many times. It was originally the personal library of Hubert Howe Bancroft, who had an early bookstore in San Francisco and became obsessed with collecting and recording early California history. Among its special collections are the Mark Twain Papers and the Oral History Center, which contains interviews of California historical figures who Bancroft had sought out.

Prior to the Internet, I would find a weekday here or there to do research. Originally it was at the Mark Twain Papers because I was planning a documentary on Twain and Ulysses S. Grant. Twain's daughter had donated everything to the Bancroft, which was right in my backyard of Berkeley. If I could find extra time, I would try exploring family history at the library.

It was supposed to be "all in the Bancroft" but where? I couldn't find a lot, just bits and pieces, until the Internet became available. Sometime in 1989 I signed up for an Internet connection with CompuServe, the first commercial online service to offer Internet connectivity. Now I could do research from my home. I typed in my great-grandfather's name, James M. Kimberlin, and did a search. I had done this in person at the library, but every collection was in a separate catalog, so it took forever. The online version searched them all at once and, bingo! It said there was a twelve-page oral history made of J. M. Kimberlin in the 1880s.

This is what I learned from those twelve pages and where they led me. My great-grandfather had also been orphaned early in life. His parents had both succumbed to yellow fever on an extended visit to Alabama from their farm in Fincastle, Virginia. James and his siblings were supported by leasing out the family slaves. Somehow, and this was fairly rare, James got a classical scholar's education, graduating from Dickinson College in Carlisle, Pennsylvania, in 1851 with a degree in the ancient languages, Latin and Greek. When he returned to Fincastle, the family not only freed its slaves, but also bought them passage to Africa at a cost of $1,000. This act did not sit well in the South and they almost lost their lives because of it, so they moved to California.

In 1847 the wages in San Francisco were about six dollars a month. Then something happened. On January 24, 1848, James Marshall discovered gold at John Sutter's millworks on the South Fork of the American River. The place was called Coloma. Shortly thereafter it was almost impossible to hire anyone to work for wages. In fact, one Colonel Richard Mason (no relation to my mother's family of Masons) found his soldiers deserting at every turn. "The struggle between right, at six dollars a month," he said, "and wrong, at seventy-five dollars a day, is a rather severe one."

The *Times* of London disapproved, writing: "The effect produced in California by this new source of wealth has been anything but beneficial to the colony or advantageous to the public service . . . From the fact that no capital is necessary, a fair competition in labour without the influence of capital, men who are only able to procure a month's provisions have now thousands of dollars of the precious metal. The labouring class have now become the capitalists of the country."

While I was only looking into my own family history, I could see in this newspaper's scolding attitude that upstart miners were upsetting the natural order of things at the beginning of a new era. Over the next 170 years or so, individuals would come here where my family had lived, and where I now lived, to defy conventional thinking. This unusual gold-rush event had kick-started something that even today is far from over. The future seems to happen where there is so little past.

Great-grandfather Kimberlin, the scholar, came in 1852 but not for the gold. He came on a mission to help found the College of the Pacific. However, when his scholarly training in the ancient world couldn't feed his family, he quit and went into farming. In 1875 he founded the J. M. Kimberlin Seed Company, which became the largest seed grower on the West Coast, owning at least 300 acres of land and leasing more. He finally found the capital in farming that those few lucky gold miners had obtained. He became wealthy and built a Victorian mansion in Santa Clara. They called him "The Seed King" and he refused to educate his children, since he felt strongly that his fancy education had done him no good. This land is now known as Silicon Valley.

By the time my father came along, the "no education rule" must have been dropped, because he graduated from Stanford Medical School as a physician and surgeon in 1911.

When I was born, my family lived in a large three-story house on a double, almost triple, lot in the Forest Hills section of San Francisco. This is where the professional class lived—lots of doctors, lawyers, and business executives. Willie Mays lived near here but in a newer section. Ours was the old section. In 1940 "The Doctor," as the rest of the family referred to him, married my mother, who was from the Mason Brewing family of San Francisco and Marin County.

In the early 1950s my father started having a series of strokes. I didn't know this until I was in my early twenties, but being a physician he knew the prognosis, and rather than being an invalid to a young mother, he went down to his large gun locker in the basement and ended it with a shotgun. My brother says that the strokes had changed his personality and they must have, because one would think that a doctor would have other less-spectacular ways of checking out. I hate to think of my mother having had to go through that.

My mother's side didn't come for gold either, but this great-grandfather, John Mason, also became a prominent man in San Francisco at this time.

He was not only a successful brewer, having established Mason's Brewery, one of the first in the city, but he also built the first synagogue in San Francisco and the first U.S. Mint. They really needed a mint because of all the gold pouring in from the mines. Between the years 1851 and 1853, today's equivalent of $9 billion had been exported out of the country as gold dust and was lost to the nation. Coinage reduced the drainage, and went a long way toward winning the Civil War for the North.

At a time when interest rates were 2 to 3 percent *a month,* John Mason was building and expanding his businesses. He had survived recessions, depressions, and bank failures. He had survived the suspension of his business during the Civil War and the vigilante committees, leaving the city in 1892 before it was destroyed by the earthquake and fire of 1906. He was a pioneer of early San Francisco and a tough act to follow.

So I had found some real history here, but beyond that it helped explain this unusual occupation I had chosen. It was all right to do this kind of crazy stuff in San Francisco, or else why would you be here?

Jurassic Park

The making of *Jurassic Park* (1993) was a major turning point in motion picture history. Spielberg was all set to make it using traditional stop-motion animation. He had hired Phil Tippett, who now had his own special effects company and was the master of stop motion and the genius behind animating the AT-AT (All Terrain Armored Transport) Walkers sequence in *The Empire Strikes Back* and many other equally impressive works. Everything had been costed out and was ready to go. Stan Winston would handle the huge robotic models that could be intercut with Phil's miniature models.

Yet, behind the scenes at ILM, our resident bad boy Steve "Spaz" Williams and his colleagues, Mark Dippé and Stephen Fangmeier, were working on what they felt was a better solution to creating what would come to be known as "full-motion" dinosaurs.

Motion is a funny thing to try to capture. Man has been trying to duplicate it in his art since the earliest cave paintings that we know about. Those ancient artists added extra legs to the animals they were trying to depict as running. When motion pictures first appeared, they were startlingly lifelike while at the same time they flickered and the images seemed to jump rather than flow. Eventually refinements in steadying the camera's speed, adding a revolving shutter, and registration pins to cement the image down briefly during exposure produced a smoothly flowing projected image.

However, there is another element to the experience of re-creating motion and that is called "motion blur." It is perhaps best understood by imagining the little tricks that a cartoonist uses to depict speed in his drawings. A rapidly turned head, for instance, might be depicted with multiple heads in different positions, with swirl marks added to suggest speed. It is that slight blur that makes the reproduction of movement look effortless in moving images. I once showed a commercial client the film we had shot of a huge model of the San Francisco city and bay. As I displayed it for him on one of our giant VistaVision viewers, I stopped the film to point out a detail and he remarked, "That frame is not sharp." Without going into detail, I simply said that he would not like it very much if all the frames were razor sharp—that's not how the magic of movies works. He seemed to buy that, and we moved on.

By the time of *Jurassic Park,* Phil and others had developed a stop-motion system called "go motion," which allowed models to move during the exposure of a given motion picture frame, rather than just clicking off frames only when the model was at rest. While not perfect, the addition of a slight blurring enhanced the smoothness of the movement when the film was projected.

Phil's expertise and the advancements in traditional stop-motion animation gave everyone confidence that these movie dinosaurs could be pulled off. Still, there was a small group in the computer graphics department that thought otherwise. They had been told that computer animation was not yet up to the task and they were not to pursue it. Besides, management thought it would be vastly more expensive even if it was possible to do it.

Somewhat undercover, Spaz and Mark built a so-called wireframe version of a walking T. rex in their computers. The movement was quite realistic-looking even in this primitive state where the dinosaur is seen only as a shape somewhat resembling something made out of chicken wire. Spaz was in the habit of letting this image run in a loop on his computer screen, especially when important visitors came on tours. One important visitor was Kathleen Kennedy, Spielberg's longtime producer. "What's that?" she asked Spaz. "Oh, just something we have been fooling around with," he replied. Of course, he also explained that he was convinced that the whole movie could be done in computer graphics.

Normally, this is the kind of conversation that management works diligently to make sure never takes place. There is justification for that. I once had a projectionist that would intervene in conversations between directors and important clients, right from the projection booth, introducing his thoughts on whatever subject might be being discussed. But this intervention was different. When you are paying a lot of money for wildly talented artists to come up with creative solutions to problems, you have to have some flexibility. It's called managing creative people, and my former colleague, Ed Catmull, wrote a whole book on the subject called *Creativity, Inc.* Unfortunately, a lot of Ed's insights were not given much credence at ILM.

But when Steven saw the tests that had been done by our bad boy Spaz, he authorized a budget for seeing if this creature could be fleshed out, literally. So a camera crew was sent out to film a background into which a much more sophisticated creature could be placed. A new wireframe was created and then muscles and skin added to an animal that seemed to be stalking its prey. Lots and lots of further detail would have to be added to make this thing work, but the basic movement was almost flawless and way beyond what stop-motion animation, even go motion, could ever achieve. As Spaz told me privately later, "When Steven saw this, he went nuts and announced that all the animation in *Jurassic Park* would now be done with computer graphics."

It was Dennis Muren who was in charge of these special effects. No matter how they were done and no matter how talented certain individuals might be, Dennis had the responsibility to make it work. While he may have been skeptical initially, he was now on board and would oversee all the small details that made those dinosaurs come to life. When a dinosaur stomped on wet ground, splashes of real, not animated, water were added to tie the creature to the landscape. When the T. rex attacks the kids in the overturned SUV, a full-size, pre-crushed SUV was produced as reference for the computer animation artists to re-create it with photorealistic accuracy.

Elsewhere I mention that I made an internal ILM documentary to immortalize all this, and in it I interviewed Phil Tippett at his studio. He told the story of how he learned on a Friday afternoon that Steven had decided to dispense with all stop-motion work and replace it with computer graphics. This was a momentous turning point in Phil's life. Everything he had ever learned now seemed to be obsolete. Phil cupped his palms together in front of my camera and then slowly opened them to simulate what he described as "bomb bay doors opening under my life" as he fell into the abyss below. Over the next decade this same thing would happen to many, many talented people.

Although Phil went through what must have been a dark weekend, he rallied on Monday as Dennis called him and said, "Look, you are still on the picture, and no one knows animal movement and the archeology of it like you." Phil adapted, changed course, and directed the computer animation. He actually got cranky computer nerds out of their chairs, making them move and imitate the animals they were going to create. They hated leaving their keyboards, but Phil was an unrelenting drill sergeant and they obeyed. As one animation painter later told me, "We started out trying to do things procedurally [draw a detail and let the computer duplicate it exactly] but it didn't look right. It was too uniform, and nature is not like that. But when we tried doing it by hand, the very randomness of that approach began to more correctly simulate a creature in nature."

In the end it wasn't all computer graphics. There were animatronic animals, models, practical effects like breakaway trees, live-action wire work that made props move on set, makeup, and tons of elements like smoke, water, dust, fire, and brush to enhance the sense that creatures were actually in the scenes. Invariably it was these little things, the small touches, that sold the big shots.

Jurassic Park was a massive hit and it changed a lot of lives, mine included. Spaz was back in business and would go on to do CG work on a scene in the restoration of *Return of the Jedi* that George had had to drop in the original version because it looked so fake. This restoration of Spaz reminded me of a comment Abraham Lincoln had made when told that General Grant was a drinker: "I can't spare this man—he fights."

Schindler's List

We had talked with Steven Spielberg in Poland every day over a secure video line that cost a fortune. Back home and summering in Martha's Vineyard, he started one conference session with, "I just had lunch on the most beautiful yacht." I could easily imagine it. The Great Gatsby had nothing on this guy.

Dailies comprised camera footage of Nazis burning dead bodies, and no one wanted to attend them because they were so depressing. Steven was essentially making two movies at the same time. He was finishing *Jurassic Park* for a summer 1993 release, and he was also working on *Schindler's List* to be released later that same year. Whether in Poland or summering on Martha's Vineyard, we communicated through a device called Image Net.

Usually we only saw the sequences that included our work, not the entire rough cut. There were exceptions, but this was the general rule, so we often couldn't make our own personal judgments about any project until much later in the process. During this time a lot of footage was coming into my editorial department every day. We all trudged to the screening room mostly in a grim mood because we knew it was going to be unpleasant to view this stuff. How else could one describe the miles of footage we had to watch of dead bodies being piled up using some kind of conveyor belt system the Nazis had designed for efficiency. It was all fake, of course, but it wouldn't look fake when we got through with it. That was our job, that's what we did for a living, to try to make you forget it is just a movie.

So how is this movie going to work for a mass audience? I was asking myself. Will he terrorize the audience to make a personal statement? My

Aunt Leonore used to say, "I go to the movies to be entertained. I have enough sadness in my life." I didn't necessarily agree with this sentiment, but I always polled my family for their opinions since they were more representative of the country than I would ever be. Yet, I still remembered something the painter Pierre-Auguste Renoir had said: "There are enough disagreeable things in life. I don't need to paint more." Who was right, if anyone?

As mentioned, we had developed a device we called Image Net, which was a secure video/phone system. This technology wasn't really new, but the way ours was tricked out was a lot more user-friendly than others at the time. Initially each viewer would see a full-screen image of the other party via the satellite linkup. This allowed each party to greet the other and engage in some small talk before getting down to business. It seems that the more you can personalize technology, the more people are comfortable using it. I had heard of many directors who abandoned these devices, but they seemed to be OK with ours.

After the greetings were over, we shrunk the images of the participants to a small window at the bottom of the screen and filled the rest of the screen with the images to be discussed. This meant you still had visual contact with the other party, which is no small part of communication. The images were sometimes artwork for approval or more often film clips of shots we were working on. Each film clip was on a video player that could be controlled to run or stop on any frame in forward or reverse. In addition, each side had a pointer that could be used to bring attention to any part of the image. Since every frame was numbered, it was pretty easy for directors to say, "At frame 143, I'd like to see such and such start to happen."

This all may seem trivial, or matter-of-fact today, but if you look at the technology that people have flocked to in recent years, such as Facebook or TiVo or Netflix, I think it is largely the user experience that is being sold here. If you try to imagine Facebook without the controlled environment for sharing photographs being central to its platform, you get Myspace.

From Poland, a portable satellite uplink was installed at whatever location Steven was shooting, so that at least once a day we could all watch whatever new work we had to show and get his direction. We were still working on the *Jurassic Park* dinosaurs at this point, so that was mostly what he was critiquing. But the trickiest assignment we had was the little girl in the red dress for *Schindler*.

Schindler's List was shot in black-and-white. Steven felt strongly that the subject matter determined that choice. Normally studios would vigorously oppose almost any film not shot in color for various worldwide marketing reasons. Peter Bogdanovich as late as his 2001 release of *The Cat's Meow* had wanted, for artistic reasons, to shoot it in black-and-white, but the studio refused. This forced him to improvise. He shot it on color film stock but dressed the actors, designed the sets, and lit the movie in such a way that it looked much like a black-and-white movie.

Steven had the power to override the studio and shoot his film in black-and-white. He had made tests using color film stock and, through film design and lab techniques, had tried a more complicated version of what Bogdanovich later did, but he was disappointed in the final result. It just didn't have that glorious tonal range that the Hollywood master filmmakers had achieved through their cinematographers in the golden era of classic black-and-white films. In fact, a lot of the techniques used by directors like Josef von Sternberg are lost to history. Von Sternberg had brought his masterpiece *The Blue Angel* to one of my film classes in the late 1960s. As the lights were dimming he said, "This print is in German, but I will shout out anything you need to know." He didn't have to shout much because it was all told visually. What a gorgeous-looking movie. Cinematographers used to sneak onto his movie sets just to try to learn how he did it. By 1993 there were not many people left alive that knew much about either black-and-white photography or the lab processing techniques that the masters such as von Sternberg had used.

Although committed to black-and-white, there were certain shots in *Schindler's List* where Steven wanted to show the little girl as the only one in the frame that was in full color. The audience would see her red dress as the only color in the film. They would see a red dress in a black-and-white movie. But how to accomplish this on film? Digital projection of movies hadn't been invented yet. We were working on shots digitally, but we were still releasing those shots on film stock.

There were few options. Some early films, made before color stock was invented, had been hand-painted. Others were tinted with blue or red dyes to suggest night or fire. But none of these were modern choices except on some experimental films. The classic way to do this would be to shoot it on color film and then to optically create a duplicate negative on color stock but with all of the color drained out except where mattes were used to preserve the red dress. But how could this work? Even creating the shot using digital techniques still produced a color image. Movies were still being released on film, and these would be black-and-white prints. If color scenes were cut into the printing negative, they would, of course, not print in color on black-and-white stock. There was only one way, and I could not imagine this happening.

At least 5,000 prints would be going out to theaters. Are they suggesting that someone is going to cut our red dress shots into every print released? That would be the only way it could be done. Yes, that was the plan. It was crazy, but that was the plan. I had a hard time believing the studio was actually going to allow this. Here was a movie going to be released in black-and-white and whatever its artistic merits, it was going to be a tough sell. The majority of the money for all films was by now coming from the release of the videotapes, and black-and-white videotapes didn't sell or rent well. Is the studio going to allow this kind of expense in light of what might just be a personal statement film? Maybe they will actually just release a few special prints for major cities around the world and the rest will not contain our spliced-in shots.

I had reason to be skeptical; directors had often seen their intended work modified for commercial reasons. Films were re-edited by powerful producers or studio heads. For instance, the original release prints of John Huston's *Reflections in a Golden Eye* had a beautiful golden hue that was expensively created by the Technicolor lab in Rome. I had seen it the day it opened at the Northpoint Theatre in San Francisco. When the film didn't perform well enough, those prints were pulled and the general release prints were not so fancy. Surely Spielberg's epic would meet the same fate.

Schindler's List was released in black-and-white with the red dress shots cut into each release print as described. It was seen as a prestige picture, and it was a critical and commercial success immediately upon release. Spielberg had pulled off a picture on the most delicate of subjects with style and grace while I had only proved that the old Hollywood adage of screenwriter William Goldman that "nobody knows anything" was still quite true. Before a film is released, no one knows what is going to happen.

The Intern

LUCASFILM HAD A PROGRAM TO ENCOURAGE THE HIRING OF INTERNS throughout all of its divisions, which now included filmmaking, visual effects, computer graphics, games, commercials, sound design, sound systems, movie theater acoustics, and business affairs. I used to borrow one of the early Hewlett-Packard portable computers over the weekends from business affairs when I was working on a screenplay.

Business affairs was where they counted the money and made all the lucrative licensing deals. In their offices was a list on the wall of all the countries in the world where *Star Wars* was distributed. The list was then broken down into areas like states, and then by cities. The number of cities on that list, that produced the ticket and merchandising sales that supported us all, was mind-boggling. Just imagine for a minute how many cities there are in the world. Then multiply that by the number of movie theaters in those cities, and you get some idea of how extensive movie profits can be.

There was a floppy disk left in the computer I borrowed that listed the oil wells the company had invested in—guess you have to do something with all that money flowing in. Of course, business affairs had an intern; we all did.

The interns would arrive in batches twice a year. For the fall program they would get college credit. For the summer one they were paid a stipend and the company helped find them temporary housing. I am not sure what hoops they had to jump through to get accepted, but by the time they got to my department, they were the brightest and whitest group of college kids anyone will ever see. Most were from the top universities in the country and all were razor sharp, but the thing that was so refreshing about them was their unbridled enthusiasm. They weren't jaded like we were, so they lifted everyone's spirits. Unfortunately, some departments took advantage of the free labor, but that was eventually corrected, or at least I think it was.

My department was largely union jobs, which our interns were not supposed to do, but I was still able to teach them valuable lessons in moviedom. I kept asking why there were no black student interns, but those in charge kept saying that none applied or something. I kept insisting that they needed to go out and find them, not wait for a knock on the door. We finally got a few black employees, but not many interns.

One kid we got came before the program had even started, and his name was John Knoll. John had been recommended by someone at USC, George's alma mater. He was a bright kid, but it took a while to find out just how bright.

While we were working on *The Golden Child* (1986), one of the gags involved the young Buddha-like child displaying his mystical powers by bringing a dead butterfly back to life. My boss, Ken Ralston, was working on this problem. He had accumulated a lot of dead butterflies but hadn't quite figured out how to resuscitate one on camera, when John came to me and showed me a mechanical butterfly that he had built. "Perhaps Ken could use this," he said. "Would you show it to him for me?" It was a great mechanical feat, as its wings flapped and everything, so I showed it to Ken, even though I knew he couldn't use it. Ken eventually drugged a butterfly and shot it so that when we printed it in reverse, it appears to wake up and fly away.

When John's internship was over, I used to see him in the front office waiting to talk to the general manager, who was trying to think of a way to keep him around. Finally they hired him as an assistant in the matte department, I think it was. Like many of the staff, he kept getting laid off as projects ended and rehired as new ones started. Gradually people began to realize that this was no ordinary, run-of-the-mill smart kid. In fact, John is the only person I ever heard George Lucas label a genius. But that was much later; for now John was spending his evenings at home working on a software project.

At least part of this project included stuff he had observed around the studio, things that were lacking or would be neat to have. Sometimes John would get stuck and have to call his older brother, Tom, back in Michigan, for help. Later, when John would have just done some amazing feat that we were all in awe of, we used to laugh and say, "You know, John has an older smarter brother back East."

It turned out that what John was working on, with his brother's help was . . . *Photoshop*. John invented perhaps the most successful software program (after Windows) ever written. Even today, if you open up the Photoshop program, the first visible page of credits starts with the name Thomas Knoll, John having sold his interests.

John, at least when I knew him, also had that special quality of being almost as surprised as you were about his gifts. He would say stuff like, "I really don't know how to do real programming, but look at this, it's something I was fooling around with last night." What else was there to say but "Wow." John is now the creative director of ILM and one of its principle project supervisors.

I finally found a black kid to bring to Lucasfilm, but I had to do it myself and he wasn't an intern, just an eleven-year-old boy who I was mentoring. Michael was from West Oakland. He had never been to a restaurant where you didn't have to pay before you ate. My goal was to allow him to see that there was another world out there beyond what he knew. His father had been in San Quentin State Prison and the whole deal was a little tricky to pull off, but I managed to do it, learning at least as much as he did in the process.

He and his buddies could beat their teachers at chess but were having trouble with reading and writing. Nothing was as I had expected it to be. His so-called ghetto neighborhood was where he felt safe, surrounded by his extended family in an all-black neighborhood interspersed with parks. A lady friend of mine thought I was brave to even go to Oakland, saying "I could never go, I have young children." She was saying that if she went to Oakland she would be leaving motherless children after she was inevitably shot down in the streets.

These were the kind of wildly exaggerated opinions each community had of the other. I took Michael to Mill Valley, a place where I used to joke the criminals not only have never been, but don't even know exists. Everywhere I took him it was totally white, and he looked around warily. I couldn't really tell what he was making of all this, but he did say things that gave me clues. After finishing one meal he said, "We could just leave." Another time he asked me what I thought about stealing a car. All I could think to say was, "Why steal one if you can just buy one?" He was feeling me out with things he probably couldn't ask other adults.

I thought I was going to be a mentor, and it turned out Michael needed tutoring. His family had told him he was stupid. My wife is a math whiz and she said, "Give me one month with that kid, and I can change the course of his life. If you know math, nobody can call you stupid." So we launched into tutoring.

I brought him to a Lucasfilm "take your kid to work" day. I really didn't know what would happen when he was surrounded by all these privileged white kids, but perhaps because the environment was so new to all the kids and so much entertainment had been arranged, it was a wash. Everyone just had a great time.

Acting Out

One of the things that movie fans are sometimes surprised to hear is that people working on what I will call genre films, like science fiction for instance, may have no interest in that genre. Nilo Rodis was one of the main designers on both *Star Wars* and *Star Trek* and he has told the tale of flunking his original job interview with George Lucas by saying he didn't read, watch, or like science fiction. George hired him anyway because of his talent.

We were all a little leery of hiring someone who was a huge fan of the movies we were making. People were hired for their talent and professionalism. This is not to say that many of us were not die-hard movie fans of all stripes, just that everyone kept their mouth shut until you got to know them. The only thing I can liken it to is going to job interviews at Xerox and Polaroid back in the early 1970s. They seemed like progressive companies to me, but on my first interview I was disabused of that fact when the recruiter said, "That's just our commercials, kid. This is just another corporation."

However, if you could just get past the well-advertised but largely absent glamour of working in the movie business, it could be a hell of a lot of fun. Sometimes one of us would even get into the act. When I worked on *Star Trek III: The Search for Spock,* I had my only chance at screen immortality when my boss Ken asked me to stand in for a guard on the bridge of a spaceship. Don't ask which one—I never could stand *Star Trek*—but I thought I might be able to sabotage the ship and bring the whole series down with it, so I agreed. They fitted me with a uniform, and I went through the entire process of being a stand-in. I spent several hours on the set while they got the lighting right for the next day's shoot. No luck in bringing down the series—it's hard to sabotage cardboard.

For the day of the real shoot, they had hired a local actor for my stand-in part. Then someone called me and said, "Ken says, just get Bill to do it—the suit fit him great." Well, I wish I'd seen that one coming, but I didn't. Now, I *wanted* to do it, but I was in a rush with my editing work and just couldn't stop. Good thing I don't believe in karma, or whatever it's called, or I might believe my thoughts of sabotage had lost me the chance to appear in a major film. My friend Mike Gleason did get to play Hitler, though. Sort of.

On *Indiana Jones and the Temple of Doom* (1984), there was a scene where Indy is undercover at some affair in Germany during Hitler's reign, and he has to ask the Führer for his autograph to escape detection or something. So Spielberg's production staff sent Indy's prop notebook up to us at ILM because Stephen felt he needed a close-up of the signing and they hadn't shot one originally. The notebook was made by the studio prop department and had all kinds of details, as if it were . . . well, a real notebook. The shot was so close, all you could see was the book, Hitler's hand signing, and a little bit of his coat sleeve. They used my friend Mike as the Hitler stand-in and they shot forty-five takes of him signing "Adolph." We sent the film down to Spielberg the next day and he pronounced it perfect.

A few days later, we got another call from the *Indy* producer: "That's not how you spell 'Adolf,' and he was left-handed, not right-handed." Oops. So Mike did the whole thing over again, but they let him do it right-handed, and he got to keep the prop book, which made a great conversation piece.

Mike kept the book in his editing room for the next twenty years, but when it came time for him to retire, he felt he had to tell the company that he still had a copy of the prop book that production had originally told him he could keep. By this time the other copy of the prop book was in a glass display case in the main house at the Ranch, along with Indy's famous hat and whip. The prop was more than just a book—it also held a treasure trove of things that the writers and producers thought it should contain, details like a mock letter from Indy's father (played by Sean

Connery), German money, etc. Lots of cool details. Being uncomfortable taking this home to retirement, Mike decided to ask one more time if he could really keep it. So he called an executive he knew at the company. The executive said no, he should give it back. It most likely resides in that executive's den now. Value to a movie memorabilia collector? Huge.

Moviemakers try to be somewhat accurate but they are making a drama, not a documentary, so story concerns often outweigh historical accuracy to the dismay of history buffs everywhere, me included. For several years after I left ILM I had an office at the Fantasy building in Berkeley. This was headquarters to Saul Zaentz's movie company as well as to his music recording company. Saul and his partners had made a fortune in the record business and then started producing hit movies like *One Flew Over the Cuckoo's Nest.* Several friends and acquaintances also had offices or editing rooms there.

Walter Murch was working on the film *Cold Mountain* (2003), based on the popular book, while I was there. When I saw the movie, I couldn't get one scene out of my head. It was where Nicole Kidman decides to take tea down to the slave cabins because it is Christmastime. I was incredulous. While it may be that some person in the South could, at one time, have taken tea to a slave, this does not correspond to the fact that the slave owners also dug holes in the ground so pregnant female slaves could be laid down, belly first, and whipped for misbehavior. I've never seen a comparable Hollywood scene in a movie about World War II and Nazi slave labor. I think it is intellectually dishonest to rewrite history that far in a movie.

On the far other end of this spectrum, we were working on *Ghostbusters II* (1989) when a fellow who worked in the purchasing department came to me with a problem. In this huge comedy story, things famously go awry and we see the Statue of Liberty triumphantly march down the streets of Manhattan. In fact, things have gone so crazy in this movie that the historic ship *Titanic* has arisen from the depths of the Atlantic Ocean and arrives inexplicably at a dock in New York Harbor. It is more or less intact and shows the ugly gash on its side where it famously hit the iceberg that sunk it. We were building all these things in the ILM model shop and filming them for the movie.

I knew a guy named Ned from purchasing. We had gone out for drinks together. He was quite smart and for a time had supported himself as a gambler. He was outside of the FX group in the sense that he worked as a buyer for the company and was not really involved in our productions. However, everyone, no matter their job, generally followed what we were working on, and Ned especially so when it came to the model we were building of the *Titanic*. You see, Ned was an expert in all things relating to this famous sea disaster. He had read every book and article ever written about this ship. He belonged to the Titanic Society and flew back East to attend their annual meetings. One might say that Ned was obsessed with the topic.

Ned came to see me. He was nervous about even mentioning something like this, he said. He knew this was a big comedy they were making and it was all just silly fun but "that huge model they are building, with the giant gash on the side that the iceberg made, well, they've got the gash on the wrong side." He didn't know what to do. Should he say something and be perhaps taken for a fool? Who in the audience would possibly know this? What difference could it make? At this point, it would be expensive to fix.

Ned wanted to get out of the purchasing department and get into production someday. His question to me was, "Should I stick my neck out and bring this up to the producers or not? I don't want my first visibility here to mark me as a troublemaker." While pointing out costly errors to movie producers can be a hazardous business, I thought he should just mention it to one of our effects supervisors and let him take it higher if he thought it worthy. That way Ned would get some internal notice as a smart fellow where it counted. He worked for us, not the studio paying the bill.

The upshot was, he told them and it went to the studio for a decision. The producers said, "Of course we want it fixed. It's a comedy, but we want it to be as accurate as we can make it." Ned got out of purchasing and worked his way up over the years, becoming a producer that I sometimes worked with. Later in a wonderful example of "no good deed goes unpunished," he and I wound up on opposite sides of most issues and he happily helped drive the final nail in my career coffin. But for now I was very much alive.

Earthquake

The only time I ever stayed overnight at the Ranch was back in 1989 when the Loma Prieta earthquake hit and caused a part of the Bay Bridge between San Francisco and the East Bay to fail, and I was concerned that I might not be able to get to work from my home in North Berkeley. My commute took me over the Richmond–San Rafael Bridge, but it occurred to me that they might either shut that one down to inspect it or the detour around the closed Bay Bridge might cause a traffic nightmare that would make me miss my appointments the next day. So I called Skywalker Ranch and made arrangements to stay there the next night; thus there would be no bridges between me and the office the next day.

Besides the Lucasfilm offices and the technical services buildings, there is also a small village-like area of the Ranch called the Farm Group, which comprises luxury apartments for visiting clients or guests. When directors are on location, they are separated from their families, so when they come back to Los Angeles to do their postproduction, they can lead a more normal life going home in the evenings, even if somewhat late. So it wasn't enough to build a world-class postproduction facility: If George wanted to attract directors to this remote location, he had to offer a resort-like experience where the director's family could come and join him. There were horses, a baseball field, restaurants, swimming pools, a lake, archery, hiking, etc. Still, it enjoyed only limited success in attracting directors. Once you drove thirty-five minutes from San Francisco, it was still many miles down a country road before you got to the Ranch entry road. Mel Brooks said, "The Ranch is all very nice, but I'm never going past San Rafael again in my life." For me, it worked perfectly.

Each apartment is like a luxury condo and has a name of either a famous film director like Federico Fellini or Clint Eastwood or some other similarly noted artist or photographer. I don't remember which unit I was assigned, but I do know that there must have been a music composer in the one above me because there was a thunderstorm that evening and he had opened wide his balcony doors and was playing a symphonic answer back at the storm. For every crack of thunder, he would roar back a response to it off what must have been a massive stereo. It was actually quite exciting.

The funny thing about this billion-dollar Ranch empire was that they never seemed to have any discretionary monies available to do things that any normal company would quickly authorize. The editorial department that I managed, for instance, held prints of Lucasfilm titles like all the *Star Wars* and *Raiders* movies. We had the Academy reels and some extra prints also. These prints belonged to ILM, but Lucasfilm headquarters at the Ranch was always borrowing them from me. We were using these titles as show reels and sales tools to attract multimillion-dollar projects so we could keep the doors open while George was pondering his next project. It finally got so bad that I stopped the new head of production, Charlie Maguire, in the hallway and said that I couldn't understand why Lucasfilm—which, after all, had made these movies—didn't own any prints of their own product. He said, "Send me a memo."

It was all about "overhead," and the company hated expenses that could not be assigned to a client billing number. So, often things didn't get done that should have been done. Here you had this massive investment in the Ranch and it was not making enough money to justify itself. It must have been a bookkeeping nightmare for the accountants to make sense of all this. In addition, when George wanted to use some facility, he didn't want to pay for it. He reasoned that it was his company and he could use whatever he wanted. So the management that was responsible for keeping the place solvent was in a tough spot. One told me that when George used a given company resource for one of his own projects, the manager not only didn't get any rent, but he also couldn't rent it to someone else. So he would get screwed financially twice in each occurrence.

This all brought about the "George said" phenomenon. Since there was no money available for a lot of projects and no one really had the authority to authorize any of these things, nothing got done unless George wanted it done. This caused people to go around pronouncing "George said [such-and-such] should be done."

This inevitably led to the following: George was walking around the Ranch buildings with a small group of people one day and he casually mentions, "There should be a door there." Weeks pass and he is again walking with the same group and notices the new door. Frustrated, he exclaims, "Just because I happen to mention something, that doesn't mean everyone should stop everything and do it!" Sure enough, the next time he passes, the door is gone and it is impossible to tell that there had ever been a door there.

A corollary to this came from my friend Mike, who had the ill-fated Indian documentary project. Mike had been a beekeeper in his earlier days and got permission to put his boxes of honeybee hives out at the Ranch. If you want to grow crops, farmers know that you have to have honeybees around to pollinate them. Mike would harvest the honey every once in a while and he had Skywalker Ranch Honey labels made up, being sure that George got plenty of honey. After several years of doing this, a ranch manager called Mike up and said he needed to get his bees off the Ranch—people were afraid of them. So Mike took them home to Petaluma, where he lives in a beautiful early 1900s Craftsman-style home. Before long George finally reached the bottom of his last jar of Ranch Honey at breakfast and called his assistant, Jane Bay, to tell Mike he was out of honey and needed more. Mike explained to Jane that he had been told to get the bees off the Ranch property. The manager got a "George said" and as far as I know, the bees may still be there.

When I arrived at the company, there were already stories about a guy who took a lot of 16mm footage of the making of *The Empire Strikes Back*. He borrowed a company camera and used "short ends" of film raw stock that often are thrown away. When management learned what he was doing, he got a severe reprimand and could have lost his job. He did, however, eventually get the satisfaction of selling the footage to the production company when they realized they needed "making of the movie" footage for publicity purposes and didn't have any.

I had my own experience with this when Patty Blau, the head of production, called me to her office, closed the door, and read me the riot act for Mike's and my making of a documentary on how the full-motion dinosaurs were made for *Jurassic Park*. These resources could have been used for other purposes more in line with company goals, she yelled at me. Fortunately, I knew George's editor at the ranch. He showed our film to George and George called the head of Lucas Digital, Jim Morris, who was Patty's boss, to say how much he liked it. Now I had my own "George said" story for battle armor, so no one ever bothered me about it again. ILM still screens it once in a while, I'm told.

Finding Boonville

In 1990 I went back to Anderson Valley, where my aunt's summer resort was located and where I had gone to high school. After eight years of production pressure, I had been looking for a weekend retreat for some time and was driving all over Northern California in my search. Returning from somewhere, I happened to stop for the night at a B&B in the Valley. When I got up I had breakfast with the couple who owned the place, and they started telling me about how much they loved living there.

That's when it hit me: How come I had never considered Anderson Valley? This could be perfect. It is two and a half hours north of San Francisco, just far enough that you feel like you are somewhere else, but not so far you can't frequent it often.

A lot of my childhood memories were slightly disastrous, but not here, not in the Valley. It was a child's paradise, whose fond memories have never left me.

As a kid the Valley was all about timber, sheep, and apples, with a few summer resorts and kids' camps thrown in. Now it was all vineyards, tasting rooms, and small organic farms, with a few apple farms and loggers. But unlike Napa and Sonoma, it is real. Best of all, my aunt's resort is still there. It's been changed by new owners, but it still looks like an old summer resort and I still swim there occasionally.

For me, perhaps the oddest thing of all is that "Shorty" Adams, the guy that drove me to high school fifty years ago, is still driving the school bus. At first I thought, how is that even possible? I spotted his hot-rod pickup and stopped him for an off-duty chat. "I've got over two million accident-free miles," he said. It is very hard to be thought of as a "local" here, but my history on Shorty's bus seems like a pedigree.

My neighbor Frank sells firewood. He runs a big operation out of another location in the Valley, but he used to sell to one customer out of the property next to mine, and that customer was Wolfgang Puck. The wood was for Spago, Puck's restaurant in West Hollywood. Puck would send a semitruck to be loaded with oak firewood twice a year from Frank's place.

Now, this is a long way to go to get oak firewood for your pizza ovens, but since it was the oak-fired pizzas that initially made Puck's restaurant successful, he must have felt it was part of his trademark brand and he kept doing it.

They loaded the trucks just below my house every six months or so. Frank kept asking me if the noise bothered me early on weekend mornings. I told him I would let him know if it ever annoyed me. It never did, because I like living in a real country town where people work at real jobs, a town where they say even if you get a wrong number, you still talk for half an hour.

Boonville is also one of the only towns in the world that has its own language, or lingo, as they call it. Boontling is a type of speech that was invented by young people in the 1880s working in nearby hop fields as a way to talk freely among themselves when outsiders were around. My uncle could speak it, and I know a couple dozen words. Linguists have studied it widely and there is a book about it, so it will never completely die out. One local speaker was on *The Tonight Show Starring Johnny Carson* several times giving demonstrations of it.

Boontling is mostly made up of nouns that represent local people or lore. People from the city are called "brightlighters." "Collar jumpy" means irritable. A "horn of Zeese" is a cup of coffee because a man named Zeese was famous for his strong coffee and a "horn" is a cup in Boontling.

I've always known the Valley as a creative place. It is here where the author Alice Walker wrote her novel *The Color Purple*. She now resides in the Valley and once said that she tried to write the book in several places, like Los Angeles and San Francisco, "but my characters wouldn't speak to me." "When I got to Boonville," she relates, "they wouldn't shut up."

Anderson Valley is a weekend home to Kary Mullis, who won the 1993 Noble Prize in Chemistry for his discovery of the polymerase chain reaction, aka DNA "fingerprinting." He came up with his breakthrough idea on the last few twisty miles of Highway 128, which leads into the Valley. His friends later uprooted the highway mile marker that symbolized the place where he conceived his world-changing revelation and presented it to him as a gift. Mullis at the time worked for the Cetus Corporation in Emeryville, California. Cetus awarded Mullis $10,000 for his discovery and then sold the patent for $300 million. In the movie business, they at least give you another movie deal for those kind of profits.

This is my place for reading books and listening to music. Lately we have gotten broadband Internet here, so I can also stream movies and run my online businesses. My brother says that Boonville is an illusion, and it certainly is. How else could I be so interested in a place with so little to do? But it is precisely that illusion that enchants me. Like a painter forever painting the same scene, trying to capture the look of sunlight falling on nature, I chase the faint charms of this little rural town. I know what they are but am hard-pressed to describe them to others.

"Unheralded" is a word that I once heard to describe it. I'm borrowing this word from a wealthy San Francisco clothing magnate that weekends on the Mendocino coast. He said, "In the Anderson Valley you can participate in the blossoming of an extraordinary, still unheralded world." There is something going on here that hasn't reached the radar screens of the chic. In the end, this may be its saving grace—that what is here ain't chic.

For instance, the other day I stopped by an organic farm that belongs to a neighbor. Usually I just select the vegetables set out for sale and count out my change from the little self-serve cash box there. But this day Vicki, who owns the place with her husband Mike, came out and said, "Would you like some corn?"

What a question. Would I like to walk with her into the cornfields with her tiny daughter Hanna trailing behind us in her birthday suit to pull ears of fresh young corn from the stalk? Corn which I would be eating at my dinner table within an hour? Like a thirsting shepherd who has wandered out of the desert and is offered water from amongst an oasis of pools, I said yes as matter-of-factly as I could. Yes, I would like some corn.

So we headed out into the fields in the warm sun of the late afternoon, first stopping to admire the giant pumpkin crop that her husband was growing for the contests he enters every year. Little Hanna marched right up to one behemoth that was approaching 800 pounds and pulled back the netting that shaded this carefully nurtured specimen. "Daddy's pumpkin," she announced triumphantly.

As I looked around this idyllic farm with its original thirteen-star American flag flying high atop a pole planted securely amongst the organic crops, I thought of the imprint this simple ritual of going into the fields on the Valley floor surrounded by redwood forests on one side and rolling grassy hills on the other will make on this little girl, just as it did on me so many years before her. Hanna's own senses were drinking it all in as she stumbled over dirt clods trailing mommy to the corn patch at golden hour in Boonville.

Are You OK?

I BELONG TO A RATHER SKETCHY GROUP, SOMEWHERE BETWEEN CARNIval barkers and real estate developers. Only now we no longer have to resort to bearded ladies and fire-breathing pigs because technology has given us dinosaurs and meteorites, not to mention titanic sea tragedies.

We are a group with a questionable reputation, which comes from traveling players and vaudevillians, I guess. We didn't always leave town having paid our hotel bills. Legend has it that that's where the term "making the nut" comes from. Businesses got so burned with unpaid bills from traveling entertainers that the local sheriff, in the days of wagons, kept the wheel nut to the main wagon in his safe until all the bills were paid. No sneaking out in the middle of the night. You had to make enough money to at least pay your expenses, to "make the nut."

Entertainers have been looked down upon since Roman times. In fact, when the Roman Coliseum was opened in AD 80, some groups were banned altogether from attending, notably gravediggers and actors.

Once we got to Hollywood, things were different. No wagons. But a common sign in the front window of rooming houses was one that said No Movies, which is what moviemakers were called. And that was really the essence of it, wasn't it? They moved. Above all else, movies moved. The wonder of it. It reminds me of the Internet. Do you remember seeing a movie on the Web in the early days? We were all so thrilled (and some not so thrilled) even though it looked worse—much worse—than an early Edison Kinetoscope. What's the famous line about the dancing bear? "The marvel is not that the bear dances well, but that it dances at all."

We are dancing very well now, and we actually have at least one PhD running a movie studio: Dr. Ed Catmull, president of Pixar and

Walt Disney Animation Studios. Is nothing sacred? Will we soon have Las Vegas casinos with PhD pit bosses? If it hasn't happened already, I predict it.

There is *one* thing about movies, however, that hasn't changed yet: They are still about people. I claim that there has never been a movie made without some variation of the line, "Are you OK?" Try to find one. That's because movies are about *us*.

It is currently popular for movie tycoons to say that they only really care about the story. To me, the story is just the conveyer belt; emotion is the package being delivered. I always thought William Faulkner had it right when he said in his acceptance speech for the Nobel Prize in Literature that the only things worth writing about were "the problems of the human heart in conflict with itself."

It had gotten to the point where I wasn't OK. I didn't want to live my life with less class than a TV dinner. The management at work actually started calling everyone artists. I had to raise my hand at a manager's meeting to say, "I am not an artist." There is no doubt that there were artists there—I just couldn't accept the cheapening of the term by including everyone. As Groucho Marx once said, "I don't want to belong to any club that will accept me as a member."

My focus had changed. I had started reading Michel de Montaigne, the famous philosopher who introduced the essay to literature and whose philosophy of life could be summarized as "slow down enough to realize that you are alive and pay attention to that." It was all well and good to work for a big-shot movie company, but what was I doing for myself? What was I doing on my own? This could all end tomorrow. I needed to make a living, but I also needed to find more about myself and where I came from. Like an adopted child seeking out his biological parents, I sought out what happened to the Kimberlin Seed Company and Mason's Brewery.

Mason's Distillery

It took me a while to figure it all out, but there had been a murder, and all the lurid headlines that go with something like that. There was also a kind of strange backstory to all this that I accidentally happened upon.

During film school I had come up to my aunt's summer resort to shoot some scenes for a student film I was working on called *Remnants*. I was attempting to portray a series of iconic images of old barns, gravestones, and abandoned farm equipment when I discovered some old trucks on the apple farm near my aunt's place. I shot film of them and forgot all about it.

Years later when I called the owner of the farm to see if the trucks were still there so I could photograph them again, he told me, "One of those old trucks is an REO Speed Wagon. It used to belong to your grandfather, Clint Mason. He had it all set with hidden compartments to haul bootleg liquor." No one had ever mentioned this to me before, so I started to look into it.

I found a large color lithograph of my great-grandfather John Mason's brewery on Chestnut Street, in the North Beach section of San Francisco. It was an advertisement for the original Mason family business, which eventually moved across the bay to the town of Sausalito in 1892. The new location was on fourteen acres, allowing for a much larger distillery that could produce Irish and Scotch whiskeys in addition to beer.

In the 1920s Mason's was selling 60,000 cases a month from the distillery. But by 1925 my great-grandfather was dead; my grandfather and his brother were running the distillery and Prohibition had arrived. However, even with Prohibition laws in full swing, Mason's Distillery was producing, under government license, nearly one-sixth of all the industrial alcohol manufactured in the United States.

There was no federal law against owning alcohol or consuming it, just manufacturing and selling it without a government contract, so it was extremely difficult to stem the tide of booze that was washing over the country. In just one 1926 shipment of 6,300 gallons of licensed alcohol from the Mason plant in Sausalito, 1,200 gallons went missing from a guarded and sealed railroad boxcar—enough to make over 300,000 drinks. I found a newspaper article saying that my great-uncle, John Mason Jr., explained to the local investigators that he was doing everything possible to comply with the law, and then invited them in for a drink.

To much of the nation, Prohibition was a joke that spawned speakeasies, defiance, and gangsters. Winston Churchill summed it up on a visit to the United States. "In Britain," he said, "we realize over 100 million pounds from our liquor taxes, an amount I understand you give to your gangsters."

In an effort to diversify from the distillery business, Grandpa Clint and his brother branched out into real estate, developed a soda works company, and built a four-story downtown garage to capture the commuters, having already contracted with the federal government to make medicinal and industrial alcohol. But it wasn't enough: Prohibition was killing their business; they needed more income.

That income came from bootlegging. It became possible to make money by merely spiriting alcohol out the back door of their own distillery. The whole country was being happily introduced to speakeasies, blind pigs,[1] and the Jazz Age. It was suddenly the Roaring Twenties, and the world had changed.

With some research, I found that they shipped the booze to San Francisco in five-gallon containers hidden in a truck designed to hold them. The truck would go on one of the car ferries leaving hourly from Sausalito.[2] That was the truck I had stumbled upon shooting an early movie. They drove that same truck right onto the ferryboats.

---

1. A "blind pig" was an illegal bar said to be so obvious that a blind pig could find it.
2. Clifford James Walker, *One Eye Closed, the Other Red: The California Bootlegging Years* (Barstow, CA: Back Door Publishing, 1999).

There was also, I learned, a new arrival in Sausalito that worked in my grandfather's downtown garage. His real name was Lester Gillis but he hid under a fake last name: Nelson. As a local man later remarked, "He was a nice-looking man, that's why they called him 'Baby Face.'" Baby Face Nelson, the famous bank robber and partner of John Dillinger, was lying low and doing odd jobs for my grandfather.

All of this was difficult to process, let alone piece together some eighty or more years later. My family wouldn't talk about it and I understood that, but it left me dangling. How bad was it?

Further research led me to a headline in the *San Francisco Chronicle* of May 23, 1930, that screamed "Gangster Killed Rum Informer, Shot Woman to Cheat Death Plot, He Charges." The subheading had photos described as "Slayer, Victim and Principals in Gang Murder, Rum Trial." My grandfather's picture was prominently featured as the "principal." No wonder no one in the family would talk about it. Grandfather Clint Mason had been arrested and was on trial on bootlegging charges when a Prohibition informer was shot and killed. No matter how much pain this history had caused my family, it was possible movie material now.

Were they gangsters? Did they actually get involved in murders? I needed to get to the truth if possible. I certainly wasn't going to allow some Hearst-type yellow journalism define my family—not if I could find a different story.

The killer had the perfect Runyonesque name of "Pegleg" Lucich. He shot a man named Nick Sturtevant near the town of Bodega, north of San Francisco, where the Masons had built another illegal still on an old ranch. Both of these guys worked for, or sold booze to, my grandfather. Aside from local producers of booze like my family, Canadian ships sat off the coast dispensing hundreds of cases of choice whiskey to rumrunners who dared to make for the shore in overloaded high-speed boats. If the federal agents didn't catch them, the hijackers would. Sturtevant was a hijacker, another source for what was now our new family business.

On the night of May 21, 1930, in the middle of my grandfather's bootlegging trial, Pegleg murdered Sturtevant. The paper said that "Sturtevant was a hijacker who had been supplying Marin County millionaires with booze." Pegleg was sent to San Quentin for life but got out in 1947, the year I was born. Was he protecting my family, or was it a personal squabble?

Looking into it more closely, the whole thing didn't make much sense. If there was a murder of a key witness in the bootlegging trial, it was a little late, because he had already given his testimony and the jurors had deadlocked and were dismissed. They were definitely selling booze, but the rest was newspaper innuendo and no other charges were ever made. However, it had its effect. Prohibition had done tremendous damage all across the country, but especially to those having businesses making wines or spirits

My grandfather subsequently lost control of the distillery to its backers, who then sold it on the day Prohibition ended to the American Distilling Company. The ultimate fate of the enterprise was not met until 1963 when it burned to the ground in a spectacular fire. Today the old fourteen-acre distillery complex is the location of a large condominium project called Whiskey Springs, and I often drive by it on my way to my boat in the Sausalito Yacht Harbor.

One curious artifact I uncovered in all of this was a letter from J. Edgar Hoover *himself* to the FBI office in San Francisco. In it he acknowledged that he was aware of what was happening in this area, but since Congress had seen fit to give the enforcement money to the Treasury Department and not the FBI, the local office was instructed to stay out of it. To me this largely accounts for the official squabbling and incompetence of it all.

Finally, I knew what had happened. A family business founded in 1854 had been destroyed by government edict. It wasn't going to bring my family back, but it did bring a sort of closure. All that was left was to find out what had happened to the Kimberlins and to see if I could somehow profit from it creatively.

Kimberlina

The only thing I knew about my father were just stories about him. He was a well-to-do older man who had had children late in life, which is why when he died we became much closer to my mother's side of the family, the Masons. However, I did know certain things. He was an avid hunter of deer, ducks, quail, and fish. This is why he had a gun locker in the basement. It was a small room filled with rifles, shotguns, and fishing gear. He was also a persistent golfer and had converted one of our garages at the big house in the city into a driving range so that he could practice his swing.

In an effort to help piece together who my father was, I convinced my brother to take a trip with me to the town where he was born, in honor of what would have been his 120th birthday.

At the center of California is a huge valley, about 50 miles wide and 450 miles long. It is very flat and produces more than half of the fruits, vegetables, and nuts for our entire country. The southern part is called the San Joaquin Valley. This valley is bisected by Highway 99 for almost its entire length. The region's farm economy grew along this highway, which links California's big cities to small, isolated towns like Tulare and Selma, where my father was born. It was along Highway 99 that John Steinbeck's fictional Joad family traveled in *The Grapes of Wrath*. This is where the Dust Bowl migrants went looking for work, and where Dorothea Lange took some of the most famous Depression-era black-and-white photos ever shot.

In *Notes from a Native Daughter*, Joan Didion wrote, "99 would never get a tourist to Big Sur or San Simeon, never get him to the California he came to see."[1] This is the authentic California of almond orchards, mangy farmyards, rusty train works, peach trees, and Depression-era hamburger stands.

There was something else along Highway 99 that the tourists didn't come to see, and this would make history. Something that no one knew anything about when my father's family expanded there in the late 1800s just north of Bakersfield.

I had always heard that my father was born in Selma, California, in 1884, but of course we soon learned that most anyone that lived in a rural area was born at home on the farm and just listed in the nearest town. We checked the county seat, which is Fresno and only about 17 miles away, with no idea about where they might have lived. Then we got lucky. We found a subdivision map that had been filed by J. M. Kimberlin for a town called Kimberlina. It was dated 1888. Slowly, with the help of vintage newspaper articles, a story emerged.

After my great-grandfather J. M. Kimberlin became wealthy from his Santa Clara seed company, he decided to expand into wheat farming near his newly proposed town. Somehow he got the Southern Pacific Railroad to construct a rail stop right next to Kimberlina. It was all laid out with street names and everything, a complete plan. This in itself was a rather startling concept. In those days the wheat farmers were at war with the railroads. Frank Norris, who wrote the famous novel *McTeague*, which was made into the legendary Eric von Stroheim film *Greed,* also wrote *The Octopus: A Story of California* about the railroads crushing the wheat farmers in the San Joaquin Valley.

Apparently J. M. Kimberlin was a tough old bird, and the railroads seemed to be no match for him. The newspapers referred to him as "Professor Kimberlin," a nod to his long history with the College of the Pacific and reputation as a scholar of ancient languages. I found a photo of him standing on the steps of his mansion in Santa Clara, and he looks like a man not to be trifled with.

Starting about 1882 the Kimberlins began acquiring land, until they were farming wheat on 10,000 acres. The farm was on Poso Creek near

---

1. Joan Didion, *Slouching Towards Bethlehem* (New York: Touchstone Books/Simon & Schuster, 1979).

a town called Poso. (I couldn't find Poso on any map, but I knew it used to be there somewhere.) With the Kimberlina railroad siding available to them, they could get freight cars to the market at Port Costa, which is just up the San Francisco Bay a little, towards Sacramento. Every year for eleven years their wheat was the first to arrive and therefore commanded the best prices. Their only problem was water, and the rains did not come. This whole thing was starting to reminded me of the mayor's pleadings in the movie *Chinatown*: "Without water the dust will rise up and cover us as though we never existed."

But there is another movie that more accurately portrays what happened to my family next. It's called *There Will Be Blood,* written and directed by Paul Thomas Anderson and based largely on the novel *Oil!* by Upton Sinclair. I had met Anderson out at the Ranch while I was working on *Gangs of New York.* I would have loved to have asked him about his research on California, but I didn't know then what I know now.

My notes from recording Aunt Neva told me that they endured seven years of drought. That was all I knew. Evidently, they sold out and left the area. What became, I wondered, of the 10,000-acre wheat farm and the town of Poso on Poso Creek, not to mention Kimberlina?

This happened over 110 years ago, and there has been no one left to ask for decades. I still don't have the whole story, but I do know this: When they left Poso Creek in about 1906, they had been standing on, or near, one of the largest pools of oil in the world. The Poso Creek oil field was discovered in 1926 by the Calipose Petroleum Company. They struck oil at *eight feet* with their first well. The original report stated, "There is practically no water apparent." Wonderful news for oil companies, disastrous news for farmers. They found eighty-eight million barrels of oil there. The Poso Creek oil field, I learned, is really an eastern extension of the Kern River Field, which is the third-largest oil field in the country with two billion barrels.

We couldn't find the town of Poso because its name was changed to Famoso in 1895, so my father was actually born in Famoso. Today one of the most famous drag strips in the world is in Famoso, where we shot film for *American Nitro* not knowing the family connection. The railroad siding is still there, but Kimberlina was never built. All that is left is a highway turnoff sign leading to Kimberlina Road. Did my family ever learn about the oil? Eight feet is pretty shallow, even for the most primitive hand-dug water well, but I don't think they ever did.

At current prices I may be out about $60 billion in oil profits, and it might have been for me like the Norma Desmond rant in *Sunset Boulevard*: "I'm richer than all this new Hollywood trash! I've got a million dollars. Own three blocks downtown, I've got oil in Bakersfield, pumping, pumping, pumping." But the reality is more like the characters at the end of *The Treasure of the Sierra Madre,* watching their gold dust blow back to the hills from which it came, and like them, all I can do is laugh.

There is something primal in losing your home, family, and dog all at once. In never knowing who your parents were. They were strangers to me, and there is trauma in that. My prescription had been to find them through my ancestors, and it seems to have worked. I was functional again.

The UFO Detector

It was the model shop at ILM that really represented the heart and soul of the company. You never knew what you might find there. A Star Destroyer being tuned up for a museum tour, the Ford Tri-Motor airplane Indy used in *Raiders 2*, a one-sixth-scale mansion designed to split in half for *Jumanji,* or just R2-D2 in for repairs.

People knew I worked on big sci-fi movies, so I thought it would be funny to have a UFO detector in my home. I drew up some ideas and had an ILM artist make it look like something that could be built. Somehow I talked the model shop into building me a prototype out of cardboard and plastic. It had dials and switches and antennas that were supposed to rotate. I even thought of producing it commercially as a sort of Pet Rock kind of gag item. It would be guaranteed to sweep the area around your home to a depth of 300 feet, setting off an alarm should aliens be detected. My own house has been alien-free for years because of this device.

This all led to an idea for a movie around 1999. What if a disgraced journalist was forced to take a job at the *National Enquirer* writing some of their elaborate hoax stories? You know, the ones with headlines like "Scientists Discover That Rome Was Actually Built . . . *In One Day.*" Let's say this reporter goes out to make up a story about a spaceship landing behind some old farmer's barn, only to find out that there actually *is* a spaceship there.

My wife had already written a very funny screenplay that was a switch on the adolescent male coming-of-age story. Hers was an adolescent female coming-of-age story. She took my story and wrote a political comedy about a private investigator who investigated extraterrestrial claims. Our idea was that this would be a great vehicle for Jim Carrey. I had ILM do a cost analysis and shopped it to a studio where a former colleague had become a big producer. Here was our pitch:

> *Titled* UFO PI, *this is an effects comedy with a role for a comic actor as a hard-boiled noir detective specializing in alien sightings. Using the Alien Detector he has invented, he uncovers a plot by an extraterrestrial to replace our politicians with kooks in an effort to gum up our national politics and slow down U.S. space exploration. Apparently it's working.*
>
> *Our hero, Jack, is a cynical Bogart type struggling to work with a group of unbalanced clients, when in walks a real client. Unfortunately, Jack gets "implanted" and must go through peculiar physical transformations as he works to crack the case. At one point he even becomes partially female, which is a real obstacle to his courtship of the girl.*

That got us a read of our screenplay and the following response: "There are some genuinely funny bits here, as well as a good deal of professionalism in the writing. [It is] cleverly written as a vehicle for a rubber-faced over-the-top comedian." (I still haven't made a sale; however, there is still interest in the project.)

When I got the budget estimate for doing the effects work on *UFO PI,* I mentioned how expensive it was to the vice president of Lucas Digital and he replied only partially in jest, "That's what pays for your big salary, Bill." That was a clear message. Come to think of it, no one had offered me a car either, like Zemeckis had demanded from Spielberg. Was my stock dropping?

Stock was an apt metaphor here. Early in my career, I had learned to make friends with the company receptionists. Like mailmen, they knew everything. One was Karen. She was smart and capable, always broke and a little rough compared to the usual college girls they hired, but I liked her. She would hit me up for twenty bucks now and then to get her to payday, and I always obliged. If she got a phone call she didn't know what to do with, she would ask me to take it. I got some great ones, but the best was from a guy who had rescued the neon sign from the original drive-in that was used as a location in *American Graffiti*. It read "Mel's" in neon script lettering and can be seen just as "Directed by George Lucas" comes on at the opening to the movie.

The guy wanted to see it go to somebody connected with the company, so I bought it for about $300. It was a little ragged from being outside over the years, but it worked and was authentic. I kept it for a while and then decided to sell it. But first I offered it to George. I sent him a letter with photos, and a few days later I got the letter back. His secretary had drawn two boxes in pen at the bottom of my letter: One was marked "Yes" and the other "No." So I guess this is how business moguls make decisions. The "No" box was marked, and I felt free to sell it myself. The restaurant chain Planet Hollywood bought it for $10,000.

Karen was a wealth of information in other ways as well. We were having some difficulties with one of the *Star Trek* movies, and the Hollywood studio suspected something. They sent a limousine full of executives to try to embarrass us about being behind schedule. Their problem was that the driver from the airport to ILM, who was one of many such drivers, was always the same guy. He didn't work for us, but Karen had befriended him and he gave her a complete rundown on what the executives were up to. People say stuff in front of cab and limo drivers as if they weren't there. We made sure we had a good presentation for them, and word got back from the driver that they were shocked to find how prepared we were.

Karen got promoted to assistant to the vice president and general manager of ILM. I didn't see her too much after that, but I do remember a time when I thought something was up and she called me to say, "Your stock is certainly rising." And it did.

I've always tried to steer clear of company politics except where survival was involved. Here it was decades later, and my stock was apparently now dropping. So I took up an offer to work some weekends out of the union hall in San Francisco. This was not an idea for a career change, just something to add to my experience. Plus I was always writing. Perhaps I could write about this line of work. As writer/director Nora Ephron had said, quoting her screenwriter mother, no matter what happens to you, "everything is copy"—fuel for your creative efforts.

When ILM originally relocated from Los Angeles to the Bay Area, the union that adopted us was IATSE, or the International Alliance of Theatrical Stage Employees. This union covers all live theater, motion pictures, television, trade shows, and concerts in San Francisco and across the nation and Canada.

Working out of the hall was a world away from Lucasfilm and ILM. I used to tell our union head that his outfit was designed to represent the equivalent of hod carriers but was representing rocket scientists at ILM. Now I was going among the real working people, the kind of people I documented in my *Nitro* movie, and I would get to see them up close again.

One of the first jobs I was assigned to was setting up video displays at booths in a large hotel's convention hall in San Francisco. First we took freight elevators deep under the hotel, down to the levels of sub-sub-basements that the general public never sees. Concrete roadways plunge deep down under these behemoth hotels, large enough for semitrucks to deliver tons of convention displays, furniture, video systems, platforms, audio equipment, whole showrooms of new model cars—whatever is needed.

Offloading the trucks using forklifts was a surly gang of teamsters that looked more like fat Hells Angels than anything else. "Don't touch my rig" was the mantra of these guys. Once it was off the truck, however, it was fair game. And we dove in, stacking pushcarts high with all manner of equipment. *Our* mantra was "put wheels under it." It was as if any problem could be solved by simply underpinning it with some wheeled conveyance. And I must say it always seemed to work. These guys lived all over the Bay Area and were lucky to have jobs with union pay scales and someday—far, far off—a pension. They were young, too young to ever imagine that that day would ever actually arrive, but I wasn't.

They were proud of their hard work and generally had a good time. This was the era when drivers were starting to talk on cellphones in their cars, to the annoyance of other drivers, and one of our guys spray-painted the side of his car with huge letters that said, "Shut up and drive." For this, he made the national news and we all had a good laugh, as we knew the feeling.

I could understand why the famous writer/philosopher Eric Hoffer continued working as a longshoreman on the San Francisco docks long after he had received acclaim and could have easily left. Hoffer called his fellow workers "lumpy with talent," and that is what I saw as well.

Next, I went out on a *Wheel of Fortune* shoot. It was going to be a special segment featured on several episodes to introduce the new line of General Motors cars as prizes on the show. Here, I was a camera assistant, while at the hotels I had been more of a video tech. All the locations were chosen because they were famous San Francisco sites with classic backgrounds for the cars, like the Palace of Fine Arts or Alamo Square where the "Painted Ladies" (beautiful Victorian houses) are the foreground to a postcard view of the San Francisco skyline.

This crew was on a different plane from the stagehands. One guy owned the "sky crane" that could float the TV camera from twenty feet in the air down to ground level. It was all on a fancy gyro, so it rendered a wonderfully steady boom-down shot. He had worked the show for years, renting and operating his rig.

All the tech stuff, like cameras and sound recorders, were still in transition and constantly changing, but all were digital. Most people in the camera crews were not experts in the fine details of the new cameras, but I met one who was.

Specialized motion picture jobs had traditionally been hard to get, but the new digital technology created loopholes in the system. The fellow I talked to said, "They love to see me coming onto the set because I know the intricate menu systems that allow digging down into the computer software that operates these high-tech cameras."

There have always been walls around the choice jobs, whether it was fresco painters at the Vatican or senior engineers at Ford Motor Company. There is a story about a craftsman from the old country that was working at a Ford plant in Michigan. He was very skilled. One day a man came up behind him at his forming machine and was impressed with his work.

"Where did you learn to do that?" the man asked.

"I learned my trade in the old country," the worker replied.

"Then, why are you not working at the Ford Rouge plant?"

"Because they told me I would have to know somebody to work there."

"Well, you know somebody now."

The man walked off and the worker asked the fellow on the next machine, "Who was that?" The other operator said, "That was Henry Ford." The craftsman later became a senior Ford engineer.

Just as in the rest of the movie world, the crew was full of gossip. On this show it was about Vanna White. "She's pushing fifty and her twenty-five-year-old boyfriend just dumped her." That was for openers. Then, "She owns three Learjets and flies all over the world giving speeches and raking in endorsement money." That was the gist of it, sex and money. All I saw was a poised and experienced player. When she came out of her trailer she knew her lines, acted like a professional, and was polite to everyone. From my observation, those are the hallmarks of big bucks and a long career.

This was one of the last places I worked outside of ILM, and I did it just for the experience. I wanted to see how the real people in my union fared. These were, for the most part, the same guys that I had documented in my movie: salt of the earth, brave, honest (for the most part), and vulnerable. I could navigate the financial markets, the real estate markets, the equity markets, and the labor markets, but I could see that they couldn't. Not all couldn't, but most. Thank God they belonged to a union. They had a pension. But what if the union collapsed?

It did eventually collapse for Lucasfilm and ILM. George hired a union-busting law firm and got the union thrown out. It was after I left, but I had seen it coming and I would not be sticking around to see that happen. So I started looking for another project I might develop for myself.

Criminal Behavior

For a short time there was a magazine called *Prison Life* and it was somewhat like *People* except it was for current and former convicts. Since the United States has the largest prison population in the world, it seemed like something that could be successful, especially considering the group included everyone who had ever served time. There are tons of these guys floating in and out of our huge prison systems. Most of them read, and a surprising number of them can write quite well. The local newspaper in Boonville, where I spend part of the year, prints their letters to the editor all the time. (Recently, I learned that a current version of *Prison Life* still exists, with articles like "Felon Friendly Apartments.")

One month the cover article in *Prison Life* was about an uneducated ex-con named Dennis McKee. He was a flamboyant small-time crook and con artist who had turned his life around while on parole, after years of crime sprees, prison breaks, car thefts, and at least one bank robbery. He was a street-smart charmer who had the gall to borrow money from the bank he had robbed to fund a business venture and invent a new life for himself.

Dennis was the flip side of the other criminal character I had written about, Willie Sutton. Sutton had attained national attention for his robberies and prison breaks. He was the real deal. Dennis was an unknown but still fascinating character. So I bought his "life rights" and in 2001 flew down to Katy, Texas, where he lived, to spend a week with him. I shot film and recorded his stories so an actor would have reference to his character, voice, and mannerisms. I really didn't know what this was going to be, but it is the kind of investment I like to make. I may have been shadowboxing with myself, with no chance at a title shot, but I didn't care, I could still be in the game. Besides, it might make a book or at least an article, maybe even a movie someday, although I knew that was the longest of long shots.

Dennis picked my wife and me up at the airport in a new black Lexus. The car had one of the first navigation screens built into the dashboard and was quite a novelty at the time, especially since it added about $5,000 to the price of the car back then. The first thing he said to us was, "I drive real fast." That Lexus was rarely under 100 mph. Dennis was part wild man, part innocent, and had a huge need to be connected to something, almost anything. He also had a mania for things that would set him apart and show his success. He had credit cards made up listing him as "Dr. McKee," thinking it would get him better seating at restaurants, for instance, and it did. But was he dangerous? We were going to be staying at his house but I didn't know much about him. I slept uneasily the first night, thinking that maybe I had jumped into this too quickly.

Things got better in the morning but no less bizarre as Dennis rolled out his story for us. "I'm not ashamed of anything I ever did. My momma was a hooker and my gramma was a drunk, who beat me half to death. We was dirt poor in Alabama when I was born. I didn't have so I stole, and stole and stole." It was a tale of poor white trash in abject Southern poverty sometime in the late 1950s, as near as I could make out.

Now he lived in a nice house with a swimming pool and luxury cars parked in the driveway. But the years of criminal activity and a revolving door life in and out of prison had taken a toll. He was an anomaly, an unexpected result of the American penal institutions. A statistical aberration who should not be free. He was the frog who at the last possible second unaccountably jumped out of the pot that was about to boil. His last stretch was in a federal prison, and at his final parole meeting they told him, almost to the month, when he would return, because they all return—except for Dennis.

I had no idea how much there was to learn about how our prison system actually functions until I talked to Dennis. For instance, when the Civil Rights Act of 1964 was passed, it didn't affect just black people—it was a sea change for any oppressed group, including prisoners. There hadn't been a civil rights act since 1875. Prisoners could be beaten, strangled, shot, or pumped full of drugs. They had no rights until sometime after 1964. It was a collateral positive for Dennis. He now had rights.

Early on Dennis faked insanity in prison in an effort to escape from a less secure facility, but the ruse backfired. Prison hospitals had become heavily staffed by Cuban doctors who had escaped the revolution that had overthrown the dictator Batista. Their methods were primitive and included shock treatments using ice and insulin injections. Patients were put on long-term treatments of the tranquilizer drug Thorazine, which puts the patient into an almost catatonic state but still able to manage a slow walk commonly called the Thorazine shuffle.

As prisoner rights slowly began to assert themselves, Dennis was noticed by a renowned criminal defense attorney named Bob Tarrant, famous for putting cops in jail on corruption charges. Tarrant ordered the prison to get Dennis off Thorazine so he could consult with his new client. He was not a person that the authorities wanted to tangle with. Tarrant was known for his withering interrogation skills and his work ethic of winning, not plea-bargaining. He had been described as "fearless and feared, a take-no-prisoners, scorched-earth defender of the damned. No case was too hard and no client was too hopeless." This then was the man who had come to the defense of the Dennis McKee who sat before me in Katy, Texas, a small town just outside Houston.

Dennis was serving a 120-year sentence for a prosecutor's briefcase full of charges. Using the novel defense that since Dennis had been declared insane years ago, he wasn't actually responsible for his subsequent actions and therefore deserved to be paroled, Tarrant was able to break down many of the charges one by one and negotiate deals on the rest. As a somewhat feared litigator who lectured on the Constitution and criminal law, he got his way. Dennis was paroled into the custody of the attorney, who eventually gave him a job as an "investigator" doing those gray-area jobs that lawyers cannot be seen doing themselves, but at which Dennis was an expert.

As Dennis took us through his life story, a powerful but misdirected personality began to emerge. He had been street smart and determined to wipe away the destitute life he was born into. Stolen cars, high-speed police chases covered by the media, bank robberies, scams, swindles, parking meter thefts, and many successful but short-lived prison breaks became his life. On the road and bored, he would randomly call up local switchboard operators and charm them into dating him. He impersonated country-and-western stars and threw honorary dinners for himself paid for by local radio stations duped into believing he was actually someone he only resembled. He also got married a lot, always to very young women that he more or less rescued from dreary lives in small Southern towns they would never have had the courage to leave on their own.

In prison Dennis had watched movies and was even in a riot precipitated by the shutdown of a movie before it was finished. He had been in jail so long that he had never heard of home video. So when his lawyer said he was going to pop into a local video store before driving home, Dennis said, "What's that?" Tarrant explained but it wasn't until Dennis visited one for himself that he started to understand. On his first visit he was impressed to see all the movies for rent, but he had a question for the store owner: "What happens to all these videos once everybody in town has seen them?" The owner replied, "What do you mean what happens to them? Nothing happens to them." That right there was the foundation of Dennis's future small empire. He had an idea.

Like most good ideas, it was rejected by everyone he knew, even his attorney. "Dennis, that will never work," Tarrant told him. Good lawyer, bad businessman. This was a time when the number of video stores in the country was about to approach 30,000. The locations ranged in size from small mom-and-pop grocery stores to large national chains. Renting videos had become wildly popular, as home video players were owned by 65 percent of households in 1988.

The source of these tapes were Hollywood sub-distributors who had a corner on the market, so the tapes were expensive to purchase, about $100 each for the studio releases, which were what everyone wanted to see. There were thousands, maybe tens of thousands, of small stores that couldn't afford to buy many tapes at these prices, and they certainly couldn't risk buying used tapes because they couldn't tell if a given tape was defective or not. There wasn't time to watch even one, let alone hundreds. Dennis had found an answer to this objection.

Dennis invented something he called a video trader. For a fee, he would swap the tapes that wouldn't rent anymore for ones that would—tapes the store customers hadn't seen. This meant several fresh rentals for their store for less than $150. That was a lot better than $100 apiece, especially since the bad-tape risk was low, as these were tapes from other video businesses, not the general public. Dennis was so broke that he started trading tapes on foot, carrying them in a paper bag. But it worked and he started making money. Still, he needed to expand, so he went to a bank.

He got the money to expand his business by borrowing it from the same bank he had robbed years earlier. His gall and charm intrigued the bank president, and instead of the $3,000 Dennis wanted to borrow, he gave him $20,000. When he purchased a van, cash flow improved and he could afford more vans to expand the areas he served throughout the South. He hired pretty girls to drive the vans since the video store owners were mostly men, and this also helped business. Soon he was opening his own video stores. "Truthfully, what made me was what made all home video, and that was porn video," Dennis said. "There wouldn't be no home video or no Internet either if it wasn't for porn video. Hell, I had police officers stop me on the highways just so they could buy them porn tapes out of the back of my vans. There's so much repression, especially in the South, that people couldn't buy them quick enough."

One of many unusual things about Dennis was his almost obsessive loyalty to the soda brand Pepsi. He signed off all phone conversations with, "Have a great Pepsi day," and his and his ex-wife's Lexus LS400s had personalized license plates that said PEPSI 1 and PEPSI 2, respectively. When he was starting to buy video stores, he wanted to have popcorn and soda to sell to the customers, just like in the movie theaters. The Pepsi district manager spent hours setting up displays in the stores, and when Dennis asked the guy why, he said, "Because we want you to be successful, Dennis." In many ways Dennis was like a lost child. His family had deserted him and he was searching for something to connect to, somewhere to belong. That somewhere became Pepsi. In convict logic, loyalty is everything. Later, when that district manager got the attention of Pepsi National and was promoted to a top executive position at Pepsi in New York, he and Dennis remained friends.

Dennis got people's attention as well. He had a powerful personality that snuck up on you without your realizing it. People wanted to help him. They just wanted to see him keep going. Local bank presidents and business executives couldn't resist befriending him because he had such a great story: bank robber to businessman. He had a nice house now but with an unusual bedroom outfitted like an S&M parlor: handcuffs, chains, straps hanging from the ceiling—he thought it was funny. "Texas ladies are a little kinky and they are mostly disappointed when they find out the chains and stuff ain't real." It was all just for show.

About this point I was starting to get worried. After all, I'm dealing with a self-admitted con man. Was all of this true? Could it be verified? If I ever do anything with this, would I wind up like one of those guys who gets exposed for research errors or fictionalizing large parts of his work? On the other hand, I reasoned, I wasn't alone on this story—there was the magazine article I had read. That author was in a better position to know than I was, and he got it published. Besides, I thought, I will verify everything I can when I get back home, and if it ever gets to be a movie, I can always open with the title, "Most of what you are about to see is true, I think."

On the day we were leaving to fly back to San Francisco, Dennis called me aside and told me that he had an idea for his funeral casket. He had designed a coffin that was a giant replica of a can of Pepsi. He was so excited that he had called his executive friend in New York early that morning to tell him about it. While he had to admit Pepsi National wasn't all that encouraging, they didn't say he couldn't do it.

Today, the long-since-reformed Dennis is a semiretired businessman still living in Katy, Texas. His is the life of any normal boring citizen, just like you or me, except not quite. He currently owns a company called International Light Bulbs. I don't know what international light bulbs are or what his angle is, but I do know that there is one.

Back in the bad old days, Dennis formed a bogus company and convinced department store managers to allow his group to pose as shoplifters to test a string of stores for what he called "security vigilance." He named it the Theft Reduction Analysis Program, or TRAP. It was a license to steal.

When I was around Dennis, his tales of adventures never stopped, and I rolled them into a screenplay that may still get made. I pitched it to the director Oliver Stone and he seemed interested. I hope so, because the story of this fascinating man shouldn't just end here on these pages.

The China Girl

Working on my own projects again lifted my spirits and reminded me why I was so interested in filmmaking to begin with. I took a lady friend to lunch one afternoon at Skywalker Ranch's main house dining room. Afterwards we walked through the living room and the library with its huge stained glass ceiling. She commented that the artwork displayed was all about the human form—the hands, the human body, the face. Over the mantle there was a large Norman Rockwell painting, *Peach Crop* (1935), portraying a beautiful young girl lying in a barn of some type. She is surrounded by ranch hands. Perhaps she has fainted, as the boys look on with a wonderful mixture of passion and concern on their faces and in their body language. A good art piece tells a story and evokes emotion. This was a movie scene.

One of the things you really have to get right in a movie is how people look: the human form, especially the face, because we are all so familiar with it. The eyes, the mouth, skin tone—we have hundreds of thousands of years of evolution in detecting the meaning of the slightest change in expression in the human face. Motion picture cameras catch all of this, and exceptional actors' faces are capable of expressing the subtlest of emotions whatever the requirements of the scene. It is really true that the camera loves some people and not others.

While we were shooting scenes for *Cocoon 2,* we were also working on the ill-fated *Howard the Duck* starring Lea Thompson. While I was heading to dailies for both films one day, I stopped by the second-floor kitchen, where there were usually some bagels or pastries, and an actress from *Cocoon 2* was the only other person in the room. She was the most beautiful woman I had ever seen in person. She had a movie star's face, with jet black hair and vividly blue eyes.

When I got to dailies, both Lea and the other actress were in the room. Lea had her hair up in curlers and may have just come from makeup. The dark-haired beauty was the one making waves in the room—that is until the projector started to roll. I watched both their scenes and Lea just jumped off the screen—you couldn't take your eyes off her, she was so attractive. The other actress just faded into the background of the scenes she was in. This is why they do screen tests. Mysterious things happen when you get people up there on the big screen.

The other actress? It was Courteney Cox, who went on to great entertainment success, largely in television. The big screen tests you, and it was testing me with all the changes that were coming to our production methods.

There is a term in motion picture making called the "China Girl." In earlier days when movies were still shot in black-and-white, every batch of film negative that was sent to the lab for printing had a reference frame or two attached of a white porcelain figure that resembled a lady's head. It was called a China Girl not because she was Chinese, but because the sculpted head was made out of a kind of china and it was in the form of a girl. The China Girl usually lay on a piece of black velvet, the two together displaying both pure white and absolute black, allowing cinematographers to easily judge the contrast quality of their prints. This image always represented for me the craft that was at the base of what we were doing. Later, it was a few frames of a female model's face shot in color that was called a "Girl Head." If the laboratory screwed up the color in printing from the negatives, it would be easy to see because cameramen had the control Girl Head back at the studio to compare it with.

This sort of Norman Rockwell view of filmmaking as a craft had been evident in the artwork I had seen at the Ranch. Now the world of model makers building rocket ships and "powder men" blowing them up was dying. The craft world itself was blowing up. By about 1987, movie production had changed with the advent of digital. The first sign of this was when it became possible to scan a film into a digital format, manipulate it in a computer, and scan it out again to film for theatrical projection. This simple technical feat would revolutionize filmmaking. The China Girl and Girl Head were replaced with the image of a gray square that could be read by a densitometer.

It took five to seven years to complete, but by the release of *Jurassic Park* in 1993, the transition was well on its way, and a film-based industry that was about a hundred years old started to collapse. Even the venerable Kodak itself would soon collapse.

Nothing quite like this had ever happened before, but the audience didn't notice and Hollywood didn't yet see the implications. They didn't realize that the creatures in *Jurassic Park* were essentially ones and zeros and that the movie business had changed forever.

Even the introduction of sound back in 1929 cannot compare with what would eventually happen to the world of motion pictures. It was painful and it turned employees' lives upside down, even forcing Oscar-winning workers into an early retirement. Yet, in my view, it was all positive.

Film to me has always been a business, a craft, and an art, in that order. While it aspires to produce art and often does, it is a business at its core. It takes a lot of investment capital to make a Hollywood film. I recently read an interview with a studio head who said, "There are not a lot of entities in the world that can throw $200 million into a movie project, but we can. That is our competitive advantage."

Hollywood has always sought a competitive advantage. When television threatened it, the movies went to wide screen, or 3-D, or even R-rated. I remember when Francis Coppola invested in something called Smell-O-Vision!

As the technology of the movie craft changes, so do the movies we make. The two are intimately bound together. Cinema follows a developmental path that straddles commerce and technology. It always has. When sound came in, it changed movies—their art was now a completely different art. The high art reached in the great silent films was gone. No one wanted to make or see new silent films anymore, no matter how great. So much for the art. Changing technology has always ruled this art form.

The invention of the typewriter didn't fundamentally change writing from the days of the pencil, but the introduction of sound did change movies. I would argue that the introduction of digital changed movies again like never before.

Digital cinema makes possible nonexistent, but realistic-looking, worlds. This is opposed to the film camera, which records the real world. The camera simply captures data that can be read back in a controlled way. The images are sequenced on a strip of celluloid, controlled by a sprocket drive and a motor. It is essentially a storage medium with a display, yet it is nonlinear. Images can be rearranged at any point in the time sequence of the stored data of film. We called this "film editing," and for years that was how I made my living.

Historically, the very first projected images were lantern slides painted by artists. Now we are returning to the artists' controlling the images with their hands. They are once again painting in movies, except this time it is from a digital paint box. How ironic that this technology should return us to our beginnings with moving images. Yet, "those wonderful people out there in the dark," as Norma Desmond referred to them, they haven't changed. They still want the emotional stories that I saw depicted above the fireplace at the Ranch in *Peach Crop*.

The Distraction

When it came time to restore the original *Star Wars* and rerelease it (1997), George called a few people together in the Building C theater and we screened his personal print. Traditionally only one or two prints like George's would be made off the original negative of any major movie. The first was called the "answer" print. People called "timers" would grade the brightness and color quality, making corrections based on tests and experience, and get their "answer" with this first print. This was also the first time picture and sound were married on one strip of film ready for projection.

The director and cinematographer would watch this print and make whatever additional corrections they wanted. If this was deemed good, the second answer print would be kept as theoretically the best and most original example of the movie. It would certainly be the sharpest, as it was made directly off the original camera negative. Many duplicate negatives would now be made off the original for mass printings that would reach theaters around the world.

As the film rolled in theater C, George made comments on the scenes he wanted to fix or, in some cases, add. From his perspective, these changes were all based on what he wanted to do in the first place but had either run out of time, technology, or money on the first go-round. Now that he had all three at his disposal, he wanted to get it exactly as he originally envisioned it.

One of the things very few directors ever got to do was make preservation masters of their films after they were completed, as it was expensive and no one wanted to pay for it, least of all the studio. But some people had enough clout and they got it done. The original negatives were protected because they were really only used to make dupe negatives, and those dupes are the ones that take the abuse. But there was another problem: The original negatives are subject to color fading and physical shrinkage over long periods of time.

Star Wars was an important film and a valuable studio property, so it got the full treatment with a process called "separation masters." Three black-and-white copies of the original negative are made, each filtered for either red, green, or blue. Since black-and-white film is essentially inert, unlike color film, which remains chemically active and subject to deterioration, long-term storage of these three strips were to provide a measure of protection, especially since they were going to be stored at the bottom of a salt mine in Nevada or somewhere.

After George pointed out all of the shots he wanted fixed, he said something I have wondered about ever since. He said that he was going to do a comedy version of *Star Wars.* It's been years since that day and it hasn't happened yet, but remember, you heard it here first!

When I got back to my office, I wrote George an e-mail saying that I thought a film should be made that documented all the people that worked on the original movie. They were all still alive, and many of them still worked for him. Surely they had great stories that shouldn't be lost forever. I reminded him that he had seen the documentary I made on the making of *Jurassic Park* and that he liked it well enough to call up my boss and tell him so. The next day my phone rang and it was George's attorney. He told me that George liked my idea and that he, Howard Rothman, would be in charge of the project. I never heard from him again.

About a month later I wrote George again and said that I guessed no one except he and I were interested in doing this project. In a few days I got a call from Lynn Hale, the head of publicity, informing me that there was going to be a documentary, but that it would be handled by the studio. I have never seen it.

Recently, I talked to my friend and fellow editor Tom Christopher, who George had hired to handle all the film and lab details of what he wanted done to the original *Star Wars.* Tom said he remembered my letter coming in because George's longtime producer Rick McCallum wanted to know, "Who the hell is this guy?"

None of the Lucasfilm executives wanted George fooling around with his old movies. "It's a distraction," they said. "We are not in the restoration business." The new movies were where the big money was. Lucasfilm's licensing was going nuts signing up sponsors and endless tie-ins. If George would commit to make three more *Star Wars* sequels, there was no limit to the money that could be made. Sales, marketing, legal—they all conspired to put on a huge show at the Ranch, to which they invited all the suitor toy, game, studio, and brand folks from around the world.

Hundreds of millions of dollars in advance money was at stake, not to mention the billions of dollars that would almost certainly flow from these deals if only the "old man," the crazy grandfather they had metaphorically locked in the attic of the main house, wasn't stirring up shit—wandering around in his bathrobe, so to speak, laying out plans and giving orders that were not in line with the juggernaut business plan of the century that business affairs was about to launch. This was a potential disaster. He owned the company outright. It was a billion-dollar enterprise but it was not a public company like Apple, where the executives could execute a coup and overnight throw out a Steve Jobs. They had to be careful. And here, I show up with even wilder ideas about doing a historical documentary. "Who is this guy?" indeed. I was seen immediately as a coconspirator and should, like Howard Beale in the movie *Network,* have been given the same famous film speech he got:

> *You have meddled with the primal forces of nature, Mr. Beale . . . There is only one holistic system of systems, one vast and immense, interwoven, interacting, multi-variant, multi-national dominion of dollars. Petro-dollars, electro-dollars, multi-dollars, reichsmarks, rins, rubles, pounds, and shekels.*
>
> *It is the international system of currency which determines the totality of life on this planet. That is the natural order of things today. That is the atomic and sub-atomic and galactic structure of things today! And you have meddled with the primal forces of nature, and* you will atone!

All was not well in the Empire by about 1996 or so. The ancillary money stream from toy deals that George had so famously bargained for with the original *Star Wars* had dwindled. The bonanza of home video sales had also dissipated. The lifetime "annuity" of cash that arrived to help smooth the balance sheets was now but a trickle. ILM was the bright spot. It was profitable most years, but the rest of the divisions were, for the most part, losing money. There had been the disappointment in the failure of *Howard the Duck,* along with a string of productions that made some money but not really enough to keep the whole studio afloat for years. *Willow, Labyrinth, The Return of Oz, Mishima, The Young Indiana Jones* television series—all did not have the blockbuster strength needed to make sense as a business plan that could underwrite the entire company like *Star Wars* had.

The original idea was sound: Make your money on the big picture releases every few years, and try to just break even during the intervening years. But when blockbusters are removed from that scenario, you are in trouble.

So, what to do? If you are a rock 'n' roll band, you go back on the road. If you are the ex–heavyweight champion, you return to the ring for one more big payday. There was really no other choice. I had walked into the middle of this scenario without knowing what was going on behind the scenes, and I would have to *atone*.

This reminded me of the time after I had first had my encounter with Francis Coppola, and I thought it would be a good idea to either write an article about him or just interview him. Maybe I could sell the interview to a magazine. So I wrote to his company, American Zoetrope, and made a proposal for an interview for *Playboy* magazine. They liked the idea but needed a letter from *Playboy* confirming it. So I wrote to *Playboy* laying out my argument for such an interview by saying that Coppola was a young, hip Oscar-winning filmmaker who had founded his own company in San Francisco. They also liked the idea but thought it was a little too early. "Let's keep our eye on him and see what develops," they wrote me.

About a year after *The Godfather* was released and became the highest-grossing motion picture of all time, I wrote *Playboy* again and reminded them of my Coppola interview project. This time they wrote back in a much firmer tone. "When people go to see a film *because* it is a Francis Coppola film, then we would consider him for a *Playboy* interview." I didn't know what to make of that. However, it seemed clear they were not going to consider my interview choice, so I moved on. In July 1975 I was at a newsstand and the cover of *Playboy* had this headline: "Big Hit Man Talks! *Playboy* Grills 'Godfather' Director Francis Ford Coppola." I didn't see my name there anywhere.

The *Star Wars* original negative was in the studio vault in Los Angeles, but there were elements important to a restoration that came from the mine shaft. With something this important, more than one location is a prudent way to insure a backup master would survive. The original plan was to only redo the wipes, those famously old-fashioned *Star Wars* transitions that literally wiped one image off the screen while bringing on the next one in an optical trick used in the old movie serials. George never liked how they looked, and he wanted them redone.

While unofficially no one wanted this restoration to happen, they couldn't really come right out and say that, but, like Congress, they could subtly defy the president's wishes by not funding it. There was a standoff for a while. George kept ordering stuff and adding to the shots he wanted fixed. For our part, ILM opened a project billing account and started charging all our time to it. Not much the executives at the Ranch could do about that. Ironically, the Ranch was a little different: That was the executives' domain, and it was under their control. So they formed a committee to oversee the restoration project, told Tom Christopher to attend, and started giving orders to mute the whole thing. But they had a problem: George asked to meet with Tom every Friday and give him a report on how things were going on the restoration. Very few people met with George on a regular basis. The power had now shifted.

Tom is a very smart, detail-oriented guy. He doesn't play politics or suffer fools gladly. He didn't argue or plead his case, he didn't threaten or pull a "George said," he just went back to the committee and simply said, "I need you to issue three purchase orders, and I will bill everything I need to them." Game over. The purchase orders were issued and the original *Star Wars* was going to get some updates and a restoration.

Tom set up a command center editing room at the Ranch and hired assistants. He found the original negative at Fox and the separation masters in a salt mine somewhere in the Midwest, but he couldn't find the original negatives for the wipes. They looked all over Los Angeles—no luck. Nobody asked me. They were in my ILM editorial warehouse. This illustrates one of the strange things about working for a large company. Information is valuable, it is power, and no one wants to give it up. Lucasfilm was a collection of fiefdoms, and all information was held strictly inside those fiefdoms. No one would tell you anything they didn't absolutely have to.

Tom knew this and decided to do the exact opposite. He told his assistants that if anyone called with any questions, they were to answer them as best they could and he did the same himself. Slowly, over time, this meant that Tom became the "go-to" guy for the entire company. Since everyone was in the dark, even the top executives, this meant that they could have their secretaries call Tom's editing room and ask, for instance, where George was. There was no downside in calling Tom because he was just an editor. Calling George's assistant and major gatekeeper Jane Bay would be noted. The question of why they wanted to know might be asked. No, it was best to just call Tom.

Finally someone called me about the missing wipe originals and I said, "Let's have a look in our warehouse." I too had the "answer all questions" policy. I'd learned that from Karen, the receptionist. Tom was a freelancer, not on staff, so it took him a while to find me. We had the negative and everything else he was looking for.

Everything should have been easy in restoring *Star Wars* because the studio had made Technicolor dye separation masters. This was the classic method of making color movies from black-and-white negatives by dyeing prints from each of the three negatives with either red, green, or blue. *Gone with the Wind* was shot in Technicolor by an enormous camera that exposed three black-and-white negatives in-camera, at once, with these primary colors. *Star Wars* had been shot with the later standard color negative made by Eastman Kodak, but to preserve the film, the Technicolor three-strip method was used because, while Eastman negatives would deteriorate with shrinkage and fading colors, the

Technicolor method would not. You just made new color prints off the bulletproof black-and-white masters.

This Technicolor process had a backstory that I discovered one day while wandering around San Rafael on my lunch hour. It's a little side note to this story of the restoration and the Technicolor elements that were used to preserve *Star Wars,* but it is typical of how things evolve in Hollywood. It turns out that in 1918 the first feature-length color motion picture was shot in San Rafael, the same city where I worked at ILM, by a man named Leon Douglas. I first learned about him while visiting a downtown area of old Marin mansions where he lived.

Mr. Douglas was a very wealthy man who had cofounded the Victor Talking Machine Company, famous for its ads that featured a dog looking into the horn of a Victrola with the line, "His Master's Voice." The Victrola was a windup record player and Douglas's version of a phonograph. He named his invention after his wife, Victoria. After Douglas encased the player in a fine furniture cabinet, so ladies would allow it in their living rooms, it became universally popular and he sold millions of them. He sold so many of them that he had to hire 7,000 cabinetmakers just to keep up with the demand.

Douglas was also a prolific inventor who held over fifty patents. For motion pictures he patented a zoom lens, the first anamorphic lens, a special effects camera which he rented to Hollywood studios, and his color film process. It was here in Marin where he produced the first American feature-length color film, starring Ruth Roland with Mary Pickford and Douglas Fairbanks making guest appearances.

When Douglas took his color process to all the major studios to demonstrate it, no one was interested. Yet, by the 1930s color motion pictures were being made using the Technicolor process, which was based on Douglas's inventions, and all the studios were distributing them. Douglas sued to enforce his patents and won a $20 million settlement in 1934. He won by default when the defendants—Paramount Pictures, Fox Film Corporation, Disney, and Technicolor—failed to respond to the suit. Needless to say, $20 million was a lot of money in 1934, arguably the bottom of the Great Depression. Still, Hollywood would often rather just buy technology than invest in its development.

In the late 1970s when the protection masters of *Star Wars,* the highest-grossing movie of all time, were made by what was now 20th Century Fox and the Douglas-inspired Technicolor, they did it on the cheap. There are two ways to make these masters: wet or dry. Either way is expensive, but the wet printing method is more expensive. Essentially the negative image from the original is rephotographed through a special liquid that makes any scratches, and some dirt, not register on the copy negative. The liquid fills up the scratch, thus letting the projector light pass straight through the film and not catch in the groove of the scratch, revealing a blemish.

Someone chose the cheaper alternative, and we were paying for that now. Eventually Tom got all of the technical challenges met by looking up some of the older lab employees from the golden era of motion picture labs. Upon their advice he had the various negatives rewashed or reprinted using the wet-gate method, all the while finding various pieces that had gone missing from this giant puzzle.

Soon all was ready to cut into the original *Star Wars* negative. Before doing that, however, Tom wanted to check something with George. He explained to George that everything was ready to cut in, but he wanted to know whether they should order a duplicate negative of the original version. It could easily be done, he said, and then there would always be an original version of this historic movie. George said, "This *is* the original version," meaning that what everyone else had described as a restoration, he considered the final version of the movie.

This brings up an interesting point. Who should decide these things? Should the public have any say in what happens to a work of art or a national treasure? After paying almost $200 million for a famous van Gogh, should the owner object if van Gogh himself showed up and said, "I always wanted to add more blue to this, but I couldn't afford it back then. Mind if I add it now?" Are there cultural treasures that are so important that they shouldn't be changed, even by the artists that created them? Franz Kafka wanted all of his writings burned after his death. Fortunately for posterity, they were not. Is the quality or historical value of a work of art more meaningful than the wishes of its author? Should Harper Lee have been allowed to publish *Go Set a*

Watchman, turning her heroic main character in *To Kill a Mockingbird*, beloved by millions, into a racist?

As we advance into the digital world of the future, where undetectable changes can be made with increasing sophistication, this question will, I think, be asked again and again.

The original *Star Wars* was rereleased in 1997 as the "Special Edition" and it skyrocketed to the number one position at the box office for three weeks, grossing over $138 million. This surprised a lot of people, even George I suspect. *Empire* and *Jedi* soon followed, all of them together grossing more than $250 million. These unwanted rereleases helped build a cash pile that could fund the new *Star Wars* films that would ultimately generate billions of dollars in new revenue. George was back in the game.

Digital City

FOR SOME TIME IT HAD BECOME APPARENT THAT ILM HAD OUTGROWN its location in Marin County, and once again the impracticality of the Ranch came up. There was certainly enough room to expand the Ranch to include ILM, but there were other problems. George had already developed an adjoining property he owned called Big Rock Ranch, but it made his neighbors unhappy, and although he later got permission from the county to build a production facility on even another ranch he owned, he wisely decided to not force it.

So, around 1999, when it came time to make a big proposal to move ILM to the Presidio in San Francisco, we made a pitch to both the board that controls the Presidio and its well-heeled neighbors. The old Presidio army base is surrounded by some of the most expensive residential real estate in the country. These neighbors had connections to politics and business, so they needed to be reassured. This move also was tantamount to admitting that the Ranch was not where all the new young talent wanted to be. The digital artists that needed to be continuously recruited had no interest in living in Lucasland or anywhere else but San Francisco. Even Silicon Valley would later have to make serious concessions, offering high-class busses to and from the city in order to be competitive in attracting talent.

George wanted to make a short film explaining why everyone should approve his building a series of structures on the old Letterman Army Hospital site on the Presidio grounds and moving a large part of his company there. They even recruited me to work on this film project. In our first meeting, the director and cinematographer, Bob Dalva, explained that he wanted to open the film with a montage of antique projection devices culminating in a modern one.

The proposed buildings were sited in such a way that they looked right down at the Palace of Fine Arts, a building designed by the famous local architect Bernard Maybeck. This beloved building was the only remnant of the 1915 Panama-Pacific Exposition, which celebrated not only the opening of the West via the new Panama Canal, but also the introduction of electric lighting and the first trans-Atlantic telephone call, which was the last link to connecting the world. So I suggested that we use some of the spectacular public-domain footage of this fair as well. It showed an entire city of exposition buildings, all lit with thousands of early electric lights. It was a magical-looking city covered with reflective globes that doubled the power of the lights, and searchlights that continuously swept the skies. This area of the Marina District had been largely reclaimed bay marsh, and it was built on fill. Importantly, the fill used was the rubble from the old San Francisco that had collapsed in 1906. By implication, we would be pointing to a rebirth of the city, whose digital future would repeat this famous analog opening of a canal. In other words, approve our proposal and help make San Francisco the center of the digital world, a world that Marshall McLuhan had presaged as a "global village."

Director Dalva shouted this idea down so forcefully that I just dropped it. It was as if I had suggested something that was uncinematic. Bob had a long history with both Lucas and Coppola and was a noted cinematographer/editor, so there was no point in arguing.

My next idea was accepted but with incredulity. I said, if you want to film some old movie projectors, I have a friend that has an amazing collection of them and she works right here at ILM. Sandra Joy Lee was our media librarian. She was whip-smart, very congenial, and, as a hobby, she collected old movie projectors from the earliest Zoetropes to beautiful, almost Deco-looking mid-1930s projectors. She also donated her time working as a projectionist at the local art house movie theater that Marcia Lucas had donated money to restore. This was the same theater to which I had ridden my bike from my Aunt Bobbitt's apartment as a child.

Sandra was yet another example of the amazing talent ILM had brought together. What other young woman is there that just so happens to collect and operate antique motion picture equipment?

Sandra's library department had absorbed my old video movie collection from the editorial department, and she had lined the archive walls with displays of her great old projectors. This was an idea that could not be just dismissed out of hand, so when I dropped by Sandra's library a few days later, Dalva had the whole place lit like a movie set and Sandra was beaming that her collection was being used to help us get awarded the coveted acreage on an invaluable site in the Presidio.

I had thought a lot about this proposed Letterman Digital Arts Center and I was strongly in favor of it because I thought it made perfect sense both historically and for the future of San Francisco. I told one of the Presidio neighbors that I didn't have a dog in this fight, I just worked for the guy, but I thought people would be crazy to turn it down, especially if you consider the quality of workmanship Lucas is known for. He was proposing an underground parking garage for all employee vehicles and had hired the foremost landscape architect in the country, Lawrence Halprin, to design a park with a creek spilling into a beautiful pond to cover the garage. Plus, this would be open to the public. Mothers with baby carriages and young children will be strolling here for decades to come.

In order to speak to the center's historical importance, I wrote a paper on the subject and sent it to the screenwriter for the film project, Matthew Robbins, an old friend of George's. The final documentary included at least some of my thoughts, and eventually the plan to build the Letterman Digital Arts Center was approved.

Today, San Francisco is awash with a tidal wave of digital success as new ventures are introduced weekly.

The Stone Age Institute

Security at ILM was always high for several reasons. One was to keep out the curious fans who were sometimes determined to find souvenirs or meet movie stars who were occasionally there. The biggest reason, however, was more industry protocol than anything else.

We were always working on several movies at a time, and each Hollywood studio expected us to protect the privacy of their intellectual property in scripts and the proprietary techniques we were using on their projects. The last thing anyone wanted was for some director or producer to divulge at a cocktail party what he or she had seen of another person's film. Since most film projects took well over a year to complete, there was a natural desire not to reveal spoilers about anyone's upcoming release. Why endanger the surprise when it's part of what the audience is looking for?

Sometimes, however, if things were slow enough, I could get permission to bring a few people in and show them around. As my interest in paleoanthropology widened, I was invited to join the advisory board of the Stone Age Institute in Bloomington, Indiana. Funded largely by Gordon Getty, the son and heir of oil tycoon J. Paul Getty, the institute fields anthropologists for worldwide expeditions to sites where early man lived, bringing back human skulls, skeletons, and tools for study and scholarly presentations. They were studying the family of man, and I was studying my family.

So I took the founders of the institute, Nick Toth and Kathy Schick, along with its vice president, Henry Corning, who with Getty is the chief financial engineer for the institute, through ILM and then to the Ranch for lunch. It turned out that Henry was so impressed with the atmosphere at the Ranch that he organized the building of a similar country complex for their institute, which gave Nick and Kathy some independence from the University of Indiana and their own stature as more than just employee professors.

The institute is now a multimillion-dollar complex on about forty acres of farmland outside Bloomington. It is a gorgeous compound built of Indiana limestone with a great hall that features, instead of the typical busts of Plato, Socrates, and other monumental intellectual leaders, all of the important skulls of our ancient ancestors such as Java Man, etc. When I first saw the new place, I remembered something Lucas had said after donating hundreds of millions of dollars to USC for a new film school building: "If you want a discipline to be taken seriously, you need a serious building." The Stone Age Institute now had a serious building.

Man is a toolmaker, and Nick invites all kinds of people who use tools in their craft to lecture and visit the institute, thus my invitation. Anthropologists learn about early man by studying his behavior and trying to reproduce his skills. The modern-day making of a stone tool is the ultimate learning experience. Nick showed me how to make what are called "hand axes" and gave me one. It's funny but they look and fit the hand just like a computer mouse.

The best examples for learning about early man are modern humans themselves. After all, as Phil Tippet, one of the geniuses behind *Jurassic Park,* taught me, existing animals are the best paleontological record we have of what the ancient ones might have been like. Since we are a type of animal ourselves, it makes sense to study ourselves in all our forms. Michel de Montaigne's *Essays* famously record his study of himself. He wrote that he used "some traits of my character" to describe the traits of man, as in, "I have never seen a greater monster or miracle than myself."

This involvement with the institute began my limited but eventful introduction to Gordon Getty. Nick called me one day and asked if I could come to Bloomington again for a convocation they were having. I was torn as to whether I could spend the time away from my own work in starting my distribution business, but when he mentioned that Gordon was flying out in his private jet and that I would be welcome to join him, that cinched it.

I can imagine no comparison in jet travel save possibly flying with a member of the Saudi royal family. Gordon and his wife had spent millions redesigning and redecorating this 727 airliner. They had chosen it because Gordon was six foot five and it was the only plane that he could stand up in comfortably. But it was not so much the luxury at play here as the simple comfort and convenience of having a personal plane of this type.

All things considered, Gordon is a fairly modest man. Having engineered the sale of his family's oil company in 1984 for $10 billion, he is well acquainted with extreme wealth. So much so that on having heard that Gordon had lost $50 million in a business venture, I asked Henry about it, since they were old friends going back to their Harvard days, and he said something I will never forget: "These things happen." That type of thinking is so far from the average person's experience, it reminds one of the famous F. Scott Fitzgerald quote, "Let me tell you about the very rich. They are different from you and me."[1]

Well, this was a different way of travel. As I pulled up to the private plane terminal at Oakland International Airport, someone came and got my bags from the car. From there I walked out onto the tarmac and scurried up the rear steps of the 727 affectionately named "Jetty" by Gordon's kids. Fore and aft were large areas with a few huge cushioned swivel chairs sprinkled about, the type you might find in an executive office except permanently attached to the floor. There were also some couches and huge video screens showing our flight path with animation as well as weather data. These screens, fore and aft, were also used to play in-flight movies or television shows. In the center of the plane was Gordon's bedroom, with a huge double bed and private bath. The kitchen was next to this towards the front of the plane.

There was a crew of five: captain, copilot, navigator, and two stewardesses. Breakfast featured fresh fruit, all kinds of juices and coffees, and the choice of two kinds of omelets. Unlike commercial flights, there was no security check and the door to the cockpit remained open, which

1. F. Scott Fitzgerald, "The Rich Boy," in *All the Sad Young Men* (New York: Charles Scribner's Sons, 1926).

meant I could talk to the pilot. I asked him if this was a dream job, and he said that the best thing for him was that while the plane had all the fancy autopilot stuff, you could still fly it manually, and because of its low weight due to so few passengers (one time it was just four people), it was a real hot rod. I can attest to this, as takeoffs were at a very sharp angle up.

I asked one of the crew where I should sit, as Gordon's limo hadn't arrived yet. "Anywhere but that chair," he said, pointing to one of the big swivels. "That's Mr. G's chair." So I sat on a couch. When Gordon arrived, he introduced himself while the crew slammed the interior cabinet doors. He never did sit in "that chair," but there was no time to ponder it, as we were almost immediately airborne. Very efficient.

Gordon was deep into writing on a yellow legal-size pad, so I poked around, noting every major newspaper and magazine either neatly folded or displayed for use. When we landed at the regional airport in Bloomington, I was told our plane was the largest one to ever land there.

Gordon may be a billionaire but he dresses like a college professor, with a saggy sport jacket, cheap wristwatch, and old wallet, all of which he laughs about. If it was about convenience or art he was interested, but petty jewelry or trinkets like cars are of little use to him. For years he drove an AMC Pacer and still talks about it fondly.

When the conference was over, I flew with Gordon to New York, where I had planned my own vacation before flying back home on a commercial flight. Landing at a private airport in New Jersey, we were still the largest plane by far. Gordon's jetliner dwarfed the puny little Learjets and Gulfstreams that all the Wall Street hotshots had squeezed into.

I hitched a ride in Gordon's limo to Manhattan, and he told me of his longtime desire to produce a movie of Wagner's *Ring* but had been told it would cost a billion dollars. When he dropped me at my cheap New York hotel, I mentioned that I would be willing to produce *The Ring* for $600 million, tops. I'm not sure if he knew I was joking or not.

I had now been turned back into a pumpkin and was no longer consorting with billionaires. Gordon was staying at New York's Palace Hotel, and I was staying at The Pod. Mine was a wonderful European-style budget hotel, just not in league with New York's finest.

My wife met me in Manhattan and, after touring the city, I suggested we drop the return airline tickets we had planned on using and drive back in a rental car that we could leave in San Francisco. Neither of us had done a cross-country drive since just after college. I vowed to take back roads whenever possible and to not eat in any chain restaurants during the entire trip. It took a month, and we had a ball.

Dropping Dead

THE LAST LINE IN THE OPENING TO ORSON WELLES'S MASTERPIECE, *Citizen Kane,* is "Then last week, as it must to all men, death came to Charles Foster Kane." Mine came on a Friday afternoon in 2002. It was not like I wasn't expecting it. They had just awarded me with a golden statue of the *Star Wars* character C-3PO to mark my twenty years. The first day of my employment, I had signed in with the receptionist, and when I walked past her, she said just loud enough for me to hear, "Day one." It was now day 7,300 and counting.

I was like the man who came to dinner—and never left. It was originally supposed to be about an eight-month gig, but the films just kept coming. I was the chief visual effects editor and was promoted to department head, which included our commercial division. Department heads traditionally didn't last very long, but I lasted nine years, which was a record. I survived four management changes and numerous political battles, but when the digital revolution hit with full force, my age began to cripple me. The company pretty much split into film versus digital. This was about the time when George announced to no one in particular that "editing on film was like scratching on rocks." I became a Neanderthal.

Although I spent all day on an Avid digital editing machine, it didn't matter. I had been using computers for writing since before hard drives; I had been on the Internet at home since about 1989 and had websites up in 1999. None of this mattered. I was "the old guy in editorial." I became the union steward and Patty, the head of production, said apropos of nothing, "That won't do you any good." Allies disappeared. I asked to see my personnel file, and in it was a statement from Kim, a producer and sometimes friend, that said, "He is an old man and should probably retire."

Fortunately I had already started preparations to retire, once again following the advice of Montaigne, "Retire into yourself, but first prepare yourself to be your own host." In December 1999 and January 2000 I had sold all the stock in my retirement account. This meant that I completely avoided the tech wreck that cost the equity markets a loss of $5 trillion.

There is a Hollywood tale that Harry Cohn once ordered the writer of *Citizen Kane,* Herman J. Mankiewicz, off the Columbia studio lot, ending his tirade with "and don't bring him back *ever* . . . unless we need him." On Friday, August 2, 2002, I walked out the door. I was back on the following Monday, because they needed me. But it was a brief reprieve, and I had decided to retire anyway. Still, it was a shock. I had worked for over thirty years—was I ready for this?

In 1919 Jess Willard, who had defeated Jack Johnson in Havana, Cuba, fought the much-feared Jack Dempsey to defend his heavyweight title. Dempsey knocked Willard down seven times in the first round, going on to win in round four when Willard could not continue. Someone later asked Willard what he was thinking as he was being knocked down so many times and he replied, "I kept saying to myself, I have $100,000 and a ranch in Kansas, I have $100,000 and a ranch in Kansas." Was there something I could say to myself? I did have a small ranch in the wine country besides my home in Berkeley. So I told myself that since I knew who I was now, I could have a life rich in writing, real estate investing, and distributing my own movies.

I love the city with its cafes and bookstores, but I also need to be in nature every so often. I find the contrast in going from one to the other immensely refreshing. Each in its own way rejuvenates my spirits, and I feel fortunate to have this option.

I bought the country place as a retreat from my high-stress job and city life in general. It is on a small hill overlooking what has become a wine region. The property contains a Sea Ranch–style house built out of clear heart redwood, a separate studio building, and a small cottage-like structure with its own deck that I use for writing. There are also lots of acres to roam around on. I can run my small businesses from there or the city, but I also try to have fun wherever I am.

Most of my friends who had also left Lucasfilm trotted off to other jobs, both in and out of the film business. I didn't feel the need anymore. I was finally ready for my close-up.

Oddly enough, one of the things I did after I retired was buy a slot machine. If there is a more clear parallel to the gambles so familiar to the moviemaker, I don't know what it would be. It's like a horoscope for real, but with no phony promises. You know you cannot win, only delay the inevitable. It's a gentle reminder of the idiot's tale we are all involved in.

Mine is one of those old-style quarter machines with a $150 jackpot. It came out of Harvey's Wagon Wheel Casino in Reno, Nevada, and is of about a 1958 vintage. I think I got it just because I could never play one when my mother occasionally took us to Reno as kids. The casinos were fascinating to me back then. Not only were there rooms full of gambling devices with bells ringing and coins crashing into payout bins, but there were also memorable displays. One casino had a museum-like room lined with artifacts from the Old West, like antique rifles, pistols, and derringers, just like I saw in the movies and on television. Another had a large glass case with a million dollars in cash on display. Cowboys and money—it doesn't get any better than that for a kid raised on Westerns.

Personally, I can't understand why anyone would want to play the new slots that have no coins and only pay out a little slip of paper. What fun is that? Even hitting a small jackpot on mine brings a neurotransmitter cocktail of pleasure to your brain, with its crash of quarters clanging into the metal tray. That sound, like a great movie moment, was carefully designed to pick up your spirits so you would play again.

Here I am, unemployed for the first time in thirty-two years, and I buy a slot machine. But that wasn't all. I bought a 1947 Lionel train set exactly like the one I lost in the chaos after my mother's death. I, like a lot of people, have a somewhat romanticized view of life. Yet, what is more appropriate? Does anyone really desire the real version? At my small ranch, my aunt's old summer resort and grandpa's booze truck, the REO Speed Wagon, are still within six miles of me. They say you can't go home again. Well, we shall see about that.

After buying the slot, I took it to a guy in San Mateo, south of San Francisco, for a tune-up. Steve Squires had been working on slot machines since he was seventeen years old, and he was then seventy-six.

This guy was amazing, and his shop was filled with antique slot machines. They were everywhere, covering almost every square foot of floor space to the extent that only footpaths were left open for navigation. The walls were hung with old slot machine faceplates like mine, from every brand and year imaginable. From the ceiling hung hundreds of old slot wheels, each with varying combinations of cherries, oranges, and plums brightly printed on them. There was room after room filled with boxes, drawers, and shelves, all overflowing with antique parts. Steve told me that Lucasfilm had once asked him to rig a slot machine for a movie so that every time the handle was pulled, there would be a jackpot. That would save a lot of time in shooting a scene. He couldn't remember the movie, and my best guess was *Tucker: The Man and His Dream.*

One thing I always wondered about was how they set the odds on a slot. I asked Steve and he said, "You can't do it mechanically, which is what everyone thinks. You have to change the order and frequency of the cherries and other fruit images that appear on a given reel." It turns out that three-reel machines have about 8,000 possible combinations of images that might appear on the payline. Alter the makeup of the reels, and you change the odds. A machine like mine could potentially earn the casino about $800 a day. A hundred working machines could pay for a lot of casino overhead back in the 1950s. The jackpot, too, was a decent payout when you consider you could buy a used car for $150 back then.

I think of my 25-cent machine as representative of the movie world's resistance to change. I don't want to play the new electronic slots, and Thomas Edison originally didn't want to project his images. He preferred to sell his Kinetoscopes for private viewing in commercial parlors, which charged 25 cents to watch a few film clips. "If we put out a screen machine [projector]," he said, "there will be a use for maybe about ten of them in the whole United States. Let's not kill the goose that lays the golden egg." My old 25-cent machine is still an un-killed goose. Edison didn't want to give up those quarters, and I don't want to submit to the electronic when the mechanical is more fun. I sometimes complain about the lack of technological progress in the world yet sometimes celebrate it, and I'm not alone. We all edit our lives to some extent. We pick and choose. Many people who drive modern cars and use the latest cellphones still want to live in Victorian houses.

When I got the slot machine home, I wondered whether I should just not tell the wife and take it to Boonville on my next trip or get it over with right now. I opened the lift back and dropped the tailgate to my SUV, invited her out, and handed her a quarter. She pulled the handle, hit three cherries, scooped up the jackpot, and disappeared back into the house saying, "That was fun." I never had a problem after that, and we both occasionally pull the handle when we are in the country. Steve had warned me to "play it often—they like that." There is something about pulling that handle and going through this little exercise of anticipation, suspense, and surprise, but I can't quite put my finger on it. I wish I could ask Montaigne what he thought.

My machine had come out of Harvey's Wagon Wheel Casino, which had been started by a former butcher named Harvey Gross. He and his wife ran a popular lunch counter with a few slots back in the 1940s. With that start, they grew it into a large casino enterprise that cleared them about a million dollars a year by the 1950s. Investor types kept pleading with him to expand throughout Nevada. He always gave the same answer: "With a million bucks a year, we are doing fine. After all, how many steaks can you eat?"

Here was another story that I could use somewhere, maybe after my distribution business runs out of gas. But it doesn't ever seem to, even though at $25, our movie is not cheap. Last Christmas alone, I mailed over 500 DVDs of *American Nitro* from Boonville in about three days, overwhelming the local post office. I don't have to wait for a royalty statement and a check from a publisher to know how I'm doing. Besides, it's more of a hobby anyway—that and my effort to keep the work alive for as long as I can. Next up to restore and distribute will be my old Jack Johnson movie.

This distribution thing all came about through a somewhat strange set of circumstances. It isn't supposed to happen. Creative people do their work and depend on a company that specializes in distribution to handle that for a fee, a large fee. And for that fee, the publisher is supposed to do advertising and promotion for their authors. This rarely works out well for the writers and filmmakers. Unfortunately there is no alternative to this for most people, but there have always been exceptions.

Mark Twain did not do what his contemporaneous authors did. Twain published his own books and sold them door to door, hiring agents for this arduous task. His methods were far outside the conventional book publishing trade. This just wasn't done by serious authors. It smacked of vanity publishing or cheap low-class books, except that this was also the way that the Bible was sold: door to door. Twain was very successful at this because he could laugh at any vanity publishing charge. He was Mark Twain.

His biggest success using this method was in publishing the memoirs of General Ulysses S. Grant, which I have mentioned before. It was one of the largest publishing successes in American history. Twain sold more of these books than anything *except* the Bible, and it brought Grant's family over $500,000 in royalties, a fortune in the 1880s. I reread the memoirs myself every few years.

In 2002 I decided to follow the Mark Twain route and distribute my own movie. Like George Lucas, I felt that now no one could tell that I was too old or uncool to make movies. I was retired and was done working on other people's projects. Besides the country house, I had a home in Berkeley, some real estate investment property, and a steady income from several sources. As Montaigne had recommended, I had prepared to be my own host.

At some point I discovered that the movie my brother and I had made, *American Nitro,* was being talked about in certain Internet chat groups. Long out of distribution, it had become a kind of cult film. This and the circus-like atmosphere of the whole thing made the movie a viable commercial entity and a historical document. One of the people in the film section of the Library of Congress told us that "your movie is pure Americana and will only get more and more interesting as time passes." That was enough for me.

We pulled the original 35mm negative out of storage and had it transferred to a digital format of the highest quality available. That's the great thing about motion picture negatives—they are of such high quality that you can keep going back to them again and again as current technologies improve. In fact, a couple of years ago I sold some of our footage to a Hollywood studio that was making a feature film on two of the characters in our movie for $100 a second.

I toyed with the idea of changing the movie, at least to the extent of trying to set it up for the non–racing fan. There was a Roman quote about bread and circuses that I tried out, but nothing seemed to improve it, so I decided to leave it as it was originally. The only thing we added was a directors' commentary where my brother and I gave our thoughts on where the movie came from and what we had tried to do.

It was a drive-in picture and almost everyone saw it as just a drag race documentary. Which it was. But if you thought about it for a minute, who in the hell would make a drag race documentary like this? It didn't hype its subject, it exposed it as a strange and somewhat hidden subculture—an outlaw sport which neither drag race officialdom nor the reviewers much appreciated. There were a few people who got it, however. On the high end, it was seen as "asphalt anthropology," and on the low, "I watched it every night for a year, just ask my wife." That's a real fan quote, and as a friend of mine pointed out, that should read "ex-wife."

Looking back, it seems that the art movement of the 1970s went through a kind of metamorphosis from abstraction to realism, or at least some of it did, and this was felt in filmmaking and still photography as well. I think of our movie as Contemporary Realism. Other examples are the movie *Derby,* a documentary on the fringe sport of roller derby, and the book *Suburbia* by Bill Owens, whose black-and-white still photos chronicled the early 1970s suburban lifestyles of Americans. I'm sure I would be hard-pressed to find any art critic to agree with me, but I really don't care—they will get to it eventually. For now, *Nitro* has well over 800,000 fans on Facebook. I looked up the ranking of our page once and at that time we were ahead of Johnny Depp, the Los Angeles Lakers, Bonnie Raitt, Starbucks, the iPhone 6, and Patsy Cline.

It is hard to find a male (and a surprising number of females) between the ages of thirty and seventy that does not have fond memories of hot rod cars in high school, or their father taking them to the races, or going racing themselves with their buddies. It was endemic to the culture, and we had attempted to chronicle this wide segment of the population. These are the guys we send to fight our wars. They drive the long-haul trucks, snowplows, and heavy equipment. They go hunting and fishing. They like guns and motorcycles and hot rod custom cars of one kind or another. They are religious and they are patriotic. They are the first to feel some of the harshest blows due to high gasoline prices, moving jobs overseas, technological change, or economic downturns.

So in an effort to find that audience and engage with them, I created a social media page on Facebook for fans of *American Nitro,* but not just the movie. I wanted it to represent the zeitgeist of this particular part of our culture as well. Since I am not a participant in this world, I can only be an observer and commentator. This makes the site an extension of the movie in a way. Yet, I have never heard of anyone else doing something like this before. Sometimes it seems more like a kind of performance piece. However, if the artist Cindy Sherman can dress up as stereotypical characters from everyday life and then photograph herself as her art, I guess I can communicate with my group through role-playing.

When I started I was only able to attract a handful of people, but as I learned how to appeal to them, it soon started to grow. We currently have a very large number of fans on the site. Many of them have purchased the movie from us, and many more will in time. People hear about the movie from the Facebook page, watch the trailers either there or on YouTube, and order it through our website using PayPal. This means we don't have to do any billing, as PayPal collects the money and deposits it in our bank before we ship the DVDs.

For the computer phobic we accept checks, and there must be some kind of economic law here or something, because we've never had a returned check in eight years. Apparently people don't bounce checks for their hobbies. They may short the grocer or the landlord, but not the discretionary items that they really don't need. Or do they? Perhaps we are just more passionate about our hobbies. Many have commented that our website is "eye candy" or even "car porn" for them. So far I have been flying completely under the radar of the studio system, hoping to remain undetected.

One thing is for sure, I've gotten to know how the fans think, as this is a window into their lives. I see pictures of their children and their homes, as well as their parents and grandparents. I know where they live and what they do, and can predict how they will react to most things. Their voting for Trump was one of those things. Politics aside, it is a fascinating group that is easy to like. As best as I can describe it, we are continuing the dialogue with the audience for the movie through a totally different medium.

This method of doing things was not even available just a few years ago, but it will expand for filmmakers, writers, musicians, and other artists with every passing year—that is if they are not reluctant to use technology. Many older artists and writers are especially timid when it comes to the vast array of digital resources now available to them, and I try to encourage anyone I run across to learn how it can be useful to them in their work. There is actually a Silicon Valley term that I've modified to describe people who shy away from these latest technologies. It's called "tech debt," and it translates into one's getting behind in those tech areas that can be of immense help to them as time goes on.

So what are my lessons? You have to make a living, but you need to also do your own work. You always need a side project: a book, a film, a screenplay, photography, painting, poetry, music, whatever it is. You must not let your job make your personal work totally subservient. You will find that what you learn from your side project eventually will either make you more successful at your career or it will become your career.

That's the story of one guy from that long list of credits at the end of the movie. It is what happened to a person who was trying to lead a creative life and still make a living. I sometimes wonder if the movie moguls I worked with ever have as much fun as I do. After all, "how many steaks can you eat?"

Index

Abbey Road, 134
The Abyss, 127–28
Ace Ventura: Pet Detective, 126
actors: accuracy as precarious for, 155–58; directors and insensitivity to, 87; visual effects as, 6; voice importance of, 51. *See also specific actors*
Adams, "Shorty," 163
Admiral Ackbar, 22
AFI. *See* American Film Institute
The Alaska Wilderness Adventure, 67
Alexander, Jane, 61
Ali, Muhammad, 119
Allen, Woody, 51
Always, 81–82
Amblin Entertainment, 103
American Distilling Company, 172
American Film Institute (AFI), 61
American Graffiti, 2, 23, 28, 88, 179
American Nitro, 2, 27, 67–79, 175, 215–18
American Zoetrope Studios, 53, 55, 56
Anchors Aweigh, 102
Anderson, Eddie, 18
Anderson, Paul Thomas, 175
Andrews, Julie, 102
animators. *See specific animators*
Annie Hall, 50
answer print, 194
Apocalypse Now, 16, 99
art director, 8–9, 20
Ask the Dust, 73
autographs, 132–33
automatic dialogue replacement, 114
Avatar, 1
Avid digital editing machine, 211

Bacall, Lauren, 11
backgrounds, 6
Back to the Future, 19, 102, 104, 109–13
Back to the Future II, 104, 112
Back to the Future III, 109, 111–12
Bancroft, Hubert Howe, 138
Barner, Dru, 112–13
Barrett, Rona, 38
Barriscale, Bessie, 13–14, 121
The Battleship Potemkin, 29
Bay, Jane, 16, 161
Beatles, 3
Blay, Andre, 37
blind pigs, 170n1
Blood Alley, 11
The Blue Angel, 148
Blue Harvest, 8
Blue Velvet, 61
Bogart, Humphrey, 48, 52
Bogdanovich, Peter, 148
Bonnie and Clyde, 68–69
Boonville, 164, 165–66, 215
Boyle, Peter, 76
Brooks, Mel, 159

Broughton, James, 46
Butch Cassidy and the Sundance Kid, 57
Butthead Lake, 5

Caen, Herb, 55
Cagney, James, 34
Caine, Michael, 51
California: gold discovery and natural order in, 137–41; Kimberlin great-grandfather moving family to, 139. *See also* northern California
Calipose Petroleum Company, 175
camera work, 24
Cameron, James, 128
Canby, Vincent, 66
Cannon Releasing, 76–77
Capra, Frank, 62
Carpenter, John, 87
Carrey, Jim, 87, 126, 178
Catmull, Ed, 115, 144, 167–68
The Cat's Meow, 148
Cetus Corporation, 165
Chandler, Raymond, 35, 125
Chan is Missing, 65–66
Chaplin, Charlie, 3, 25, 34, 35
Chase, Chevy, 87
China Girl, 191, 192
Chinatown, 175
Christopher, Tom, 195, 198–99
Churchill, Winston, 170
cinematography, black and white, 148
cinema verité, 71–72
Cinerama, 6
Citizen Kane, 100, 123, 211, 212
Civil Rights Act of 1964, 184–85
Clark, Desmond, 42
Cline, Patsy, 217
Clinton, Bill, 112
clouds, 32
Cocoon, 88–89, 90
Cocoon 2, 190
Cohn, Harry, 62, 212
Colbert, Claudette, 62
Cold Mountain, 157
Cole, Lester, 45–46
The Color Purple, 164
Columbia Studios, 61–62
Compulsion, 61–62
CompuServe, 138–39
computers: interns for, 151; Lucasfilm Building C for, 115; Lucasfilm hiring Lasseter for, 116; Oracle system database, 94; Pixar imaging software with, 116; *Young Sherlock* as first shot by, 95
Conway, Don, 115
Coppola, Francis, 28, 45, 53–54, 63, 89, 192, 197–98
Corning, Henry, 206
costumes, 8
Cow Palace, 31
Cox, Courteney, 190–91
Creativity, Inc., 144
Cronyn, Hume, 88
Crowther, Bosley, 68
Cruise, Tom, 101
Cummings, Bob, 67
Curtis, Garniss, 42

Dallas, 64
Dalva, Bob, 203–4
Darth Vader, 8
The Day the Earth Stood Still, 54
death, of Kimberlin parents, 11–12
Deauville American Film Festival, 76–77
The Deer Hunter, 78
DeLorean, 19
DeMille, Cecil B., 8, 14
Dempsey, Jack, 212
densitometer, 192

Depp, Johnny, 217
Derby, 217
Desmond, Norma, 14
Dial M for Murder, 67
Diaz, Cameron, 126
Dickinson College, 139
Didion, Joan, 173–74n1
Die Hard and *Die Hard 2*, 81, 82
DiFrancesco, David, 115
digital cinema: Avid editing machine for, 211; early process for, 115; filmmaking changed by, 191–92; *Jurassic Park* as, 192; Letterman Digital Arts Center for, 203–5; as story telling, 190–93; visual effects before, 30–31
Dillinger, John, 171
DiMaggio, Joe, 49
Dippé, Mark, 129–31, 142–43
directors, 29, 85–90. *See also specific directors*
Disney, 32, 102, 103, 106, 107, 116–17. *See also* Walt Disney Animation Studios
distribution rights, 78–79
documentary films, 2, 20, 26, 55–56, 96
Doheny, Edward, 61
Dolby Stereo, 10
"do or do not," 2
Douglas, Leon, 25, 200
Dova, Dickie, 133
drag racing, 71, 175
Dreyfuss, Richard, 81
Driving Miss Daisy, 89
Droid Olympics, 16–18
Dr. Strangelove, 65, 72–73;
Dumb and Dumber, 126

Eastman Kodak, 115, 192, 199
Eastwood, Clint, 101
Easy Rider, 68, 98
Ebert, Roger, 66, 108
Eclair movie camera, 72
Edison, Thomas, 24, 167, 214
Edlund, Richard, 22
Eisenstein, Sergei, 24, 29
Eisner, Michael, 106
The Elephant Man, 61
Ellsberg, Daniel, 42
Elstree Studios, 6
The Empire Strikes Back, 3, 16, 17, 31, 41, 161–62, 142
employee compensation, Silicon Valley rigging, 118
Endless Summer, 75–76
England, Chrissie, 83
Ephron, Nora, 179–80
Eraserhead, 61
Escape from Alcatraz, 78
E.T., 9, 38
Ewoks, 9, 109
exploitation films, 67–68
explosions, 6, 31

Facebook, 79, 147, 217–18
Fahrenheit 9/11, 68
Fairbanks, Douglas, 34, 200
Fangmeier, Stephen, 142
Fante, John, 73
Farnsworth, Philo T., 25
Faulkner, William, 92, 96, 168
Feature Film Making at Used Car Prices, 65
Feldman, Edward S., 86
Filmex, 77
film festivals, 65, 76–77
film reels, 35, 41
Fincher, David, 1
Fitzgerald, F. Scott, 5, 122, 208n1
Flash Gordon movie serial, 2
Fleischer, Richard, 61–62
Foley, Jack, 114

Ford, Harrison, 10–11
Ford, Henry, 18, 24, 181–82
Ford, John, 29
Forrest Gump, 1, 39, 104
48 Hrs., 81

Gable, Clark, 34, 51, 62
Gance, Abel, 24
The Gangs of New York, 27, 175
Garland, Judy, 51
Gates of Heaven, 73
Getty, Gordon: Getty, J. P., 42, 206–7, 208–9
Getty, J. Paul, 206
Ghostbusters II, 157
Gibson, Mel, 68
Gillis, Lester, 171
Gladwell, Malcolm, 41
Gleason, Mike, 133, 156
The Godfather, 16, 28, 53–54, 89, 61–62, 92
The Golden Child, 85, 86, 107, 152
Goldman, William, 150
gold rush, 139, 140–41
Gone with the Wind, 48, 199
Goodman, John, 81
Good Morning America, 38
Go Set a Watchman, 201–2
Grand Theft Auto, 88
Grant, Ulysses S., 55–56, 138, 145, 216
The Grapes of Wrath, 173
Great-Aunt Bobbitt, 11–12
The Great White Hope, 48, 53, 54
Greed, 35, 174
Griffin, Marcia, 2, 4, 122, 204; divorce, 117–18; as film editor, 9, 114; Lucasfilm Building C designer, 114–15; *Raiders of the Lost Ark* input from, 117
Gross, Harvey, 215, 219
Guggenheim, Ralph, 115

Haack, Warren, 47
Hale, Lynn, 195
Halprin, Lawrence, 205
Harlin, Renny, 82
Harrah, Bill, 110
Harvey's Wagon Wheel Casino, 213, 215
Hearst, William Randolph, 14
Hemingway, Ernest, 55–56
Hickman, Mrs., 12, 13–14
High Noon, 112
Hitchcock, Alfred, 48, 67
Hoffer, Eric, 181
Hoffman, Abbie, 46
Holden, William, 123
Hollywood hierarchy, 137
Hollywood movie making, 57–64
Hollywood studios, 2–3
home video, 37, 78–79, 186–87
Honey, I Shrunk the Kids, 1
Hoover, J. Edgar, 172
Hopper, Dennis, 98
Howard, Ron, 88, 90
Howard the Duck, 190, 197
How to Film the Impossible, 20
Hughes, Howard, 34
Hunter, Holly, 81
The Hunt for Red October, 10
Huston, John, 29, 61, 149

IATSE. *See* International Alliance of Theatrical Stage Employees
ILM. *See* Industrial Light and Magic
Image Net, 146–47
Ince, Thomas, 14
independent films, 45
Indiana Jones and the Temple of Doom, 156–57
Industrial Light and Magic (ILM): black interns lack at, 152–54; cash flow fading for, 197; creativity voyage as, 114–20; Dalva as Presidio

location leader for, 203–4; as Dolby Stereo logo for trust, 10; England as producer for, 83; *The Golden Child* visual effects by, 85; Hollywood directors offered use of, 80; IATSE as union for, 180, 182; *Jurassic Park* motion models by, 142–44; Kimberlin as head editor at, 102–8; Knoll, J., as intern to creative director of, 152–53; Lee, S., as media librarian of, 204–5; Lucasfilm division as, 1; Lucas plans countered by business of, 196; in Marin County light industrial zone, 4; Marin County location outgrown by, 203; McAlister as visual effects supervisor at, 82; McCartney, P., music video by, 132; model shop of, 177; Roger Rabbit goofiness of, 102–8; Spielberg on, 118–19; *Star Trek III: The Search for Spock* visual effects by, 85; *Star Wars* rerelease producing cash for, 202; Toth, Schick, Corning touring, 206; *Who Framed Roger Rabbit* and visual effects of, 105. *See also* Lucasfilm

interactivity, 24

International Alliance of Theatrical Stage Employees (IATSE): ILM union as, 180, 182; Kimberlin working weekends for, 180–82

International Raceway Parks, 70

interns: for ILM, 151; tutoring and, 151–54

It Happened One Night: Capra directing, 62; Gable, Colbert starring in, 62

Jack Benny television show, 18

Jackson, Michael, 3, 101

Jaws: Spielberg as director of, 2, 90; Zanuck, R., as producer of, 90; Zanuck, R., on audience reaction to, 51

Jeffries-Johnson 1910: Cole assist for sales of, 46; Coppola inquiring about, 53–54; *The Great White Hope* as feature version of, 48; Kimberlin as director of, 2; McGraw-Hill release of documentary, 2, 55; SFIFF not showing, 55

J. M. Kimberlin Seed Company, 140, 168

Jobs, Steve, 196; Pixar return on investment for, 116–18

Joe, 76

Johnson, Jack: black boxing champion as, 2, 46–47, 53; Kimberlin to restore movie of, 215; Willard defeating, 212

Johnson, Joe, 1, 8–9, 20

Jones, James Earl, 8

Joplin, Janis, 58

The Joy Luck Club, 65

Jumanji, 177

Jurassic Park, 162, 192; making of movie footage for, 162; Muren on lack of flaws in, 44; Tippett as animation director for, 142, 145, 207; visual effects in, 43–44, 142–45; Williams, S., as animator on, 127–28

Kael, Pauline, 46, 68

Kafka, Franz, 201

Keach, Stacy, 61

Keaton, Buster, 3

Kellerman, Sally, 35

Kelly, Gene, 102

KEM film editing machine, 1, 28, 32

Kennedy, Kathleen, 143

Kimberlin, J. M.: as College of Pacific founder, 140, 174; Kimberlina subdivided by, 174; as Kimberlin

great-grandfather, 139; slave emancipation by, 139–40
Kimberlina: Kimberlin finding self through, 173–76; in San Joaquin Valley farms, 173–74
Kinetoscope, 167, 214
Knoll, John: as ILM creative director, 153; as ILM intern, 152; Photoshop co-created by, 1, 153
Knoll, Thomas, 1, 153
Kovács, László, 98
Kubrick, Stanley, 65, 72–73
Kurosawa, Akira, 100, 101

Lake Ewok, 5
Lange, Dorothea, 173
Lasseter, John, 95, 115, 116
Leaky, Mary, 41
Learjet, 31–32
Leary, Timothy, 129–30
Lee, Harper, 201–2
Lee, Sandra Joy, 204–5
Lennon, John, 132
Lethal Weapon, 81
Letterman Army Hospital, 203, 205
Letterman Digital Arts Center, 203–5
Lincoln, Abraham, 145
live sync sound, 72
Lloyd, Harold, 3, 61
Lombard, Carole, 34, 51
The Lone Ranger, 46
Los Angeles, 35
Lucas, George, 1, 4, 7, 10, 23, 29–30, 39, 53, 194–202; on age 30 accomplishments, 119; on autographs, 132–33; Bay as secretary for, 16, 161; cinematography as not reputation for, 99; as director from film school, 29; film school attended by, 45; Griffin as wife and business partner for, 2; Griffin divorce from, 117–18; ILM business groups countering plans by, 196; Johnston as art director for, 8–9, 20; *Raiders of the Lost Ark* and, 3–4, 20; regret for selling Pixar, 118; *Star Wars* opening scene by, 20; *Star Wars* rerelease by, 201–2; *THX 1138* as protest film by, 47–48, 53–54; 20th Century Fox granting toy rights to, 3, 197; VistaVision utilized by, 6
Lucas, Marcia. *See* Griffin, Marcia
Lucasfilm: computers and visual effects in Building C of, 115; creative people met at, 97–101; creativity voyage as, 114–20; Edlund as supervisor at, 22; employee communications board for, 119; Griffin as Building C designer at, 114–15; home video format for clients of, 79; *How to Film the Impossible* as documentary on, 20; ILM as division of, 1; Johnson as art director at, 8–9, 20; Lasseter hired by computer division of, 116; movie prints for, 160; Norby as president and Ross boss at, 129–31; Oracle for creativity and history of, 94–96; Oscars for visual effects of, 40n1; Ralston as effects director at, 19; screening rooms as public place, 97, 98
Lucasfilm games division, 24
Lucasland, 5
Luxo Jr., 95, 116
Lynch, David, 61

Maguire, Charlie, 160
The Maltese Falcon, 48
Mankiewicz, Herman J., 212

Marin County: ILM in light industrial zone of, 4, 203; Kimberlin family history in, 109–13
Marx, Groucho, 87, 168
Mary Poppins, 102
*M*A*S*H*, 35
The Mask, 126; Williams, S., as animator on, 127–28
Mason's Brewery, 140–41, 168
Mason's Distillery, 169–72
The Matrix, 81
Matsushita, 120
McAlister, Mike, 82
McCallum, Rick, 195
McCarthy, John, 54
McCarthy, Joseph, 45–46
McCartney, Linda, 132, 134–35, 136
McCartney, Paul, 3, 132–34
McEwen, Tom "The Mongoose," 74
McGraw-Hill Films, 2, 55
McKee, Dennis, 183–89
McTeague, 174
McTiernan, John, 10
Meader, Fred, 67
Medavoy, Mike, 58, 59–60
Memoirs of an Invisible Man, 87
Milius, John, 99, 100, 101
Millennium Falcon, 6
Miller, Arthur, 91
Mill Valley, 153–54
The Misfits, 91
Miwok Indian tribe, 109
Mix, Tom, 35
Monroe, Marilyn, 29, 49
Montaigne, Michel de, 168, 207, 212, 215, 216
Moore, Michael, 68
Morris, Errol, 73
Morris, Jim, 162
Motel 6, 121
movie dollar take, 39
movie guns, 112
movies: digital cinema as painting, 193; dropping dead as box office failure of, 2; Hollywood hierarchy of, 137; home video culturing interest in, 37; made, or not, 132–36; Muybridge horse photo creating, 24–25; reviews making or breaking, 69
movie sound, 28
Moviola editing machine, 17
Mullin, Jack, 52
Mullis, Kary, 164–65
Murch, Walter: *Apocalypse Now* editing and sound by, 16; *Cold Mountain* edited by, 157; Droid Olympics at house of, 16–18; as editor, sound engineer, screenwriter, 16; *Empire Strikes Back* sound by, 16; *The Godfather* editing and sound by, 16
Muren, Dennis, 138; *Jurassic Park* lack of flaws by, 44; *Jurassic Park* visual effects by, 144; Oscars held by, 40
Murphy, Eddie, 85–86
Musso & Frank's, 34
Muybridge, Eadweard: with horse photo creating movies, 24–25; Stanford horse photo in north California by, 24–25

Nagra tape recorder, 72
Nelson, "Baby Face," 171
Network, 196
The New Centurions, 61, 62
Newman, Paul, 57
Nicholson, Jack, 68
Nixon, Richard, 47
Nobel Prize, 168
Norby, Doug, 129–31
Norris, Frank, 174
North, Edwin, 54

northern California: Chaplin exit scene in, 25; Douglas patenting Technicolor in, 25; Farnsworth inventing television in, 25; Lucas moving to, 24; Mason family truck and bootleg booze in, 170; Muybridge and horse photo in, 24–25
Notes from a Native Daughter, 173–74
Not My Sister, 14

The Octopus: A Story of California, 174
O'Fallon, James, 63
"Off the Ground," 132–34
Oil!, 175
Olivier, Sir Laurence, 16
One Eye Closed, the Other Red: The California Bootlegging Years: Mason family truck and bootleg booze in, 170; Walker, C., as writer of, 170n2
One Flew Over the Cuckoo's Nest, 157
Operating Engineers Union, 111
Oracle computer, Lucasfilm history on, 94–96
Oscars: digital cinema obsoleting winners of, 192; for Lucasfilm visual effects, 40n1; Muren holding nine, 40; *Patton* providing Coppola an, 54; Ralston accepting for crew in, 36; Ralston winning five, 19; visual effects presentations for, 40
Owens, Bill, 217

Palmer, Bill, 52
The Passion of the Christ, 68
Patton, 54
PayPal, 79, 218
Pearl Harbor, 41
Penn, Arthur, 69
Pentagon Papers, 42
The Phantom Menace, 29–30
photographs, Kimberlin and, 96
Photoshop, 1, 153
Pickford, Mary, 34, 121; first American color film with, 200; *Secrets* star as, 14
Pickins, Slim, 65
Pixar, 116
Pixar Animation Studios: Catmull as president of, 167–68; creativity voyage as, 114–20; Disney purchase of, 116–17; Jobs return on investment from, 116–18; Lasseter as creative officer of, 95; Lucas regret on selling, 118
Platoon, 79
Portman, Natalie, 51–52
Poso Creek, 175
Presidio location, 203–4, 205
Prince, 86
Prison Life, 183
producers: Hollywood players as, 85–90; Lucasfilm screening rooms and, 97. *See also specific producers*
Prohibition: American Distilling buying Mason's after, 172; blind pigs in, 170n1; Churchill on, 170; Kimberlin Mason Distillery destroyed by, 169–72
Puck, Wolfgang, 164
Puzo, Mario, 92

R2-D2, 8, 177
Rabbit, Roger, ILM goofiness of, 102–8
race issues: Civil Rights Act of 1964 for, 184; *Cold Mountain* and, 157; ILM lack of black interns as, 152–54; Kimberlin ancestor slave emancipation and, 139–40; Mill Valley and, 153–54; U.S. Mint of California gold coins and, 141; West Oakland and, 153; white interns, mentoring, tutoring and, 151–54

Raiders of the Lost Ark, 3–4, 20, 117, 177
Raitt, Bonnie, 217
Ralston, Ken, 85, 152; on *Back to the Future* and DeLorean, 19; Oscar accepted for crew by, 36; as Oscars visual effects winner, 19; Sony Pictures Imageworks hiring, 19; *Who Framed Roger Rabbit* effects tests by, 103; Zemeckis getting along with, 104
Reagan, Ronald, 47
Red Dawn, 99
Reflections in a Golden Eye, 149
Remnants, 169
REO Speed Wagon, 169, 213
Return of the Jedi, 30, 33, 36; complicated effects shot for, 20–21; *Revenge of the Jedi* as original title for, 18; Williams, S., pardoned with, 145
reviews, 69
Riefenstahl, Leni, 43
The Ring, 209
Ritchie, Michael, 85
Ritt, Martin, 54
Robbins, Matthew, 205
Rockwell, Norman: filmmaking craft compared with, 191; *Peach Crop* painting of, 190, 193
Rodis, Nilo, 155
Roland, Ruth, 200
Romancing the Stone, 102
Rose of the Rancho, 14
Ross, Scott, 129–31
Rothman, Howard, 195
rough cut, 27–28
Russell, Chuck, 126

Saboteur, 67
Sackler, Howard, 53
Sanders, Don, 64
San Francisco, 31, 203–4, 210, 214
San Francisco International Film Festival (SFIFF): *Chan is Missing* rejected by, 65; *Jeffries-Johnson 1910* not shown by, 55; Medavoy talk at, 58
San Francisco State, 45–46, 47
San Joaquin Valley, 173–75
Sarandon, Susan, 101
Saving Private Ryan, 43
Schick, Kathy, 42, 206
Schindler's List, 146–50
Schmidt, Rick, 65
Scorsese, Martin, 45
Scott, George C., 61
screenwriters. *See specific screenwriters*
secrecy: *Blue Harvest* as phony film for, 8; Lucas filmmaking in, 7–8
Secrets, 14
separation masters, 195
70mm prints, 33–34
SFIFF. *See* San Francisco International Film Festival
Sherman, Cindy, 218
Silicon Valley, 4, 25, 30, 36, 129, 140, 203, 219
Silliphant, Sterling, 61
Silver, Joel, 80–84, 106
Sinatra, Frank, 82–83
Sinclair, Upton, 175
16mm film, 30
Skelton, Red, 11
sky crane, 181
Skywalker Ranch, 4, 5, 128–31, 159–60, 203, 206–7
Smell-O-Vision, 192
The Social Network, 1
Solnit, Rebecca, 25
Sony Pictures Imageworks, 19
sound engineer, 151. *See also specific sound engineers*
soundtracks: 70mm prints as superior for, 33–34; ADR utilized for, 114;

Foley for creating, 114; Hollywood studios changed by, 2–3
Southern, Terry, 72–73
spaceship battles, 1, 6
special effects. *See* visual effects
Spielberg, Steven: *Always* directed by, 81; as director, 29; film school attended by, 45; on ILM, 118–19; Indiana Jones director as, 1; as *Jaws* director, 2, 90; on *Jurassic Park* animation, 144; Kennedy as producer for, 143; Milius as friends with, 99, 101; *Raiders of the Lost Ark* as homage by, 3–4; *Schindler's List* in black and white by, 146–50; *Who Framed Roger Rabbit* go-ahead from, 103–4
Splash, 88
Squires, Steve, 214
Stallone, Sylvester, 101
Stanford, Leland, 24–25
Starkey, Steve, 1
Star Trek, 155
Star Trek III: The Search for Spock: ILM on visual effects for, 85; Kimberlin with bit part in, 155
Star Trek II: The Wrath of Khan, 38
Star Wars, 38; Admiral Ackbar as character in, 22; Christopher accomplishing restoration of, 198–99; "do or do not" as quote from, 2; *Empire Strikes Back* as sequel to, 3; *E.T.* surpassing, 9; as ode to Flash Gordon movies, 2; ILM and cash from rerelease of, 202; Kimberlin working on, 27; Lucas as series producer of, 1, 20; Lucas rerelease success with, 201–2; Lucas slotting dogfight footage in, 29–30; *Millennium Falcon* at Elstree Studios for, 6; models as stationary for, 19; restoration of, 194; Rodis as designer on, 155; rough cut as amateurish, 27–28; screenplay as long, 50; separation masters for, 195; Zsigmond not hired for, 99
Stein, Gertrude, 55–56
Steinbeck, John, 173
Stone, Judy, 55
Stone Age Institute of Anthropology, 42, 206–10
storyboards, 6
story telling: digital cinema as, 190–93; filmmaking as, 190–93
von Stroheim, Erich, 35
sub-distributors, 76
Suburbia, 217
Sunset Boulevard, 14, 123, 176
Sutton, Willie, 57
Swanson, Gloria, 14, 34
Syufy, 76

talent, movie business keeping, 126–31
Tandy, Jessica, 88
Tarrant, Bob, 185
Taxi Driver, 9
Taylor, William Desmond, 14
Technicolor, 149, 199–200; Douglas with patent on, 25, 200; *Gone with the Wind* shot with, 199
Techniscope, 99
television: 16mm film usability for, 30; Farnsworth inventing, 25; *The Young Indiana Jones* in 16mm film for, 30, 197
The Ten Commandments, 8
Terminator 2, 127–29
Tevis Cup, 112–13
There Will Be Blood, 175
35mm negative, 216–17
Thompson, Hunter S., 65
Thompson, Lea, 190–91

THX 1138: American Zoetrope as banking on success of, 55; Lucas first feature film as, 47–48, 53–54
The Tin Star, 112–13
Tippett, Phil, 142, 144–45, 207
The Tipping Point, 41
Titanic: *Ghostbusters II* with model of, 157; historically incorrect gash in, 158
To Kill a Mockingbird, 201–2
The Tonight Show Starring Johnny Carson, 164
Tora! Tora! Tora!, 61
Toth, Nick, 42, 206
toy rights, 3, 197
The Tramp, 25
The Treasure of Sierra Madre, 176
Triumph of the Will, 43
Tucker: The Man and His Dream, 214
Twain, Mark, 28, 138; Grant memoirs as self-published by, 55–56, 216
20,000 Leagues Under the Sea, 61
20th Century Fox: Blay licensing for home video from, 37; *Die Hard 2* studio as, 82; Lucas granted toy rights from, 3, 197
Twin Peaks, 61

UFO PI, 177–78
UFOs: Kimberlin detecting aliens with, 177–82; Kimberlin idea for movie about, 177–78
United Artists, 58
University of California, Berkeley, 25, 42, 138

Vertigo, 48
video tape rentals: McKee business of, 186–87; pornography as business basis for, 187
VistaVision, 18–19, 22, 103; Learjet and filming clouds in, 31–32; visual effects film format as, 6
visual effects, 1, 151; as backgrounds, fields, spaceships, monsters, explosions, actors, 6; as digital painting, 193; *The Empire Strikes Back* reel of, 41; *The Golden Child* and ILM for, 85; Hollywood studios changed by, 2–3; in *Jurassic Park*, 43–44; *Jurassic Park* and Dippé for, 142–43; *Jurassic Park* and Fangmeier for, 142; *Jurassic Park* as turning point in, 142; Kimberlin as editor of, 137–38; Lucasfilm Building C rooms for, 115; motion depicted in, 142–43; movie business influenced by, 37–38; Oscars for Lucasfilm, 40n1; Oscars presentations from, 40; *Pearl Harbor* reel for, 41; in pre-digital days, 30–31; *Return of the Jedi* shot for, 20–21; in *Saving Private Ryan*, 43; VistaVision film format for, 6; *Who Framed Roger Rabbit* and ILM, 105
von Sternberg, Josef, 148
von Stroheim, Erich, 24

Walker, Alice, 164
Walker, Clifford James, 170n2
Walt Disney Animation Studios, 167–68
Wambaugh, Joseph, 61
Wang, Wayne, 65
Warner, Ty, 124
Wayne, John, 11
Welles, Orson, 62, 211
Wellman, William, 11
Wheel of Fortune, 181–82
White, Vanna, 182

Who Framed Roger Rabbit: Amblin Entertainment as studio for, 103; Disney as studio for, 102, 103; Disney keeping rough language in, 107; Ebert review of, 108; frames drawn for, 104–6; ILM visual effects for, 105; Kimberlin as editor of, 102; Ralston creating effects tests for, 103; Silver in, 106; Spielberg go-ahead for, 103–4; Zemeckis as director of, 102
Willard, Jess, 212
Williams, Robin, 87
Williams, Steve "Spaz": *The Abyss* animations by, 127–28; *Jurassic Park* animations by, 127–28; *Jurassic Park* as pardoning, 142–45; *Jurassic Park* motion models from, 142–44; Kennedy with T. rex inquiry for, 143; *The Mask* animations by, 127–28; Ranch trouble for, 129–31; *Return of the Jedi* restoration as pardoning, 145; *Terminator 2* animations by, 127–29
Wilson, Colin, 1
Wilson, Edmund, 55–56
Winston, Stan, 142
Wisdom of the Elders, 133, 134–35, 136
Wolfe, Tom, 74–75
writers. *See specific writers*

Xerox PARC, 116

The Young Indiana Jones, 30, 197
Young Man with a Horn, 54
Young Sherlock, 95
YouTube, 79, 218

Zaentz, Saul, 157
Zanuck, Daryl, 88
Zanuck, Lily, 88–89
Zanuck, Richard: *Cocoon* producer as, 88–89; *Driving Miss Daisy* producer as, 89; *Jaws* audience reaction for, 51; *Jaws* producer as, 90; as son to Daryl, 88
Zemeckis, Bob: *Back to the Future* directed by, 102; *Forrest Gump* directed by, 104; Ralston getting along with, 104; *Romancing the Stone* directed by, 102; Silver hired by, 106; *Who Framed Roger Rabbit* director as, 102
Zoetrope, 204
Zsigmond, Vilmos, 99

About the Author

Bill Kimberlin has worked on dozens of films (imdb.com/name/nm0453863/?ref_=fn_al_nm_1) and is sought after as a lecturer and speaker on the subject of special effects. He is the director of the film *American Nitro* (the film that nabbed him a coveted spot in Lucas's studio), which has a strong cult following, including close to 800,000 followers on Facebook. *Inside the Star Wars Empire* is his first book.